Yours Truly

James Bradley

The Confederate Mail Carrier

OR

FROM MISSOURI TO ARKANSAS,

Through Mississippi, Alabama, Georgia
and Tennessee.

An Unwritten Leaf of the "Civil War."

Being an account of the Battles, Marches and Hardships of the
First and Second Brigades, Mo., C. S. A. Together with
the thrilling adventures and narrow escapes of
Captain Grimes and his fair accomplice,
who carried the mail by "the underground route" from
the Brigade to
Missouri.

BY JAMES BRADLEY,
Mexico, Mo.,
1894.

DEDICATION.

To his dear wife, and children, Mrs. M. Bettie Bradley; Miss M. Mayer Bradley; Miss Zettie B. Bradley; Richard A. Bradley; Miss Maggie W. Bradley and Isaac C. Bradley, who have shared with him the fortunes of life. To G. N. Ratliff, his companion in war; his messmate in camp; his comrade in battle; his associate in peace, and never failing friend. To the confederate soldier, who fought for a never dying principle. To the noble Daughters of the Confederacy; and to the memory of the Confederate Home, this work is most respectfully dedicated by

THE AUTHOR.

CONTENTS.

CONTENTS.

CONTENTS TO PART II.

ILLUSTRATIONS.

CHAPTER I.

THE WAR INEVITABLE.

It is not the purpose of the writer, in giving a sketch of the stirring events set forth in this volume, to enter into a detailed account of the causes that led up to them. These are matters of history, and have gone upon record, according to the prejudices and passions of the contending parties : or they have been given from the different points from which men view them.

Whatever the causes, or whoever was to blame in inaugurating the bloody contest, much has been done since the close of that dark drama, to break down former prejudices; to change the nature and relationship of the contending parties, and to bring them into closer union, and thereby make them understand the motives of each.

When Mason and Dixon's line was first blazed out, the country was divided into two powerful, distinct and widely diverging factions, differing radically in the policy of the government and financial interests; and these of such magnitude as that the casual observer will understand at once, must not only lead to a disruption of the government, but to war and blood-shed. From that very hour the two factions began forming their ranks for the final conflict; the coming of which was as fixed as fate itself. Nor did either think of grounding their arms. True, one was aggressive, and the other defensive. But if the aggression was persistent, the defense was determined. In both the North and the South the worst passions of men were appealed to, and in the name of patriotism each was called upon to stand for their homes, their firesides, and their country. South of Mason and Dixon's line were the homes and firesides of the Southerner, and north of it the homes of their former Northern brethren.

True, there was a large element, both North and South, whose patriotism rose above sectional lines and who looked with dark forebodings upon the coming conflict and who were ready to interpose in behalf of peace and good government, and whose love of country reached beyond the sectional strife that was raging. But in the great whirl of passion and prejudice their efforts proved in vain; their voice hushed, and they found themselves powerless to avert the inevitable. The die had been cast; the line drawn; the decree had gone forth, and no mortal hand could stay the tempest or arrest the calamity. And when, at last, the crash came, even the conservative element had nothing to do but to drop into line, according to their feelings or natural interests.

There was no half-way ground to occupy; war knows nothing but decision, and if one could not decide for himself, there was a fate to decide for him. "He that is not for me, is against me," is an inexorable decree of battle, and to that decree men were compelled to bow whether they would or not. Thus, as the mighty avalanche, or the terrible whirlwind, were they swept on.

America was young, and filled with younger sons, sons each of whom felt himself a king. With him to be an American was to be a freeman, and he stood proudly upon his royal rights; to dare to trample upon these inherent privileges was an insult to his honor, to his Americanism. The fires of seventy-six were re-kindled into a blazing, burning flame, as each pictured to himself the long catalogue of grievances. The cannon of 1812 echoed and re-echoed over the plains of South Carolina, while its defiant tones were hurled back from the mountains of New Hampshire, rousing the young blood of the sons of New England. The young men, full of martial fire, pictured the American flag, borne with proud victorious arms, into the very halls of the Montazumas, showing that our arms had been victorious on every battle field; that never had we crossed swords with any foe but that victory followed. They sat down and read of the Spartan band at Thermopolæ; of the Roman guard; of Lexington, and Bunker Hill; of all the valorous deeds of the buried fathers, while the young blood darted with a bound through his veins, and his cheeks glowed with the burning flame of martial fire, and each pictured himself charging the battlements of his foe and wreathing around his brow the laurels of victory. The American Eagle, proud, victorious bird, belonged to each, and each felt called upon to see that that bird soared unfettered the clear, bright sunlight of heaven. Each thought himself the special guardian of freedom, and the protector of American liberty. None stopped to ponder the old adage, "When Greek meets Greek then comes the tug of war."

With such a spirit animating each heart, it was not surprising that, when the bugle sounded to arms, from the prairies of Texas to the cotton and rice fields of South Carolina and the blue-tinged hills of the "Old Dominion," men sprang to arms by the thousands eager for the battle to begin. If the Southerner felt his arm strengthened and nerved for the conflict, the Northern son as confidently rushed to the front at his country's call. The muttering thunders of war rolled out over the vast sweep of country from the Atlantic to the Pacific, and was echoed back from the Gulf to the Lakes. The hour for calm, sober reflection had passed; no time to reason now, but from hill-top to valley echoed the tramp of war, till a nation trembled beneath the tread of armies. As the drunken, frenzied rabble rolls on, moved by they know not what, so the gathering hosts shouted, "To arms! to arms!"

From the time of the election of Abraham Lincoln in November, 1860, until the conflict actually begun, the whole country was thrown into a fever of excitement, and this was increased in intensity with every floating breeze. One startling event followed another in quick succession; reason was dethroned and the great whirlwind of passion and prejudice swept the whole land, kindling the fires of conflict in all the States. On the 20th of December, 1860, the Legislature of South Carolina unanimously declared that that State no longer belonged to the American Union. In January, 1861, Florida withdrew, followed by Mississippi, on the 9th of the same month, Alabama on the 11th, Georgia on the 20th, Louisiana on the 26th, and Texas on February 1st. Thus, in less than three months from the time of the election of Abraham Lincoln to the Presidency, all the cotton States, proper, had, by a unanimous vote withdrawn from the Union, and had taken possession of all the Federal fortifications except those in Charleston harbor.

While the sympathies of the people of Missouri were overwhelmingly with the South, yet her condition, surrounded as she was upon three sides by free States, made her hesitate

before she took a decided stand. She even tried to throw herself into the breach, and, if possible, heal up the differences
and wounds of the past, and thus, avert the terrors of war.
But her effort was not only vain, but futile. The storm had
already gathered; the dark clouds of passion and hatred had
already formed, and each hurled black defiance at the other.
The two volcanoes, one at the South and the other at the
North, whose pent up fires had been hissing and struggling to
break loose from their smothered furies, were now belching
forth fire and flame, and the burning lava rolling on, but
mocked the feeble efforts of the Middle States for peace. Hot
blood was up, and the furies were all turned loose and an inexorable fate led them on. What Missouri could not settle for
herself was soon settled for her and she was compelled, whether
she would or not, to action.

CHAPTER II.

PREPARING FOR THE BATTLE.

On the 11th day of June, 1861, those passing along the road leading from Huntsville, Randolph county, Mo., to Keytesville, Chariton county, would have passed a little frame school house near what is now known as Clifton Hill. On looking in they would have seen a company of intelligent, bright-looking little boys and girls all intent upon their books, apparently little dreaming of the terrible days that were soon to follow. This school was presided over by a young man about twenty-four years of age, full of vigor, manhood and a look of fixed determination. While his voice was pleasant enough to his students, yet there was a tinge of sadness in it that seemed to communicate to the pupil the thought of the trouble within. There was a restless tramp to and fro across the long floor, a troubled sigh, and anon, a step to the door as if expecting some important news. That evening, when ready to dismiss school, he said to the children, "Children, these are strange and troublesome times; we know not what a day may bring forth, that war *will* come there can be no doubt, the only question is; when will it begin?"

The children cast strange glances at each other, and looks of inquiry to the teacher. "War," said they, "war, what is war?" Little did those innocents know that they were soon to learn the full meaning of that terrible word.

The teacher seeing those questioning glances said, "Well may you ask this question. Oh, that I knew you would never learn the terribleness of its meaning. This evening you will have a little taste of its bitterness, for I must tell you that I feel that our school is over."

"Oh! oh!" cried the little voices all over the room, "will you leave us? why leave us?"

"I cannot explain, just now, why, but you will learn before many days and then you will forgive. God bless you, farewell," and Mr. George Tracy (for that was his name) hurried to the door and was gone before his pupils could comprehend the meaning of his words.

When he reached home his mother met him at the door with such a look of love and sadness that, divining something of the cause, he said, "What is it, mother?" She answered, "The war has begun, your father has just come in from town and says that yesterday, June the 10th, camp Jackson, near St. Louis, was surprised and taken; that General Lyon, with a force of Federal troops, is coming up the Missouri River, and that Governor, C. F. Jackson, has fallen back to Boonville, and he has called for 50,000 men to defend their homes and fire-sides. *You*, my son, are a true Southerner; we know you will stand by the Governor, and we have made ready. The forces must reach Boonville quickly, and no time to be lost. You will meet the boys by 9 o'clock to-night at the cross roads; this is the word that has been left for you, and they all know you will be there."

"Yes, mother, they all *know*." "Ah!" she replied, that is the pride of my life, my boy is such a true man that men *know* where he will be found in the hour of need."

A hasty supper, a few parting words, and the clatter of horse's feet is heard down the old lane, where, from childhood, the rider of that noble steed had skipped and played and gambolled in happy days now gone forever. The meadows, the flowers, the trees and the brooks lying in the bright moonlight of that balmy June evening, spoke to that lone rider as never before. Strange thoughts, strange feelings arose and swelled the bosom. "Farewell, farewell," he involuntarily said, "to the scenes of my childhood." It may be that the scene is shut out forever. And he felt, as never before, that there is a hand that shapes our ends and moulds the purpose of our lives.

But it was not the purpose of the lone-rider to go at once to the cross roads. There was yet a word to be spoken and a farewell to be said to another whose life and happiness were wrapped up in his own and whose plighted faith had linked their lives as one. Reining up before a pleasant, cozy farm mansion, now wrapped in the mellow moonlight, and from the windows of which gleamed the light of burning lamps our prospective soldier hurriedly dismounted, and hitching his steed walked hastily to the parlor door.

"She is home," said he to himself, "and expects my coming. But how will the parting be?"

A gentle knock at the door was quickly answered from within; the door swung open and two hands were extended to bid him welcome. "I knew you would come," were the first words of greeting.

"Yes," was the reply, "it could not be otherwise. To go forth into the dark unknown without your blessing, to me, would be impossible."

"Then," said she, anxiously, "You go in answer to the call of the Governor?"

"You know," answered Mr. Tracy, "the grounds I have always occupied upon this question, and what my feelings have always been toward the two sections, the North and the South. *I must act my convictions.* Time and circumstances have proven that there is, and can be, no middle ground to occupy. 'He that is not for me, is against me.' Our State will soon be a field of bloody conflict, and to a man of conviction even neutrality is utterly impossible. The South is my native, my loved land; there all my fathers found a home, and there their bones lie buried. Against them my arm can never, no, never be raised, and as it cannot be against, it must be for them. I know we have pictured a bright, happy and glorious future together, but for the present that has been swept away in a few brief moments. We cannot have that happy home, now, seek it as we might. Amid the clash of arms, the shock of battle, there is, there can be, no happy, peaceful homes, or sunlit hours. How long the dark and gloomy clouds will hang over us, only the God of all battles knows; or, amid its storms, whether you and I will be swept away and forgotten, or, whether we shall live to see the rising of a brighter sun, only He who holds the destinies of peoples and nations in His hands and lifts up and casts down, as He well can tell. And while knowing, that knowledge belongs to His hidden wisdom."

"But," answered Ella Herbert, "do you believe that slavery is right, and is it to defend this that you go to join the fortunes of the South?"

"That," he replied, "is not a question to be answered by me. I am not going to fight for slavery, though if the negro is to remain here he ought to be a slave. I'm a Southerner; this

is my native land, and I go in obedience to its commands.
Every tie of earth binds me to these people. - Their homes,
their firesides, their altars are mine, and their destiny shall be
mine."

"But," returned Miss Herbert, "do you believe in the right
of the States to secede?"

"Whether I do, or do not, has nothing to do with my
action. A country has a right to defend its rights. But the
point with me is this. This is *my* country; these people are
my people, and if they have blundered it is not for me to for-
sake them. If they have done wrong it is not for me to sever
the tie that binds us one. It is theirs to command and mine
to obey. If my people erred the error is theirs, not mine, and
for it they shall answer. I deem it the first duty of a citizen to
obey the calls of his country, and I leave it to Him who does
all things well to decide the issue."

"Right, right," returned Miss Herbert, with a glow of satisfaction upon her face. "Your first duty is to your God, the
second to your country. And now that God only knows when
we shall meet again, if ever, but I trust in Him; in Him I have
an abiding faith, and to Him I intrust all my future. He sees
the end from the beginning and however dark the clouds to
you and me His eye penetrates the gloom, and He sees the
graves of all that will sleep, and thick as the leaden hail may
fall He has marked the course of every ball, and remember that,

> " 'Not a single shaft shall hit,
>   Except the Lord of love sees fit.'

"Yea, He has marked out in his unchanged and unchange-
able mind, the turn of every path, and in his mind is laid the
footprints of your feet on every hill, and He has treasured up
every sigh and measured the depth of every groan. Go, then,
trusting in Him who makes no mistakes, and whose presence
may be seen and felt in the midst of every conflict, and know
that He cares for us.

"I, too, am Southern born, I love her sunny vales, her sunlit hills and her vine-clad homes. And it may be, in the fortunes of war, that I can be of service to that land I love so
well. If such should ever happen, that my help is needed, for
you, for my State; or for the sunny South, it shall not be found

wanting. But remember, George, I have an abiding faith that we shall meet again. Go now, and the blessings of God go with you."

Each looking the stern, stubborn realities of war in the face, felt that it was no time for sentimentalities; each grasped the other's hand in a warm, affectionate farewell; each felt the throbbing of the other's heart, and each with an abiding faith in the Ever-present One, plighted to the other that faithful love that binds us one on earth, and symbolizes the bride and groom as one on the eternal shore. Her last words were, "let me hear if I am wanted."

CHAPTER III.

THE ARMY GATHERING; IN SEIGEL'S CAMP.

For the next few days all was bustle and stir all over the State. The news of the capture of Camp Jackson spread like fire over the broad prairies, and at the call of the governor thousands flew to arms.

The meeting at the cross-roads was a brief one. After a temporary organization, men were detailed to go in different directions and ordered to bring in by the next evening all the fire arms they could collect. By Saturday night, June the 15th, they had gathered a company of sixty-three men, all armed with common rifles or shot guns. Early on Sunday morning they all met at the school-house, where, the Friday before, the young children had been so happy together, and where the school had closed so abruptly, never to open again.

On this June Sunday morning there were assembled young men and maidens, old men and matrons; fathers, mothers; brothers, sisters; lovers and the loved. There were partings to be taken, last words to be spoken, and farewells to be said, that would never again be repeated. Eyes look into eyes that would be closed upon each other till the resurrection morn.

And this was the Sabbath day, God's own hallowed day, to be given to His service. In this hour it was not forgotten that there was a God that held in His own good hand the destiny of men and nations. There were present those whose life had been spent in the service of the great Captain of Salvation, men who had tasted that He was gracious, and could bear testimony to His care over the lives of men. And in that company there were none so steeped in sin but that wished the parting blessings of these gray-haired fathers, and matron mothers, and to hear their intercessory pleadings at the Father's throne for them.

The little school-house was packed with anxious, throbbing hearts, as never before, and men spoke to each other in whispered tones as if feeling they were in the presence of death, or bordering on the other land, where the light of the bright day just flashes across the narrow stream.

At last an old father in Israel, with locks silvered over by the frosts of many winters, and whose eyes had grown dim in the long looking across the shadowy vale, and whose way-worn frame seemed tottering, ready to lie down and take its long rest, arose, and in a trembling voice, began the tune "Old Hundred" to the words,

> "Before Jehovah's awful throne,
>   Ye nations, bow with sacred joy;
>   Know that the Lord is God alone;
>   He can create, and He destroy."

And as the words dropped from his lips his soul seemed to catch the kindling fires of divine's thought and the song rolled out in sweet and awful melody, until it was caught up by every tongue in that assembly. When the last lines were reached:

> "We'll crowd thy gates with thankful songs,
>   High as the heavens our voices raise;
>   And earth, with her ten thousand tongues,
>   Shall fill thy courts with sounding praise."

It seemed the very hearts of all that throng were turned to praise, and the sweet music echoed back from the shining shore. As the last words died away, and while lingering yet upon the lips, the old man lifted up his trembling, feeble hand and said, "let us pray." And as the sweet recollections of the glorious song in its echoes seemed ascending the hill of Zion, the old man prayed. "God of all grace and mercy be with us now," he said. And then he magnified the name of God; the power of God, the wisdom of God, and the goodness and mercy of God. And he prayed Him to comfort the fathers; to bless the mothers; to be with the sons and daughters, and to give victory to the right and blessings to the faithful. Oh, such a prayer, and offered in such a way. Its last echoes died away amid the sighs and tears of all that people, and when the last word of blessing was spoken, it had an answering amen from every heart. The old father's hand dropped feebly by his side, and to many in that company his tongue was still forever; it was to them his last hymn and his last blessing. But who knows how many sad hearts have been cheered, and souls comforted by the remembrance of these last words.

The song being sung, the prayer offered and the blessing sought; the command was given to mount. Quick good-by's were said; little words of love were spoken; precious tokens of affection were given and the soldier was off for the war.

It was the purpose of the Federal Government to over-run and take possession of Missouri as rapidly as possible, and to cut off, as far as could be, recruits to the Confederate army. To this end General Lyon, a very brave and determined officer, with a force of 7,000 men, came up the Missouri River in transports to within five miles of Boonville, and landed on the 20th of June, with his whole force. The force to meet him, of armed men, was about 800. Col. Marmaduke commanded the Confederate forces. A battle ensued, lasting an hour or more, but the Confederate forces fell back in the direction of Lexington with but little loss.

General Sterling Price, the commander-in-chief of the Confederate forces, by appointment of the Governor, Claiborne F Jackson had been taken severely ill; and on the 19th, had been placed on a boat and sent up the river to Lexington, one of the points at which he had ordered a part of the forces to congregate.

The bold move of the Federal forces into the very heart of Missouri had its disastrous effect upon the gathering hosts that were pouring from all quarters into Boonville. Missouri had hoped and struggled for peace until the fall of Camp Jackson. Here it was clearly developed that the Federal government had determined her subjection to the Federal authorities, and that all hope of an honorable and peaceful adjustment of difficulties was out of the question. It was only left for Missourians to decide which side they would take. The time from the fall of Camp Jackson to the bold attack upon Boonville had been so short that there could be no concert of action. The forces gathering upon the north side of the river with the intention of crossing at that place, had been delayed, by word being sent to them to gather all the guns and ammunition possible, so as to arm all the forces. So that they were not ready to cross the river till

Your friend
J M Allen

the morning the battle begun. Besides the eight hundred armed men already at Boonville, there were three or four thousand without arms. The force that had been collected at Franklin some six or eight miles from the river, in Howard county, numbered on the morning of the 20th, about three thousand. These were without a leader, or, every man was a General, and every General had his orderly. To cross the river after the battle began was impossible for lack of transports. Under these circumstances the forces scattered so soon as the result of the battle became known; some returned home and some moved up and crossed the river at Glasgow, and took up the line of march in the direction of Lexington.

In this general break up, our school teacher, George Tracy, and five others determined to strike directly for Arkansas, their main purpose being to see what preparation the South was making for the defense of Missouri. Missourians felt that it was a great mistake upon the part of the South that they did not move at once to the help of General Price. For had such decisive action been taken, it would have been worth 50,000 men to the Southern army. This inactivity upon the part of the South had left the impression that she cared but little as to whether Missouri was identified with her or not. It was to determine this that induced these six men to make this long journey. Crossing the Missouri River at Glasgow, the evening of the 21st, found them in Marshall, Saline county, where most of the forces were gathering preparatory to moving to Lexington. But our six men pushed ahead to Arkansas. At Carthage, Mo., they fell in with General Price, who, with a small force, was making directly for the southwest part of the State. Here he stopped for a day or two collecting what force he could. Leaving General Price, on the evening of the 27th of June, the 28th found them in the State of Arkansas. They found General McCulloch at Camp Walker with a force of about 3,000 Confederate troops. Receiving from him an assurance of co-operation with the forces of Missouri, they determined to return and join the forces under Governor Jackson, who, before this, had left Lexington with a force of about 5,000, and was falling back to join General Price. In the meantime, General Price had left Carthage and had fallen back to "Cow Skin Prairie," in Newton county.

General Lyon had rapidly followed up his success at Boonville, and seemed determined to prevent the Confederate forces from collecting. To this end he dispatched General Seigel with a force of 3,000 infantry and about six hundred cavalry from St. Louis to Neosho, Mo., while he, with his force of 7,000, set out from Boonville in close pursuit of Governor Jackson and his little army. Besides this, General Sturgis was moving down from Kansas with a force of 3,000. The design was to attack the Governor's forces from three different directions and thus capture the little army.

General Seigel, with his whole force, had succeeded in reaching Neosho in a day or two after General Price with his small force had passed through. Our six men were not aware of all these military movements, and were, therefore, subject to surprise. They knew their old acquaintances were with Gov. Jackson, and leaving the camp of Gen. McCulloch, they started directly back in the direction they had gone, expecting to meet the Governor's forces. When they were within five miles of Neosho, they were told that General Seigel's forces were in the place, but they could not see that such a thing could be possible. Yet, they deemed it necessary to use a little caution. They divided off into pairs, two and two. It fell to George Tracy and his companion to bring up the rear. But who can imagine their surprise when, on making a sharp turn at the foot of the hill, into the valley road running into town, they found themselves inside the line of Federal pickets. Tracy argued, as they went on into town, that the town was guarded and it would be useless to attempt to escape at that time of day. But they determined to go on, traveling the main street till they were halted. After passing the Public Square, they were halted by a guard and informed that they must apply to General Seigel for a pass. This, they at once resolved to do. Tracy went into General Seigel's headquarters, while his companion took care of the horses. Before going to General Seigel, they had fallen in with a man who loved to be of importance, and who, after questioning them for a short time, agreed to vouch for their loyalty. General Seigel was a very gruff looking officer at best, and he spoke, indeed, as one having authority. He was busy writing some military order, but notwithstanding, the accommodating gentleman who had agreed to vouch for Tracy and his companion, informed him that "this gentleman," pointing to Tracy, which the General did not see as he did not raise his eyes from his paper, "and his partner have been traveling South, and owing to difficulties, are now returning home to North Missouri. I have talked with them and think they are all right. I recommend, therefore, that you give them a pass." The General wrote on, as though he had not heard a word for some moments, and then suddenly raising his head and fixing his savage and piercing eyes upon Tracy, said, in his severest and most commanding tone, "Where have you been, sir?" The question almost stunned and staggered him. He was not prepared for it; and yet he knew it must be answered at once. This all flashed over him in an instant. In that instant he decided his course, in what he would say, and at once recovering from the confusion into which he came near being thrown, he answered with decision: "We have been to Arkansas, sir."

"What was your business there?" was the next question.

"We," said Tracy, "had been teaching school, and being thrown out of employment by the difficulties, were looking at the country."

To this the General replied very sarcastically, "*Yes*"; as much as if he said, I'll believe all of that I want. But if the answer to this question was to be received with doubt, the answer to the next removed the idea of equivocation.

"Have you been to General McCulloch's camp?"

"Yes, sir," was the astonishing reply.

"How many men has he?"

"Three thousand."

By the quick answer to these questions, and the appearance of no evasion, Tracy was glad to note that the General's tone was moderating and to see that the fierce look was giving place to kindness and friendship.

The next question was, "Did you see, or do you know anything of General Price?"

The reply was, that Tracy "had heard that General Price had gone down on Cow-skin Prairie."

After some further conversation, the General agreed to give the two men a pass at six o'clock, as he stated that he was giving no one a pass before that hour.

In the meantime, their other four companions had not been so fortunate. Finding themselves in the enemy's camp, they had undertaken to make their escape, and had been captured. Soon after Tracy and his partner had left the headquarters of Gen. Seigel, they saw their companions brought in under guard. They thought best not to recognize them, as it would only get them all into the same difficulty, and more, Tracy thought they might get some one to intercede for them.

Six o'clock being so very late, Tracy determined to stay in town over night. Having an old acquaintance in the place, he made arrangements with him for a place for the horses and a bed.

Having disposed of all their side arms, papers and so forth, in safe keeping till morning, they made themselves as pleasant as they could, until after all the people living in the country had been given a pass; then they applied for theirs. The General asked if they would take an oath to support the constitution of the United States. "O, yes," they replied, "that is all we ask of anyone, and were we at home, such questions would not be asked us."

The General seemed to forget that there were different constructions put upon that important instrument; and that the South believed that a proper construction of it would secure to them all they were contending for. He had forgotten that the South held that the North were the people that were violating that sacred compact. He seemed to take it for granted that the sympathies of these two men were with the Federal government, and that they were ready to join the Northern forces so soon as they reached home. Without further questioning, he gave them a pass, and next morning, finding they had not gone, rode with them through the camp, showing them his strength, and boasting that he would take dinner with the "Rebel Governor," Jackson, the Fourth of July; that he had cut off his retreat and that General Lyon was coming up in his rear and that escape was impossible. Thus Tracy and his companion came into full possession of the strength and condition of the enemy and their intentions. They also received instructions as to how to avoid Jackson's forces, and how to reach General Lyon. But after passing Gen. Seigel's pickets and being assured by the General himself that they would meet with no further opposition, they made a bee line for Jackson's camp.

It was the 31st day of June when Tracy and his partner left General Seigel's camp. The next morning their four friends, who had been taken prisoners, not coming up, Tracy's partner returned to see what he could do for them while Tracy pushed on to Jackson's camp. He reached the Governor's forces that evening and brought to him the first authentic information of the force that was in front of him. Here Tracy attached himself to Captain Elgin's company of volunteers, and from that day on became a fixed part of the army.

On the morning of the 5th of July, the Governor's forces took up the line of march in the direction of Neosho. It seems that upon the same day, General Seigel moved out with his force in the direction of Jackson's camp. That night General Seigel camped at Carthage, while the Governor's forces camped within ten miles of that place. The next morning, July 6th, both armies took up the line of march, advancing to meet each other. By 9 o'clock the two armies were in full view of each other upon the open prairie. General Seigel's forces had crossed a little creek called "Bear Creek," and formed in line of battle. The Governor's forces were commanded by Generals J. B. Clark, Parsons and Slack, the whole being under command of the Governor himself. He formed his men on the brow of the ridge about six hundred yards in front of the enemies' lines.

The Governor's force, infantry and cavalry, amounted to about 5,000, but not more than half of these were armed, and these armed only with small rifles and shot-guns. The battle opened with an artillery duel, which lasted for some minutes, when General Seigel's force fell back across Bear Creek and formed along a skirt of timber running along its banks, while his batteries occupied the bluffs beyond. The whole Confederate line was then ordered forward. When they came in range of the enemies' guns upon the bluffs, he opened upon them with grape and canister. The Confederate forces were then ordered to charge at double-quick, and dashing into the skirt of timber occupied by Seigel's infantry, they were soon hotly engaged with small arms. But nothing daunted, the Confederates pushed forward, crossed the stream and drove the Federal forces flying before them. A running fight was kept up to Carthage where General Seigel attempted to make a stand in order to collect his demoralized forces. But here he was again charged by the victorious Confederates, and driven flying in the direction of Rolla. The pursuit was kept up till night fall, when the Confederate forces were called back and went into camp at Carthage, on the very ground on which General Seigel had camped the night before.

The loss of the Missourians was about fifty killed, and one hundred and fifty wounded. The loss of the enemy was estimated to be two hundred killed and three hundred and fifty wounded. The Missourians captured a large number of muskets, which were greatly needed.

CHAPTER IV.

BATTLE OF WILSON'S CREEK AND LEXINGTON.

On the day following the battle at Bear Creek and Carthage, General Price, having formed a junction with General McCulloch, came into camp. General Seigel had left a garrison of one hundred men at Neosho; these Generals McCulloch's and Price's forces captured.

The next day the Confederate forces took up the line of march for Cow-skin Prairie, where they went into camp for several days, drilling, and perfecting their organization. Price's army continued to receive recruits till the 26th of July, when his force numbered about 10,000, still poorly armed.

After the defeat of General Seigel at Carthage, General Lyon turned his course in the direction of Springfield, Mo., where he was joined by Generals Seigel and Sturgis, their combined force numbering about 11,000 men, well armed and equipped for war.

Generals McCulloch and Price now determined to unite their forces and take the offensive. On the 26th, the Missouri troops, under General Price, took up the line of march for Cassville, where they were to form a junction with the Confederate forces under McCulloch and Pearce. On reaching Cassville, General McCulloch was placed in command of the army. The army was divided into three columns; the first under General McCulloch, the second under General Pearce, and the third under General Price. In this order it moved in the direction of Springfield, and on the night of August the 9th, camped at Wilson's Creek, and within ten miles of Springfield. It was the intention to take up the line of march at 12 o'clock that night, and to attack General Lyon early next morning, and if possible, surprise him in his camp. To this end the pickets of

23

General McCulloch's army were called in, but, owing to the threatened rain and to the fact that the troops had no way of protecting their ammunition, it was determined not to move till day-light; but unfortunately the pickets were not again sent out.

If the Confederate forces were expecting to find the Federal General Lyon sleeping, they were greatly mistaken. He was not only not sleeping, but was wide awake to the condition of the Confederate army. They were camped in the low ground on either side of Wilson's Creek, and could he attack them in their camp, it gave him the heights above them, both in front and rear, thus securing a great advantage. While it had been determined by the Confederates to surprise General Lyon at Springfield, it was also the determination of General Lyon to surprise General McCulloch at Wilson's Creek. The difference was that General Lyon put his plans into execution, while General McCulloch did not.

General Lyon moved out of Springfield at 12 o'clock at night, sending General Seigel with nearly half his force to the right flank and rear of the Confederate army, while he, with the remainder of the force moved up to attack them in front. General McCulloch having called in his pickets, General Lyon's army gained its position without molestation, and awaited the dawn to begin the battle.

Little did the Confederate forces dream of the terrible beginning of the next day, the memorable 10th of August. But just at the day dawn, and just as the men had begun to arouse from their peaceful slumbers, and were beginning to stir around a little, they were startled by the crack of cannon upon the hills just across the creek, and the shells came shrieking and plunging through the camp. For a time the Confederate forces were thrown into the most terrible confusion. There were cannons in front of them, cannon to the right of them and cannon to the rear of them, pouring a terrible fire into the confused mass. But after the first shock had subsided, and the men took in the fact that a great battle had begun, and that it was now or never, for home and country, they began rapidly to form into line to meet the now advancing column of infantry. General Pearce was commanded to attack the force under Seigel, who had gained the rear. This he did with such spirit and gallantry as completely drove General Seigel from the field, capturing all his artillery and a great many of his command.

But the main attack was made upon that part of the Confederate line occupied by the Missourians under Generals Slack, Clark, Parsons and Rains, the whole force commanded by General Price.

. Generals Lyon and Price had held a conference before the taking of Camp Jackson, the purpose of which, upon the part of General Price, was to secure, if possible, for Missouri an armed neutrality. General Lyon refused to entertain such a proposition, and the two men parted in no friendly mood, each declaring vengeance against the other. And it seems the fortune of battle had placed these two men face to face in mortal combat. To each of them death was preferable to defeat. Each was in the front of the fight cheering their men, and while the other part of the Confederate forces were routing and driving from the field the flanking parties on the right and rear, the battle in front raged with varying changes. General Price, bareheaded, dashed from point to point, cheering his men and urging them on to the contest; while General Lyon, equally determined, was seen leading charge after charge. The two contending armies with a determination seldom witnessed on the field of battle, surged back and forth over the same ground; sometimes one stubbornly giving way and sometimes the other. Col. James A. Pritchard, who was in the thickest of the fight and witnessed it all, says: "Here the fortunes of battle ebbed and flowed for hours. We had the same ground we formed on in the morning in our possession seven times during the day." General Lyon determined to fight to the last, and General Price with equal determination stood his ground.

General Lyon collected all the scattered force of General Seigel and concentrated it upon the force of General Price in front and prepared for the last desperate charge. As rapidly did General McCulloch throw all his available force to General Price.

General Lyon, placing himself at the head of his men, said: "I will lead you." General Price, with his gray locks floating out to the breeze, stood in the fore-front to receive the desperate onset. The Federals came on gallantly, and the battle became general and raged furiously. General Lyon had already been wounded, and just before this last desperate charge had expressed a fear that the day was lost. He now seems in mere desperation to be leading "a forlorn hope." In the midst of this last terrible charge, he is shot from his horse right in the fore-front of the battle. His fall decides the day. The Federal forces, learning that their General was killed, gave way all along the line until they broke into a general rout and fled in the direction of Springfield.

The battle that began before sun up had raged around "Bloody Hill" till 2 o'clock in the evening. The Confederates camped upon the battle ground and only pursued the Federals with the cavalry.

The body of General Lyon fell into the hands of the Confederates, but was treated with the respect it deserved. It was delivered into the hands of friends and finally sent to St. Louis, where it was buried with military honors.

The loss of General Lyon was a great blow to the Federal forces in Missouri; for to his activity and courage more than any other one man they owed the subjugation and humiliation of the State.

Men are strange beings; they claim to be ready to sacrifice all upon their country's altar, and yet when the fate of that country is trembling in the balance, and its success depends upon the united action of its defenders, these same men will sacrifice it all for a little personal glory. For some reason that will probably forever remain unwritten, General McCulloch refused to co-operate with General Price in an advance into Missouri, and this too in the face of an order from the Confederate General Polk, commander of the western department, directing such an advance.

Immediately after this decisive victory, General McCulloch fell back with his force to Arkansas, while General Price took up the line of march for Lexington, Mo. The victories of Carthage and Wilson's Creek had enabled General Price to arm most of his men, and had added to his command several pieces of artillery and ammunition.

General Seigel fell back with all the Federal force to St. Louis. Late in August, General Price set out with about 10,000 men and seven pieces of artillery for the Missouri River, designing to strike it at or near Lexington. On the 7th of October he met General Lane, about fifteen miles from Fort Scott on a creek called Drywood, where, after a brief engagement, he defeated the Federal force, and with a small detachment drove it beyond Fort Scott, capturing that place.

He thus moved rapidly with his whole force towards Lexington, where General Mulligan was stationed, and strongly fortified with a Federal force of 3,500 men, five pieces of artillery and two mortars. By the first of September General Price's forces had reached the neighborhood of Lexington, where they were reinforced by about 3,000 men under Generals Harris and Martin E. Green. General Price's army now recruited rapidly, so that within a few days he found himself at the head of about 15,000 men, part of whom were well armed. The Federal force was soon surrounded and a siege began. But the siege was shortly brought to an end by the strategy of using of hemp bales. These were dipped into the water to prevent their taking fire and then rolled in front of the men as a moving breast work in the advance upon the enemy's works. General Mulligan, seeing that it was impossible to hold his position against the force collecting against him, ordered the white flag to be raised, and, on the 20th of September, surrendered his whole force to General Price. This gave General Price about 6,000 muskets and five pieces of artillery. With these new arms added to those already armed, he had an effective force of 15,000, with twelve pieces of artillery. Learning that General Fremont had collected a force of about 30,000, and was moving up the river by way of Sedalia to attack him in the rear and cut off his retreat, General Price determined to again fall back in the direction of Springfield. General Price's force, all told, was now about 20,000. Managing to deceive General Fremont as to his real intention, he passed by him, and having put all enemies in his rear, marched leisurely on till he was again at Neosho.

Here the Legislature had been called together and passed the ordinance of secession, and elected delegates to the provisional government at Richmond, among whom were General John B. Clark, Col. E. W. Price and General Harris.

General Fremont, in the meantime, had moved to Springfield at the head of about 40,000 men, well armed and finely equipped. General Price took up his position at Pineville, to await the advance of General Fremont. At this juncture an order from Washington relieved General Fremont of his command, and the Federal army was withdrawn from Southern Missouri, followed closely by General Price to Osceola, where he remained in camp for over a month.

CHAPTER V.

ORGANIZATION OF THE CONFEDERATE BRIGADE.—RETREAT FROM SPRINGFIELD.

Up to this time the whole force of General Price's army was known as the "Missouri State Guards." General Price seeing the need of perfecting an organization upon a firmer and better basis, began the organization of Confederate troops. A special camp was laid out for Confederate recruits, and the organization of companies, battalions, regiments and brigades began.

The first battery organized was that of artillery, with William Wade as captain. On the 30th of December the First Missouri Cavalry organized; electing Elijah Gates, colonel. On the 11th of January the first regiment of infantry was organized, with John Q. Burbridge, colonel. But soon after the organization of this regiment it was learned that John S. Bowen had organized a regiment at Memphis which was justly entitled to the first place, therefore, Burbridge's regiment was called the second. On the same day of the organization of the second regiment, the third was also organized, with B. A. Rives, colonel. The second battery commanded by Captain S. Churchill Clark, was added, and these forces formed, for a time, the First Brigade of Missouri Confederate troops. They were placed under the command of Brigadier-General Henry Little.

During the stay of General Price at Osceola, or his camp on Sac River, near that place, his force was greatly depleted, by he expiration of the time for which many of his men had enlisted. While he was actively engaged, his men were in good spirits and his force was continually augmented. But the rigors of the winter had compelled him to retire into winter quarters.

General Price had promised his men to winter upon the Missouri River. But in this he had expected the Confederate force collecting in Arkansas to co-operate with him. And with such co-operation this might have been done. The action of the Southern forces under General McCulloch, retiring to the Boston mountains and remaining inactive from the time of the battle of Wilson's Creek, August the 10th, while General Price with his little army of gallant Missourians, were standing guard, will ever remain a mystery. But this indifference of the South to the interest of Missouri, greatly dispirited the men, and, as their time of service expired, many returned to their homes.

General Price saw, with forebodings, the necessity of a retrograde movement. Generals Curtis and Seigel, with a force of about 30,000, had moved out from St. Louis and was threatening his position on Sac River; and had General McCulloch moved up to his support, he would have been able to have met this force and to have hurled it back to the Missouri River, under cover of its gun boats; but, as it was, he was powerless to meet it. In this extremity he determined to fall back to Springfield. On the 19th of December, the army, now numbering over twelve thousand all told, evacuated their camp at Osceola, and, on the 23rd, went into quarters at Springfield. Here the army remained in camp till the first of February, General Price still vainly hoping to be supported by the Southern army before being compelled to leave the State. With this hope, he held his position at Springfield till the very last moment. By the first of February it was known by General Price that General Curtis was moving from Rolla, with a strong force, while another was moving, under Lane, from Fort Scott, Kansas, to attack him in his position. On the 10th the pickets reported the force of General Curtis to be within seven miles, and orders were at once issued to prepare to move. This order was given at 3 o'clock in the evening and by 5 o'clock the army was falling back. That night the Confederate army camped on the old battle ground at Wilson's Creek, while the enemy entered Springfield. The weather had turned very cold, and there was much suffering among the poorly clad and poorly shod soldiery. The Confederate forces, consisting of two regiments of infantry, one of cavalry and two batteries, were given

the post of honor. They covered the rear of the rapidly retreating army.

There was an immense army train of every kind and condition, and this greatly retarded the movements of the army.
On the evening of the 12th, they had just gone into camp, on
Crane Creek, and began to prepare for supper and a night's
rest, when the booming of cannon in the rear told them that
the enemy was upon them in force. Snatching a half prepared
supper the men fell into line, and the retreat was renewed.

It was now developed that while General Curtis attacked
the Confederate forces in front, General Lane, with his force,
was to move to Cassville and cut off Price's retreat to Arkansas.
General Lane had the inside track, as it were, being nearest to
Cassville, and now began a race for that point. General Curtis
was pressing on, hoping to check Price's march; while General
Price was hurrying everything forward as rapidly as possible.
Colonel Gates with his cavalry veterans, supported by Confederate infantry, and batteries formed a line of battle in front of
the enemy, holding him in check till Price's whole force was
full on the road and moving rapidly south.

About 9 o'clock at night the rear guard of Confederate
forces were drawn off and began falling back, Gates' cavalry
keeping guard. And now began a scene of hardships and suffering, which can be known only by those who endured it.
The night was intensely cold, the men poorly clad, footsore
and supperless. They were compelled to build up fires by the
roadside to keep warm; the rear guard having frequently to
stop for the wagon train to get out of the way. All night they
marched on. The next morning the enemy was pressing closely and no time was given for breakfast. Captains Wade and
Clark, with their batteries, divided honors; one being in the
rear one day and the other the next. The little brigade stood
like a stone wall, hurling back every effort of the enemy to
break through their ranks. Col. Gates, with his regiment of
cavalry contested every inch of ground, and again and again
did the two regiments of infantry double-quick back and form
line for his support. Just as the rear of General Price's army
was entering Cassville, about 3 o'clock on the evening of the
13th, the enemy made a desperate effort to break through the

rear guard and scatter it. But they were met with such spirit and determination as threw them back in confusion.

This was, indeed, a close race for the salvation of General Price's army. For while he was passing through Cassville, General Lane was only seven miles away where he had stopped his force for a hasty meal. But by the time the rear guard was well on its way out of town, the columns of Curtis and Lane were entering it. Thus, General Price had narrowly escaped the trap set for him and now had the whole Federal force in his rear.

After night-fall, the rear guard was given supper, and then again took up the line of March till about 4 o'clock in the morning, when they were given an hour's sleep. They had now been marching and fighting for two days and nights with no sleep and a very little to eat. Under these circumstances, the hour's sleep that morning was very sweet. But they were awakened at sun-up with orders to fall into line and prepare for action; the enemy was upon them in force, and during this day made the most determined efforts to break through the rear guard. There were no less than three separate engagements, in all of which the enemy was repulsed with loss, especially in the last one. Their cavalry charged Col. Gates' regiment with such determination, that their front became mixed up with his rear and dashed past the Confederate battery and line of infantry. But so soon as the Confederate cavalry were out of the way, the infantry and battery opened fire, and the Federals were driven back with considerable loss in killed, as well as about twenty five taken prisoners.

The army camped that night upon Big Sugar Creek, in the State of Arkansas. The rear guard of Confederates came into camp about nine o'clock, and after a good meal, the first for four days, they had a good sleep. Next morning, the 15th, the rear had hardly reached the bluffs on the other side of the creek before the enemy appeared on the opposite bank. The Brigade immediately formed in line for his reception, but he cautiously drew back and the Confederates pulled off and moved on. But they had not gone more than a mile before the rattle of small arms called the infantry back on double-quick. The enemy had charged Gates' cavalry in great force and drove it back with some confusion. Clark's battery was brought

Miss Belle Morris.

down the road on double-quick, and Burbridge's regiment took position on the right, and Rives' on the left. The Federals opened upon the Confederate line with artillery, and for a time it seemed that the Confederate forces would be forced to fight. The artillery of the Confederate force did not reply to the enemy's guns for some time, but at a given signal Clark opened with his six guns with such a well-directed fire as to dismount two of the enemies' guns and blow up their caissons.

After this brisk engagement of the morning the enemy followed the retreating army no further, and that evening they reached Cross Hollows. At this point they met General McCulloch, and the next day, the 16th, being Sunday, the army rested. On the morning of the 17th, the army was again put in motion, falling back through Fayetteville and to Cove Creek at the foot of the Boston Mountains, which place was reached on the evening of the 22nd.

CHAPTER VI.

BATTLE OF PEARIDGE, OR ELKHORN.

In January, 1862, General Earl VanDorn was appointed Commander of the Trans-Mississippi Department, then a part of the great territorial department of General Albert Sidney Johnston. He reached the headquarters of General Price on the 2nd of March, and, after a consultation with him and General McCulloch, it was determined to move at once and attack the Federal army, under Curtis, on Sugar Creek. The Confederate force all told amounted to about 17,000.

On the morning of the 4th of March, in obedience to the command of General VanDorn, the army broke up camp and took up the line of march in the direction of the enemy, leaving all the baggage behind; the soldiers being provided with five days' rations. It was with joy that the Missouri troops hailed the coming of Gen. VanDorn and the order to move in the direction of their own loved State. There being no incumbrance of baggage trains, the army moved off rapidly and after a march of twenty-two miles, passing through Fayetteville, they went into camp. The next day they reached Elm Springs and on the next morning, the 6th of March, came in sight of the enemy, under Gen. Seigel, retreating rapidly through Bentonville. General McIntosh, commanding the mounted men, charged Seigel's retreating infantry, but was repulsed. Shortly after this the cavalry of the First Brigade charged the Federal line killing fifty of Seigel's men and taking twenty-five prisoners and a wagon loaded with minnie rifles, together with six mules and the driver.

The Confederate army was now divided into two parts. Generals McCulloch and McIntosh were sent to attack the enemy in front, while General Price, with his Missourians, accompanied by General VanDorn, went to the rear. General Martin E. Green guarded the wagon train.

To say the least of it, this division of the forces proved disastrous to the Confederates. Never before in all the history of war was it ever known that the commanding General went with a flanking party to the rear. Gen. Price and his men had covered themselves all over with glory, in the last year's campaign, so that the name of his veterans was known from the North to the South. General McCulloch was overheard to tell Gen. VanDorn that if General Price, with his force was sent to the rear, he, Gen. Price, would get the glory of the victory. This explains the whole of Gen. McCulloch's indifference, and his wish for the defeat of Gen. Price. To obviate all of this, General VanDorn himself went with the flanking party to the rear. Thus the fruits of a great victory were destroyed by the jealousy of one man.*

---

* I append the following from Dr. J. M. Allen, who, at the time was principal surgeon in the brigade, and in that part of the army commanded by Gen. Price. Dr. Allen held such a position that he had the opportunity of knowing whereof he speaks, and his statement is so well authenticated, that it need scarcely be called in question.

He says that he occupied such a position on the battlefield at Wilson's Creek, that he could observe any important movement of the Confederate army, and that during the battle he frequently saw Gen. McCulloch; that his generalship was the most magnificent and grand that he ever witnessed; that the handling of his troop in the routing of Curtis and the destruction of Gen. Seigel's division was most superb, and to that generalship the Confederates owe the victory. He further states, and on good authority, that it was no fault of Gen. McCulloch that the pickets were not replaced after being withdrawn for the advance; that Gen. Price was in the advance and Gen. Rains commanded the pickets.

In the history of this affair we have given what has been the generally accepted view of this battle, but we deem it but just to Gen. McCulloch to correct any mistake that may have been made, either in the mind of the men or the written histories.

So far as the battle of Pearidge or Elkhorn is concerned, the doctor says, that in the counsel of war held before and also after the arrival of Gen. VanDorn that Gen. McCulloch opposed an attack upon the Federal force, and that too for the very best of reasons. The army was very poorly disciplined; that he had but three regiments upon which he could depend, these were the third Louisiana, and Arkansas, and a Texas regiment. Gen. Price had no disciplined troop except the Confederates under him, which consisted of but two regiments of infantry, two or three battalions, and one regiment of cavalry. He took the ground that should any accident happen in that imperfectly organized state of the army defeat must follow. That very accident happened in the death of McCulloch himself, and his second in command, and the very thing took place which he had predicted would occur under such circumstances.

McCulloch's plan was for Price and VanDorn to remain wher

By 9 o'clock on the morning of the 7th of March, Gen. Price's men were pouring into the road running from Fayetteville to Springfield, known as the "old telegraph road," while the cannon of General McCulloch told that the battle had opened hotly in front. The attack in the rear was a complete surprise to General Curtis, as many of his foraging wagons were captured. But he soon sent a force back to meet Price's advance. The Missouri State Guard, under Gen. Parsons, occupied the left; the First Missouri Brigade, under Gen. Little, the centre; while Gen. Slack, with some battalions of Missouri Confederate troops, occupied the right. (Slack's was called the Second Brigade).

The battle was opened with spirit, both in front and rear. The army of Gen. Curtis was in a critical condition; every avenue of retreat was cut off, and with him it was either conquer or surrender. The First Brigade was formed, reaching across the road running up a ridge to Elkhorn Tavern, with Clark's battery occupying the road. Scarcely had these two regiments, Rives' and Burbridge's, taken their position when a Federal Brigade was seen moving down upon them. But to deceive the Confederates, the Federals shouted to them not to fire, they were friends, and to deceive them more, Col. Gates' cavalry regiment had just dashed up the road and the Confederates knew not what had become of them. But they, seeing the enemy advance in such force, deployed right and left and formed on each side of the two infantry regiments. Orders were given to the men not to fire, but seeing the enemy would, they lay down and the fire passed over their head. Col. Rives, still believing them Confederates, ordered the regiment flag to

---

they were and to thoroughly organize and equip the infantry and to collect together all the available force possible, while he, with a cavalry force, swung around Curtis' army and striking his rear would capture Springfield and Rolla and press on to the Missouri River, thus destroying the supplies of the Federal army and forcing him to retreat. The sequel shows, as well as the after movements of the Confederate cavalry, that McCulloch's plans were really the right ones, and that in their conception he was in advance of VanDorn, Forest, Steward and other cavalry officers. The condition of the Confederate army was just such as Gen. McCulloch described it to be, and so well authenticated are the statements made above, that we deem it but just to a brave man who proved his devotion to his country by giving his life to its cause, that we would be faithless to the trust reposed in us as a historian did we not give them.

be raised, but no sooner was it up, than it was riddled with bullets. Col. Rives then ordered a charge, and a roll of small arms echoed out over the hills. In five minutes' time the Federal force was driven back. Gen. VanDorn then ordered Gen. Little to hold the position at all hazards. Soon after this Col. Burbridge was attacked upon the right of Rives, and a continued roll of musketry was kept up for nearly an hour. General Burbridge's regiment was suffering considerably and was contending against heavy odds. In this extremity Col. Rives was ordered to advance to his help; the Federal force was soon driven back and took shelter behind a fence near the Elkhorn Tavern. Clark's battery moved up and taking position, opened upon the enemy. This was replied to with spirit by the Federals, and an artillery duel was kept up for an hour or more.

During all the morning the news from the front was of the most cheering nature; couriers reported the Federals giving way all along the line and the prospect of a glorious victory. Generals VanDorn and Price had been steadily advancing all the morning, and no doubt was entertained, but they were able to hold their position against all odds. Hearing such glorious news from the front, they had determined to advance the whole line and complete the victory. Just as General Van-Dorn was in the act of ordering this advance a courier dashed up to inform him that Gens. McCulloch and McIntosh were both killed and for lack of a commander operations had ceased in front. At this news and unexpected turn in the tide of battle General VanDorn turned pale. But, nevertheless, he ordered the line forward. The State Guard, under General Parsons, began the advance, which was soon taken up all along the line. The Confederates sprang forward with a yell and an impetuosity that drove the enemy flying before it. In less than fifteen minutes from the time the charge began, the Confederates had possession of Elkhorn Tavern, with an abundance of commissary stores, also seven pieces of artillery. Nor did the charge stop till the enemy were driven far beyond the Tavern, and night coming on put an end to the battle.

But to counteract this glorious victory upon the part of Gen. Price's forces, the death of Generals McCulloch, McIntosh and Hebert had placed that part of the army out of the fight.

From the lack of thorough organization there was no one to take command and that part of the army, though by no means defeated, had no commander, and all operations from that direction stopped. The ammunition train, by some frightened officer, had been ordered to Bentonville, and the commissary department followed suit. During the night a part of McCulloch's forces came around and joined the forces of VanDorn. Could Gen. VanDorn have supplied his men and artillery with ammunition, he could still have maintained his position, but to his utter dismay, the next morning, the ammunition train could not be found, and most of his artillery was left without ammunition, as was also his infantry. General Curtis, being no longer pressed in front, had concentrated his whole force upon the Confederates in his rear. Under these circumstances it was impossible to maintain the battle. Leaving the First Brigade under Gen. Little and the Second under General Slack to hold the enemy in check and cover his movements Gen. VanDorn put his force upon the Huntsville road and began swinging around the enemy's right. These two brigades met the whole force of General Curtis and held it in check till VanDorn's force was well upon the road, and then, after pulling back slowly for a mile, drew off in perfect order. Their daring and bravery commanded the admiration of the enemy. This was shown by their giving them three cheers as they moved off in such splendid order.

Captain Wade's battery had been drawn back so far in falling back before the enemy that it was impossible for him to cross the hills to the Huntsville road, and taking two of the captured guns and gathering together the scattered forces in the rear, he fell back into Missouri by the way of Keytesville, and then around by Huntsville, and finally succeeded in joining VanDorn's army. General Price had thus swept completely around the Federal army; had beaten them at every point, and carried off seven pieces of artillery. The enemy did not follow the retreating army. Indeed, the Missouri troops did not know they were retreating till they were well on the way. They thought they were only changing position to renew the fight.

CHAPTER VII.

ACROSS THE MISSISSIPPI.

It was now determined by the Confederate authorities to withdraw the whole force, under Gen. VanDorn, from the Trans-Mississippi department, and transfer them to the army under Gen. P. G. T. Beauregard, at Corinth, Miss., where he was assembling a magnificent army. General Albert Sidney Johnston had left Murfreesboro and joined his force with that of Beauregard, and had taken command of the army. Also two divisions of the army, under Gen. Polk, had been sent from Columbus to this point, with also several regiments from Louisiana and a force from Mobile.

"General Grant occupied a position at Pittsburg Landing, awaiting the arrival of Gen. Buell, who was rapidly hastening from Nashville to join him." (Civil war, page 83). It was the purpose for General VanDorn's force to arrive before the great battle of Shiloh was fought. But General Johnston having collected a considerable force and seeing the rapid concentration of the force of the enemy, deemed it best to strike the army under Gen. Grant before Buell's force could arrive. The sequel shows that he waited one day too long, or that the delay of one day lost to the Confederates the fruits of a great victory.

The order to cross the Mississippi and unite with Johnston's army was a trying ordeal to the Missouri troops. This little army had presented a spectacle of courage and endurance without a parallel in the history of warfare. They were surrounded upon three sides by hostile States; Illinois on the east, Iowa on the north, and Kansas on the west, with a great river running through the center of their State. Besides this, the enemy had all the appliances of modern warfare, money, men and arms at their command, and possession of all the boats on the river. And while Missouri was honestly and earnestly pleading for peace and an honorable adjustment of the difficulties, this enemy suddenly, and without notice, threw its army into her very midst.

Missouri was without arms, ammunition, or any of the appliances of war, and unsupported by a single State. Being so suddenly plunged into war, the men came together as best they could. They made their way through the enemy's lines singly, in pairs and squads, without arms, without discipline, in a word without anything but an indomitable will, and an unconquerable devotion to what they conceived to be the eternal principle of right.

Under these conditions the struggle began, and for one whole year the unequaled contest was maintained. During that time this little army, without a single dollar to its credit, armed itself from the enemy's arsenals, fed itself in a great part, from their commissary stores, took their artillery, and was able to equip 20,000 men. This little unarmed army had collected in the southwest corner of the State, had met and defeated General Seigel at Carthage, had destroyed the force under General Lyon at Springfield, had swept down through the State, and driving the Kansas force before it, had captured Lexington, and had held at bay an army of 40,000 of the best armed troops in America, under Fremont. Starting out with two little pieces of artillery, they had captured fifty-five guns, and had a well armed, well equipped artillery army corps, and in the last battle at Elkhorn they had saved the Southern army from annihilation. And all of this had been accomplished against overwhelming numbers.

The Missourian naturally felt piqued at the supreme indifference of the Southern army that lay hidden in the Boston Mountains and looked on with a spirit of indifference, while they were struggling to defend the homes and firesides of their loved State. To turn their backs upon all these scenes of conflict, to abandon the homes and firesides of all they had loved, and for which they had toiled that long and bloody year; to abandon it all to the enemy and join arms with those who had, apparently, been indifferent to their pleadings, appealed to a manhood that displayed a spirit of bravery and devotion that reaches far beyond the clash of arms, and rises above the mere conquests of the sword. The man who can bring his passions and prejudices under subjection to principle has won a victory

more glorious than ever crowned the hero on the bloody field.
It is a spirit of devotion that rises up in such grand propor-
tions as to command the admiration of men and nations. The
man who can conquer himself, can conquer a host, and may be
trusted to do or die before the opposing enemy.

These men were Missouri's noblest blood, and every soldier
was fit to command an army. It is not the purpose of this
history to perpetuate the names of particular men, but of a
grand, noble body of men, who, from general to private, are
moved by one impulse; actuated by one spirit, and who stood
as one solid phalanx as the representative of a principle. Men
who endured hardships without a murmur, who made sacrifices
without complaint, and each courted the rigors of discipline.

Such were the men that were called upon to abandon the
scenes of all their grand achievements and glorious victories,
and more, to leave the scenes of their childhood and the homes
of their loved in the hands of the enemy. But when the call
came, they answered *ready*. They knew that one of the first
qualifications of a soldier is to obey his superior officer, and
with a devotion born of patriotism they said to their grand old
general, "*Lead on.*"

On the 22nd day of March, 1862, the army received marching orders and started in the direction of Des Arc, on the
White River, in Arkansas, at which place the Missourians
arrived on the evening of the 7th of April, after a march of
sixteen days. On the next morning they were taken on board
boats and started down White River for Memphis.

The boats entered the great "Father of Waters" about
sun down; and, indeed, it was a mighty river. The streams
all up and down its banks, flushed by the spring rains, were
pouring into it great floods of water, and at the mouth of
White River it spread out like a great rolling sea. The vessel
rode proudly its waves and plowed grandly its waters, and the
quivering groaning puffs of steam, as they answered the pon-
derous strokes of the engine, telling the power of that mighty
current that was sweeping beneath. As the night settles
down, the soldiers, weary of that long and tedious march,
spread out their blankets and lay down to rest. Nothing is
heard but the heavy breathing of the sleeping soldiers, the
rushing of the mighty waters and the labored surges of the

great wheel as it forces its burden against the current. As far up and down as the eye can reach are the great waters, and on either side is the shadowy fringe of a bordering forest, while from overhead the million stars are looking down as so many eyes of the Eternal, keeping watch over the sleeping army, or directing the course of the mighty river, while He holds all in the hollow of His hand.

CHAPTER VIII.

AROUND CORINTH.

The forces under VanDorn landed at Memphis, on the evening of the 10th of April, and slept on board the cars, and on the next evening reached Corinth, Miss., and joined the forces under Gen. Beauregard. Reaching this place, the Missouri troops were sent out to Rienzi, a station on the Mobile & Ohio R. R. and about ten miles in the rear of Corinth, where they went into camp.

It would be proper to state here that before leaving Frog Bayou, in Arkansas, that the Second Brigade of Missouri Confederate troops was placed under command of General Martin E. Green, he having received his commission from the Confederate government. Hughes', Erwin's and Rosser's detachments were organinized into battalions under Lieutenant Colonels Hughes, Erwin and MacFarlane. Such of the State Guard as were willing to follow General Price were organized into a brigade under General M. M. Parsons. The remainder, staying west of the river, were assigned to the command of Brigadier-General J. S. Rains. All the artillery of the Missouri army was organized into a brigade, under command of Brigadier-General D. M. Frost. Col. Gates' cavalry regiment had been dismounted and became a part of the Second Brigade.

General Beauregard's army had been divided into three divisions, the right commanded by General VanDorn, the center by General Hardee and the left by General Bragg, his whole force numbering about forty-seven thousand men. After the battle of Shiloh, Gen. H. W. Halleck was placed in command of the Federal army, his whole force numbering about ninety thousand. Yet with this greatly superior force, General Halleck was not willing to risk another pitched battle, but began approaching Corinth by parallel lines, keeping himself continually under cover of his intrenchments.

43

On the 8th of May, General Pope, commanding the advance of the Federal army, moved up with two full brigades and occupied Farmington. General Beauregard determined to accept the gage of battle thus thrown down to him and at once moved out to the attack; Generals Bragg and Hardee, to attack the right and center, while General VanDorn attacked the left and rear. General Price's division of VanDorn's corps was sent to attack the rear. General Price moved out with his force the night of the 8th to within an easy march of the rear of Popes' command without molestation or even the knowledge of the enemy. Early on the morning of the 9th the signal guns were fired and the whole army began its advance. But General Hardee attacked the enemy with such spirit as drove him at once from his line of works, and the Missourians coming in contact with one of those Mississippi swamps that is almost impassable, the enemy made safe his retreat before his rear could be reached. But he left his headquarter tent telegraph operator and office, with tents and wagons, with all his dead and wounded, in the hands of the Confederates. General Halleck, although with more than double the force of the Confederates, absolutely refusing to come out into open ground and give battle, General Beauregard withdrew his forces inside the fortifications around Corinth. This battle was familiarly known as "*The Farmington Races.*"

The camp at Rienzi was completely broken up and the Missouri troops given their place in the line of defense. The enemy continued to approach under cover of his guns. By the 28th, the lines had been drawn so close together, that heavy cannonading was opened up all along the front and continued throughout the day. The army lay in line of battle all night. Next morning, just before day, the shooting of sky-rockets called the entire army to attention. So soon as it was light the cannonading was renewed with vigor upon both sides and kept up till about 4 o'clock in the evening, when it was ascertained that the ammunition was all gone; wagons all gone, commissaries all gone, in fact, everything gone save the men with three days' rations. For a description of the evacuation of Corinth. I quote from Col. R. S. Bevier's History, pp. 121–124:

At midnight of the 29th of May, the Missouri brigades moved out of their position to follow the evacuating army of General Beauregard, so silently that the Yankees within eight hundred yards of them, knew nothing of it until noon next day.

A Northern man, writing of this event at the time, says:

"The Confederate strategy since the battle of Shiloh has been as successful as it has been superior. Taking the enemy's stand-point, and writing when and where I do, I cannot possibly imagine how it could have been more eminent for perfection and success. Taking our stand-point—the stand-point of the Union's hopes and Halleck's fame—I cannot possibly imagine how it could have been more mortifyingly disastrous. If the attack at Shiloh was a surprise to General Grant, the evacuation of Corinth was no less a surprise to General Halleck, and has laid out in pallid death the military name and fame of Major General Henry W. Halleck. Corinth has been searched in vain for a spiked or disabled gun. Shame on us! what a clean piece of evacuation it was!"

General Beauregard, in his official report, says:

"The purposes and ends for which I had held and occupied Corinth having been mainly accomplished by the last of May, and by the 25th of that month having ascertained definitely that the enemy had received large accessions to his already superior force, whilst ours had been reduced day by day by disease, resulting from bad water and inferior food, I felt it clearly my duty to evacuate that position without delay. The transparent object of the Federal commander had been to cut off my resources by destroying the Mobile and Ohio, and the Memphis and Charleston railroads. This was substantially foiled by the evacuation and withdrawal along the line of the former road, and if followed by the enemy, remote from his base, I confidently anticipated opportunity for resumption of the offensive, with chances for signal success."

On the ensuing morning, the enemy opened a heavy fire on our lines from formidable batteries of long range guns, blissfully ignorant that there was no one to reply save a scattered cavalry picket.

"The troops moved off in good spirits and order, prepared to give battle, if pursued, but no serious pursuit was attempted. Whilst at Rienzi, half way to Baldwin, I was informed that on the morning of the 13th ult., a detachment of the enemy's cavalry had penetrated to Booneville, eight miles south of Rienzi, and had captured and burned a railroad train of ammunition, baggage and subsistence, delayed there forty-eight hours by some mismanagement. I regret to add that the enemy also burned the railroad depot, in which were, at the moment, a number of dead bodies, and at least four sick soldiers of this army, who were consumed; an act of barbarism scarcely credible, and without a precedent, to my knowledge, in civilized warfare. Upon the opportune appearance in a short time, however, of an inferior force of cavalry, the enemy left in great haste and confusion, after having received one volley."

This "inferior force" of cavalry was seventy-five of Colonel McCullough's men from the gallant and chivalrous Third Missouri cavalry.

"I desire to record that one Colonel Elliott, of the Federal army, commanded in this raid, and is responsible for the cruel death of our sick," adds General Beauregard.

General Pope evolves the following version of this affair:

"It seems proper for me to state here that the day previous I sent out the first of the cavalry raids which I believe was made during the war. Colonel (now brevet Major General) W. L. Elliott, was instructed to proceed with his own regiment (the second Iowa cavalry) and the second Michigan cavalry, commanded by Colonel (now Major General) P. H. Sheridan, and make a descent upon the Mobile & Ohio railroad, if possible, as far as forty miles south of Corinth. This raid was conducted with great vigor and complete success by General Elliott. He struck the railroad at Booneville, twenty miles south of Corinth, tore up the track and the telegraph lines and captured a train of cars loaded with ammunition and small-arms, which they destroyed. He also captured, and for want of means to bring them off, paroled two thousand of the enemy, mostly convalescents."

The Federal general fails to add that he did not do any such thing—only four hundred sick men were captured, and these were involuntarily and speedily released when the seventy-five brave Missourians attacked and drove away in dismay and confusion this "first cavalry raid of the war"—these thousand moss troopers commanded by Major Generals W. L. Elliott and P. H. Sheridan.

The truth of history has long since fully corroborated the Southern version of the evacuation of Corinth and its results.[*]

On the 1st of June, the Missouri Brigades went into camp at Baldwin—remained there until the 7th, when they were moved to Priceville—from thence, on the 7th of July, to Tupelo, and finally, on the 29th of July, to Saltillo, where they remained until the movement against Iuka. From Tupelo the remains of the Missouri State Guard, under command of General Parsons, left for the Trans-Mississippi Department.

Col. J. T. Hughes was commissioned as a brigadier-general and left for Missouri, where he raised a brigade and attacked and captured Independence, but was killed just as victory had perched upon his banners.

---

[*] "Lost Cause," p. 329. "Official Reports to Confederate Congress," p. 436. General Pope's Reports "Conduct of the War," part 2d. Anderson's "Memoirs," p. 200. Covell's "Diary," p. 120. Hubbell's "Diary," p. 81.

At Priceville Col. Burbridge resigned, F. M. Cockrell becoming Colonel of the Second Infantry, Major Dwyer Lieutenant-Colonel and Pembroke S. Senteny, Captain of Company A, was promoted to the position of Major.

About the first of August the commands of Generals Polk and Hardee were sent off to the Department of Tennessee, under General Bragg, operating from Chattanooga. General Breckenridge's corps was sent to reinforce VanDorn, who had been placed in charge of a Southern department comprising Vicksburg and Baton Rouge. General Beauregard was sick at Bladen Springs, and General Price was left in command in North Mississippi. General Little commanded a division composed of Hebert's (Louisiana), Martin's (Mississippi), the First Missouri, commanded by Colonel Gates, and the Second Missouri, commanded by General Green. The Second Missouri Regiment of Cavalry, Colonel McCulloch was operating under General Frank Armstrong in the vicinity of Corinth and along the Tennessee border.

CHAPTER IX.

A DYING SOLDIER: THE MAIL SENT OUT.

If the thought had not occurred to the soldier before, the conviction was forced upon him now that the war was not to be a thing of an hour or a day. The fire that was the inspiration of a moment had died away, and the impetuosity of the first flush of battle had given place to a solemn and stern reality. From East to West, and from North to South, a nation trembled beneath the tread of mighty armies, and the roar of conflicting arms shook a great continent, and a fixed determination seemed to actuate both parties to fight on to the finish—that is, to fight on until one party or the other, or both were exhausted. This, it was fully realized, would take weeks, months and doubtless years of toil and hardships. The Missourians had been promised that so soon as the emergency was over, they would return to the Trans-Mississippi Department, and again drive the enemy from their native State. But the soldier had learned that every day and hour of war was an emergency, and that in its shifting scenes and changing fortunes no one could tell what a day would bring forth.

To no one was this a more solemn reality than to the First and Second Brigades of Missourians. These brigades were composed of the noblest blood of the State; young men of promise, of pride, of honor, of manhood, of expectation; young men who loved home, country, and whose ambition was to be an ornament to one and a blessing to the other; men who were proud of their State, and of whose courage and devotion the State will ever boast. Many of them had stepped right out from the first colleges of the land to enlist in the army; young lawyers had left their practice, and those who were taking the front rank in every profession, had joined their fortunes with the fate of battle.

Such men as these loved the sacred altars of home, and the

48

Yours

G. N. Ratliff

social circle of life. But here they were, not only many miles from these homes and firesides, but between them and these hallowed precincts there was a line of bristling steel that not only barred the way, but shut out all knowledge of what the condition was in the land of their nativity. Occasionally a paper might fall into the hands of some soldier that gave an account of the doings in Missouri, but if it did, it was only of some poor "Rebel" being led out to his death, or some innocent being murdered, some household being laid in flames, just enough for him to know that over all those once fair prairies walked the grim visage of war; that the hills were infested with robbers, and that death was borne upon every breeze. But that did not answer his longings. Many of them had left their plighted faith, the bond that locked their lives in one, and oft in their pictured dreams, or waking fancy, those loved days gone, returned again, and the love spoken was repeated. O! what would not the soldier give to have fancy's picture realized, to have one sweet word from her own hand, to see that hand-write once more.

Or it may be a young man that was mother's pet, the dear boy whom mother loved, and whose soul thrilled at mother's words. Reader, did you ever see a soldier die on the battle field? You maybe have. But in the solitude of the camp, in the lone, weary, dreary hours, did you ever sit by the cot of a dying boy, where none but soldiers kept watch, and see the young life pass out? If not, you know not the soldier's trying hours; you know not what it is for strong men to weep, nor for stout hearts to dissolve in tears.

The writer stood picket once over such a scene. It was a boy, young, tender and brave; mother's pet and sister's darling. When he bade his mother farewell, she gave him a Bible with God's blessings, and smoothing back his shining locks, planted a kiss on that manly brow, and offered up one short prayer to God for his safe return. The Bible is by him now, and the worn and faded leaves tell of how the pages have been scanned, and the marks here and there of the sweet promises that have been a blessing in those long, dreary days. And in these folded pages lies a withered flower, a faded leaf. It was sister's gift when he said farewell. It was the flower of affection and the emblem of hope. Just before he died, he called for mother. ."Mother, can't you come? May I not see you once more?" and the tears trickled down his cheek. And then he said, "She cannot come," and taking up the Bible he said to the soldier, "Read to me one more chapter, and if you can, just as mother read; the same sweet, gentle tone, and yet with the same blessed inflection of hope. Ah, yes," he said, "those are sweet words, but 'tis not mother's voice. But the words are true, 'In my Father's house are many mansions,' and I'll see her there. I will just cross over and wait."

Around that dying couch stood the grim warrior who had never wavered in the shock of battle; who had seen his comrades fall on every hand, sometimes bleeding and torn limb from limb; who had walked unmoved amidst the field of death, where palid faces and glaring eyes and open mouths gaped upon him at every turn, but standing by this death scene, where is re-called all the sacred, sweet and blessed memories of home, he is overwhelmed with grief.

The boy's last words were calling mother, and when not long after he died, news came into camp that his mother had died some weeks before, the soldier understood that sweet smile that played so lovely upon his parting lips. The mother had come, and in those blessed mansions they had "met to part, no, never!" Gently they put the boy to rest, and there his body sleeps in a lone grave, far, far from the old home.

Yes, the soldier thinks of home, and often in his dreams he wanders through the sweet fields that had been his delight in days now gone. And how he would prize a message from the dear, precious loved ones. As the days drag heavily by, he sighs for home. Not that he was home-sick, as the meaning of that word implies, or that he would for one moment think of abandoning his undertaking for a return to its hallowed precincts. No, he felt that he was fighting for home; for the rights and blessing of home, and that for all of these he had staked his life upon the altar of home. But to get a word from the dear ones, a line from mother, a word from father, a thought from sister or brother; or, it may be a sweet flower from her, whose life seems to be a part of his own. Such a word, such a token, would help to bridge the broad chasm, or burst through the bristling bayonets and bring home and the scenes of better days nearer to him, and would nerve his arm, raise his spirits, infuse new life, and cheer his heart for the battle.

Occasionally some soldier, who was fortunate enough to be informed of an exchange of prisoners, or of a flag of truce being sent out for some purpose, might get a letter through the lines. Or, it sometimes happened that a rebel soldier met a Yankee soldier, by agreement, between the lines and intrusted him with a letter for the home friends. It often happened that the lines were so close together that the soldiers talked one to another. And often agreements were made to meet and have a mutual exchange of compliments. But then he knew it was simply at the option of the Federal authorities whether it went to its destination or not. And if it reached the point for which it was designed, there was no chance for an answer. Besides all this, it must be opened and read by different officers, thus robbing it of all its sweetness, and blotting out all that was sacred, and only intended for the home eyes, or the idol's fingers. More than this, there was danger that this missive might reveal something of the actions or feelings of the best friend that would be taken as a pretext for setting a spy upon their lives and actions and prove the means of their persecution and death. As these chances of sending letters were only some of the fortunes and circumstances of war, the soldier longed for a better and a more private way.

Under all these circumstances, strange and dangerous as it was, it was determined to open up a line of communication with Missouri, a kind of an "underground mail rout." True, the mail might not be regular, or it might be long delayed, or it might be captured and robbed, but if it did succeed these sacred missives would be free from curious eyes. The mail-carrier might be captured and killed, but suppose all this happen? The soldier has taken his life in his own hand; it has been placed upon his country's altar; he knows how, and is not *afraid to die*. He has stood and looked death square in the face without a tremor, and why not face him upon the bosom of the great "Father of Waters," or if need be, in the prison, or facing a platoon of soldiers with musket and ball. Conscious of the blessings he may carry to many homes, and the comfort he may bring to many hearts, the mail-carrier goes armed to do or die.

The question was not so much as to who will undertake for us, as it was as to the one upon whom this honor, this privilege should be conferred. There were a thousand men ready and anxious for the service. But after consultation and due deliberation, the honor, for honor it was, was conferred upon Captain Ab Grimes, as he was familiarly called. He was a man of tried and known courage, besides an acquaintance with all classes of men. He had, before the war, been a steamboat pilot, and was, therefore, acquainted with every crook and turn of the river, and this was a great advantage, as the greater part of the journey must be made by water. He was of medium height, somewhat heavy build, a little inclined to the corpulent, and yet not an overburden of flesh; of fair complexion and pleasing address, really a jolly good fellow, making himself agreeable in any circle. His hair was light and a little wavy, and his plump hand was the tapering finish of a well shaped arm.

So soon as these arrangements were made and the captain had received his commission to labor in the new field, for he would not act only as a regular soldier of the Confederacy; he wished still to be considered a soldier as he was; word was given out to the men that all who wished to send a message home must have it ready by the third day as then it would start upon its mission.

Such a stirring around then as there was for pen, ink and paper. Every camp was visited, every tent was raided, and every knap-sack searched, and paper was brought out from its long hiding place. The sutler's store was soon emptied of pens, ink, paper and envelopes, and even the commissary and quartermaster's wagons were ransacked. Nor was the commander's tent unnoticed; he divided as long as he had a pen or sheet, until, by dividing sheets and parceling out envelopes, all were supplied.

As one passed through the camp during the following day, a strange sight met him. On every stump and log, by every camp-fire and upon every stool was a soldier with paper in some position before him, and pen in hand drawing out the long lines of love and affection to home friends. Or, perchance, some soldier holding the ink bottle dictating to one more expert in letter writing, or, maybe, waiting patiently for his brother soldier to complete his message that he may receive the loan of the pen and ink-bottle. All night the camp-fires burned and men wrote and the hours of writing lengthened out into another day. But by the middle of the third day the writing was all done and the letters were all ready for packing and embarkation upon their long journey.

There was one more difficulty to overcome. Each letter must be stamped with a three cent U. S. postage stamp. To the Confederate soldier greenbacks were a rarety and U. S. postage stamps were entire strangers. If there is any one thing that especially marks the life of a soldier, it is his generosity, it is one of his first duties. And a man without this principle is always set down as an arrant coward. Nor was the soldier ever mistaken in his man. While hundreds had no money that was current in the Federal government, yet a few were fortunate enough to have a dollar or two, maybe some relic they had kept as a reminder of other days. But be that as it may, it all, with a noble generosity, came from its long retreat and was appropriated to the needs of the destitute. The letters were counted, the estimate made and the money furnished to purchase the necessary stamps. Each one who wrote, put in a P. S. "Please inclose a few stamps when answer is returned." These things being completed late in August, Captain Grimes set out on his arduous and dangerous task of carrying the mail to friends in Missouri.

CHAPTER X.

BATTLES OF IUKA AND CORINTH.

We are now approaching the time when the little army again begins active operations. If its rest through the long summer months had been quiet, healthful and peaceful, the months that were soon to follow were marked with blood, carnage and the rapid shocks of battle. For a full description of the campaign, the reader will allow us to quote from the "Recollections" of Major General Dabney H. Maury. We do this the more readily because he was commander of one of the divisions of the Southern army, under General Price, and was a man highly respected and may be relied upon as perfectly accurate, so far as that standard could be attained.

"I am the senior surviving general of those who took part in the whole campaign in North Mississippi in 1862, against the forces of General Grant, and it is proper I should place on record my knowledge of those operations. In doing this, I must rely on my own recollections and memoranda, and upon those of such comrades as I may be able to confer with. There are no official records open to us now, which may perhaps be regretted less on this occasion because the campaign under discussion was outside the grand movements of the war; but it was of deep concern to important communities in the South, to the soldiers who bore an active part in it, and to the Southern widows and orphans whose nearest and dearest died on those battle fields, as bloody and as honorable as any that were ever illustrated by Confederate valor. Therefore I write about it. Of the general officers of our army, who took part in those operations, VanDorn, Price, Martin, Green, Rust, Little, Villipique and Bowen have all gone to their rest, leaving but three or four of us to toil on until our summons comes and we shall go to join them again; I shall therefore tell my story in no spirit of detraction. Indeed, I have neither inclination nor occasion to detract from any of them; their honors in those fights were hard-earned, nor can I blame any of them for the disasters which came upon our army. They were brave men, who devoted all to their country, and among them were commanders of a high order of ability.

"On the 30th of May, 1862, General Beauregard evacuated Corinth in the presence of Halleck's army, and in June, 1862, his army was lying around Tupelo, cantoned ·on the Mobile and Ohio railroad. Late in June, VanDorn was detached from command of his corps, known as the Army of the West, and sent to take command at Vicksburg, which was then threatened with attack. You will remember how well he acquitted himself in that command. He repulsed the enemy from Vicksburg and occupied and defended Port Hudson, thus securing to the Confederacy for nearly a year free access to the Trans-Mississippi Department and the unobstructed navigation of Red River, by which vast supplies of meat and grain were contributed to the maintenance of our armies east of the great river, which already began to feel the want of good provisions.

"General Beauregard having fallen into ill health, the supreme command of our army at Tupelo devolved upon General Bragg. In August, 1862, Bragg threw his main army, by rail, *via* Mobile to Chattanooga, leaving Price in command of the Army of the West, with orders to observe the Federal army at Corinth, under Grant, with a view to oppose him in any movement down into Mississippi; or, in case Grant should move up into Tennessee to join Buell, then Price was to hinder him in that movement, and was also to move up into Tennessee and unite his forces with the army of Bragg.

"VanDorn and·Price were thus left independent of each other. Each commanded a corps of two strong divisions, both were in the State of Mississippi, and, as events proved, it might have been for the good of all had one of them been in supreme command over the whole military force of that State.

"VanDorn, after placing Vicksburg and Port Hudson in satisfactory condition of defence, attacked the Federal forces in Baton Rouge. He sent General Breckenridge to conduct the expedition, (with whom was General Bowen and the First Missouri Infantry). It seems altogether probable that he would have captured the place and the enemy's army in it, but for the accidental loss of the iron-clad Arkansas, and the extraordinary epidemic of cholera which reduced his force to one-half its original numbers.

"As soon as VanDorn had refitted his forces after this attack, his ever-restless, aggressive spirit drew him up toward the northern line of the State, where Grant commanded a considerable force, occupying Corinth, Bolivar, and other points in West Tennessee, Northern Mississippi and Alabama. VanDorn having superior rank, but not having command over Price, sent Colonel Lomax, early in September, to urge upon Price that they should combine their forces and drive the Federals out of Mississippi and West Tennessee. At the time he made the proposition their combined forces would have amounted to about twenty-five thousand infantry, with about three thousand cavalry. Price replied that he could not comply with this request without departing from his instructions and the object for which General Bragg had left him where he was. And just here were developed the bad consequences of having these two commanders present in the field without a common superior; for, had Price been justified in placing his forces under VanDorn's command at this time, there is scarcely a doubt that the enemy would have been driven in a few days entirely beyond the Tennessee river. Then would have followed the reinforcement of Bragg's army by the corps of VanDorn and Price, and without extraordinary misconduct or misfortunes, the Confederate army of Tennessee might have crossed the Ohio. But such speculations are vain and sad enough now; my present business is to tell the sorrowful story as it was, not to dream about what might have been.

"Within a few days after Price declined VanDorn's invitation, he learned from spies in Corinth, that Grant had commenced his evacuation of that line, and was then actually throwing his supplies across the Tennessee, and would soon be on his way to reinforce Buell. Therefore, to intercept him, or that failing, to join Bragg, Price marched from Tupelo to Iuka. Tupelo is on the Mobile & Ohio railroad, fifty miles south of Corinth. Iuka is on the Memphis and Charleston railroad, seventeen miles east of Corinth. Our army consisted of Maury's First Division and Little's Second Division of infantry, and Armstrong's cavalry brigade." (Maury's Division consisted of the brigades of Generals John C. Moore, William S. Cabell and Charles Phiffer, and Little's Division of the First and Second Missouri Brigades, commanded by Colonel Gates and General Green respectively, and Hebert's Louisiana, and Martin's Mississippi brigades.)

"We numbered in all, near sixteen thousand effectives, viz.: about fourteen thousand infantry and near two thousand cavalry.

"On the 19th of September we entered Iuka. Armstrong's cavalry advanced, found the place occupied by a force of the enemy, who retreated toward Corinth, abandoning to us a considerable amount of stores.

"On the 21st of September I placed the First Division on the march, intending to move close up to Burnsville, the station on the Memphis and Charleston railroad between Iuka and Corinth, where we now ascertained the enemy was in strong force. At about three P. M., the enemy advanced upon me from Burnsville with so much boldness that I believed it to be an attack in force; but deploying three battalions of sharpshooters, forced him back by them alone, and proved him to be merely a reconnoissance in force. It was handsomely conducted, and was pushed with a boldness not usual in my experience with the Federal troops, so that I formed a line of battle and awaited with confident expectation the attack of Grant's whole army.

"From this time we began to receive such information about Grant's position as indicated that he had moved none of his forces over the Tennessee, but that he still held the line of Corinth; and this conviction was much strengthened in the mind of General Price, when, on the 24th of September, he received, by flag of truce, a summons from General Ord to surrender! General Ord stated in his letter that recent information showed that McClellan had destroyed Lee's army at Antietam; that therefore the rebellion must soon terminate, and that, in order to spare the useless effusion of blood, he gave Price this opportunity to lay down his arms! Price replied to Ord that he was glad to be able to inform him that we had late and reliable information which justified the belief that the results of the battle of Sharpsburg had been highly satisfactory to us; that the army of Northern Virginia was still in the field, and that as for himself, duly sensible of the kindness of feeling which had inspired General Ord's invitation, he would lay down his arms whenever Mr. Lincoln should acknowledge the independence of the Southern Confederacy, and not sooner.

"On the same day Price received another urgent request from VanDorn to come with all his forces, meet him at Ripley, and move their combined forces against Grant in Corinth. At this time Little and I were occupying with both our divisions a line of battle about two miles west of Iuka. We faced Burnsville, our left resting on the Memphis and Charleston road. About ten A. M. we were called by General Price to a council of war. He then disclosed to us Ord's and VanDorn's letters, with other important information, and it was evident to us that the enemy was not moving over the Tennessee at all, but still lay in heavy force on our immediate left, and in position to cut us off entirely from our line and base of supplies on the Mobile & Ohio railroad. He decided to march back next morning toward Baldwin, and thence unite with VanDorn in a combined attack on Corinth. Orders were at once issued for the trains to be packed and the whole army to move at dawn in the morning on the road back to Baldwin.

"Since an early hour on this day our cavalry pickets had been sending reports of a heavy force moving on us by the Jacinto road. General Little moved, soon after mid-day, away from the line facing Burnsville, and took position to command the approach by the

Jacinto road. And he was just in good time, for about four o'clock P. M., Rosecranz came upon him with a sudden and heavy attack, striking our advanced line, which was composed of new troops, most of whom were now in their first battle; he forced them back, and came triumphantly onward without a check. He had advanced almost within sight of Iuka, when Little met him with his glorious First Missouri Brigade; the Third Louisiana Infantry and Westfield's Texas Legion were there too. And then they rolled back the victorious tide of battle. The Federals were driven before them; our first line of battle was restored, and when night fell the Confederates held the field. Nine cannon had been captured from the enemy, and every man in Little's division was confident of victory should Rosecranz resume his attack on the morrow.

"But one reflection saddened every heart. General Henry Little had fallen dead in the very execution of the advance which had won that bloody field. He was conversing with General Price when he was shot through the head, and fell from his horse without a word. He was buried that night by torchlight in Iuka. No more efficient soldier than Henry Little ever fought for a good cause. The magnificent Missouri Brigade, the finest body of troops I had ever then seen, or have ever seen since, was the creation of his untiring devotion to duty and his remarkable qualities as a commander. In camp he was diligent in instructing his officers in their duty and providing for the comfort and efficiency of his men, and on the battlefield he was as steady, cool and able a commander as I have ever seen. His eyes closed forever upon the happiest spectacle they could behold, and the last throbs of his heart were amidst the victorious shouts of his charging brigade.

"The night had fallen dark when the battle closed. It had been brief, but was one of the fiercest and bloodiest combats of the war. The Third Louisiana regiment lost half its men: Whitfield's Legion also suffered very heavily. These two regiments and a little Arkansas battalion of about one hundred men, had charged and captured the enemy's guns.

"While Rosecranz advanced by this Jacinto road, which enters Iuka from the south, Grant was to attack by the Burnsville road from the West. As generally happens in combined movements, there was want of concert of action. Rosecranz had been beaten and forced back by Little, when, at about sunset, Grant deployed in front of me. He was then too late to attack me that night. At dark General Price withdrew me from before Grant, and intended to attack Rosecranz at dawn with all his forces. At ten o'clock that night Rosecranz dispatched Grant to the following effect: 'I have met with such obstinate resistance that I cannot advance further by the

Jacinto road; but there are some heights on my right which command the town, and at dawn I shall occupy them.

"'*L'homme propose Dieu dispose*,' is often true in war. At dawn *I* held those heights. Before midnight I had received from pickets, prisoners and others, satisfactory information that Grant had deployed a heavy force, estimated at ten thousand men, in front of my skirmish line, across the Burnsville road. I had at dark withdrawn my division, except the cavalry, under General Wirt Adams, and the skirmish line under Colonel William P. Rodgers, and now we lay in the town, with purpose to take part in the attack on Rosecranz in the morning. Rosecranz's force on the Jacinto road was estimated at over seventeen thousand men. Our army lay between Rosecranz and Grant, and if the battle were renewed in the morning, placed as we were, our total destruction seemed inevitable.

"About two hours after midnight, accompanied by General Armstrong, who commanded our cavalry forces, and who was one of the cleverest of our cavalry commanders, and by Colonel Thomas Snead, General Price's clever chief of staff, I went to the old General's quarters, aroused him from a sound sleep. laid before him the information I had received, and urged upon him the necessity for our carrying out, without delay, the decision we had formed at 10 A. M. that morning, to return to our base on the Mobile and Ohio railroad.

"The old man was hard to move. He had taken an active personal part in the battle that evening; his Missourians had behaved beautifully under his own direction, the enemy had been so freely driven back, that he could think of nothing but the complete victory he would gain over Rosecranz in the morning. He seemed to take no account of Grant at all. His only reply to our facts and our arguments, as he sat on the side of his bed in appropriate sleeping costume, was:

"'We'll wade through him, sir, in the morning. General, you ought to have seen how my boys fought this evening; we drove them a mile, sir!'

"'But,' said I, 'Grant has come up since then; and since dark you have drawn me from before him. My brigades are lying in the streets, with their backs to Grant; and the whole wagon train is mixed up with us, so that we can't get into position promptly in the morning. As sure as we resume battle, placed as we are, we shall be beaten, and we shall lose every wagon. You can't procure another wagon train like this, not if you were to drain the State of Mississippi of all its teams. We have won the fight this evening. We decided on going back anyhow, in the morning, to Baldwin, and I don't see that anything that has happened since we published that decision should detain us here any longer.'

"Armstrong and Snead both sustained my views. I think Governor Polk, of Missouri, was occupying the same chamber and was present during our interview.

"After decided opposition, General Price admitted the prudence of our executing our return to the railroad, instead of assuming the aggressive in the morning. Orders were issued accordingly for the wagon train to move at three A. M. I was instructed to send one of my brigades to escort the wagon train, and to remain with the other two brigades as rear-guard of the army.

"Accordingly, before dawn, I had occupied the commanding heights referred to by Rosecranz in his last night's dispatch to Grant, with the brigades of Moore and Cabell. Phiffer's brigade had gone on with the train.

"I think Rosecranz must have thought our army was changing front to offer battle from those heights, and the concerted plans of Grant and himself were so disconcerted that before they could rearrange any, the wagon-train was safe on the road toward the Gulf of Mexico. The army, too, disappeared over the hill and into the forest-screened road, while the commanding heights were occupied by my line of battle with colors flying and guns unlimbered, offering battle to all their combined forces.

"Soon after eight A. M., Colonel Snead galloped up to me and said, 'General, I am ordered by General Price to say that the train and army are now well on the road, and you will please follow immediately with the rear-guard.' We moved at once; Armstrong covered my rear with his cavalry, and it was about two P. M., at a point eight miles from Iuka, that the last collision occurred between us and Grant's army during the Iuka affair. I held the Second Texas sharpshooters, Rodgers commanding, and Bledsoe's Missouri battery in rear of the rear-guard. Armstrong had been followed all day by the enemy's pursuing force, who were very cautious in their pressure upon him, but kept close up to his cavalry constantly. About two P. M., the movement of our army had become quite slow. The teamsters, having no longer the fear of the enemy before them, had relaxed their energies, and the rear-guard halted.

"Just at this moment the enemy was coming confidently on; Armstrong moved on with his cavalry past the rear of the rear-guard of infantry, Rodgers and Bledsoe were lying in ambuscade at a good point in the road, and Colonel 'Bob McCullough's' Second Missouri cavalry regiment was formed ready to charge. On came the confident Federals—I think a General Hatch was commanding them—until they were within short range, when the Second Texas rifles and Bledsoe's canister and old McCullough's cavalry all broke upon them at once. We laid many of them low, and then pursued our march to Baldwin without a shot."

In a letter to Gen. Joseph E. Johnston, Vice-President of the Southern Historical Society, Gen. Maury says:

"In my narrative of the battle of Iuka, I related how General Price, acting on information received from General Bragg, and from our scouts, had moved as far as Iuka on his way to prevent Grant's forces in Mississippi from effecting a junction with Buell's in Tennessee; how at Iuka we had been attacked by Rosecranz; how we had repulsed him, capturing nine cannon and many prisoners, and had next morning returned to our proper base upon the railroad, with purpose to join our forces to VanDorn's and make a combined attack on Corinth.

'"This attack had for some time occupied VanDorn's mind. Several weeks before General Price moved upon Iuka, General Van-Dorn had sent a staff-officer, Colonel Lomax, of Virginia, (since Major General Lomax) to invite and urge General Price that they should combine their forces in an attack upon Corinth. The plan was wise, while it was bold and characteristic of VanDorn's aggressive temper. The enemy occupied West Tennessee and the Memphis and Charleston railroad at Memphis, Bolivar, Jackson, Corinth, Rienzi, Jacinto, Iuka and Bethel, with garrisons aggregating forty-two thousand men, and was preparing with extraordinary energy to reduce Vicksburg by a combined attack of land and naval forces.

"To prevent this, his expulsion from West Tennessee was a military necessity, while it was our obvious defensive policy to force him across the Ohio, occupy Columbus, and fortify the Cumberland and Tennessee rivers. This policy induced General Bragg to move his army into Kentucky, and VanDorn felt that he could force the enemy out of West Tennessee and contribute to its success.

"Corinth was the enemy's strongest and most salient point. Its capture would decide the fate of West Tennessee; and the combined forces of Price and VanDorn in the month of August could have captured Corinth, and have cleared West Tennessee of all hostile forces. When VanDorn first invited General Price's co-operation in this enterprise, his command embraced two large divisions under Breckenridge and Lovell, numbering about twelve thousand infantry, with over one thousand cavalry under Jackson; and he expected to receive about five thousand veteran infantry just exchanged from the Fort Donelson prisoners, in time for the movement. This force, added to General Price's army, would have given an effective active force of over thirty thousand veteran troops; and it is most unfortunate that General Price could not then have consented to unite with General VanDorn in a movement so auspicious of great results.

"But, as I have told you, Price was constrained by his orders to decline all part in that enterprise until he made his movement to

Iuka, after which Price's forces were greatly reduced by the results of the battle, while VanDorn's were diminished by the detachment of Breckenridge with six thousand men, and by the unexpected delays in fitting out the 'Donelson prisoners' for the field; so that when on the thirtieth of September we marched from Ripley against Corinth, our combined forces were but a little over half of what Van-Dorn had justly calculated upon when he first proposed the enterprise. The disastrous results which ensued brought censure upon VanDorn, and have left a cloud upon his military reputation which I hope the publication of this narrative will aid to dispel. There are few of those who criticised his conduct who knew the great objects he sought to accomplish, or the means with which he proposed to march to a certain and brilliant victory by which the State of Mississippi would have been freed from invasion, and the war would have been transferred beyond the Ohio. Such results justified unusual hazard of battle, and after VanDorn's forces were reduced by near one-half, he still felt he ought to strike a bold and manly blow for his native State, and did not hesitate to attack the enemy with all the energy and force he could bring to bear upon him.

"We marched from Baldwin to join VanDorn at Ripley on the morning of the 27th, and our whole effective force was made up of— Maury's division, 4,800; Hebert's division, 5,000; Armstrong's cavalry, 2,000; light artillery, 42 guns.

"We reached Ripley on the evening of the 29th. General Van-Dorn, with his staff, was already there. He had sent his cavalry forward to cover our front, and his infantry and artillery, under General Lovell, were close at hand and marched into Ripley in fine order the day after our arrival.

"On the morning of October 1st, our combined forces moved from Ripley to attack the enemy in Corinth. We marched with a total force of nearly nineteen thousand effectives, viz.: Maury's division, about 4,800; Hebert's division, 5,000; Lovell's, 6,000; Armstrong's cavalry, including Jackson's brigade, 2,800.

"VanDorn threw his cavalry forward so as to mask his movements, and marched directly with his infantry by way of Davis' bridge upon the enemy in Corinth.

"On the evening of October 2d, we bivouacked at Chewalla, on the railroad, eight miles west of Corinth. At dawn of the 3rd of October, we moved from Chewalla to the attack. Jackson had been sent towards Bolivar, where he captured a large regiment of cavalry, and our advance was covered by Armstrong's brigade alone, Wirt Adams' brigade having been detached towards Davis' bridge.

"General VanDorn was assured that the whole force of the enemy in the works at Corinth numbered about twelve thousand men, and he resolved to 'assault with all his forces. His purpose was to dismount his cavalry and attack with the whole army, and had he executed this intention in the spirit in which he conceived it, there is not ground for a reasonable doubt of his success.

"Soon after daylight our cavalry became engaged with the enemy's advanced pickets, and forced them back, until, just after crossing to the north side of the railroad, we formed in line of battle. We were then more than three miles from Corinth. Our line was perpendicular to the Memphis and Charleston railroad. Lovell's division was formed on the right (south) of the railroad; Maury's division was formed on the left (north) of the railroad, Moore's brigade touching the left of Lovell's division on the railroad; Cabell's brigade was formed as a reserve behind the left of Maury's division; the Missouri division touched Maury's left; and in this order we moved forward at ten A. M.; and soon found ourselves confronted by the enemy's line of battle, which occupied the defences constructed by General Beauregard during the previous spring against the army of Halleck. All the timber covering the slopes which led up to the works had been felled and formed an obstructing *abattis* to our advancing line; but, at the signal to advance, our whole line moved forward, under a heavy fire of artillery and musketry, across the space which divided us from the enemy, without any check or hesitation, and drove him at every point from his position. We captured five cannon and put the whole force to rout. Our loss was not heavy in men, but we had to mourn the death of Colonel Martin, a young officer commanding the Mississippi brigade, who was killed while gallantly leading his men.

"The division of Maury and Hebert, composing the Army of the West, as Price's corps was designated, continued to advance towards Corinth, preserving an alignment perpendicular to the Memphis and Charleston railroad. We were repeatedly and obstinately encountered by the opposing lines of the enemy, and during the day several fierce combats took place, which necessarily delayed our arrival before the place, but did not cause our troops to lose one foot of the ground we had won.

"During the advance of Price's corps on this day, the right brigade of Maury's division was commanded by General John C. Moore, an officer of fine ability and courage. Close on the railroad, but on the south side of it, was an entrenched camp of the enemy. Moore, advancing with his right on the railroad, would have soon been enfiladed by this force, but instantly perceiving his situation, he threw his brigade across the railroad, and attacking the camp, drove the Federals who were occupying it back into their heavy works about College Hill; he then recrossed to the north of the railroad, resumed his position in the line of Maury's division and soon encountered a Federal brigade, which after a fierce conflict he drove before him into the works of Corinth. The Missourians and Phiffer's brigade of Maury's division were also hotly engaged during this advance, and Cabell's brigade acting as reserve was repeatedly detached to reinforce such portions of the line north of the railroad as seemed in need of support.

"At sunset the enemy in front of Price's corps had been driven into the town at every point along our whole front, and these troops had established their line close up to Corinth. After a hot day of incessant action and constant victory, we felt that our prize was just before us, and one more vigorous effort would crown our arms with complete success. VanDorn felt all this, and wished to storm the town at once, but General Price thought the troops were too much exhausted. They had been marching and fighting since dawn; the day had been one of the hottest of the year; our men had been without water since morning, and were almost famished; while we were pursuing the enemy from his outer works that morning, several of our men fell from sunstroke, and it was with good reason that General Price opposed further action that evening. He said: 'I think we have done enough for to-day, General, and the men should rest.'

"VanDorn acquiesced in this, and gave his orders for a general assault in the morning. They were of the simplest nature. At an early hour before dawn, all of the artillery of his army was ordered to open upon the town and works, and at daylight the whole line was to advance and storm them. During the night the enemy was actively moving his trains and baggage out on the roads to the Tennessee River, and all night reinforcements were pouring into Corinth.

"Under the direction of Colonel William E. Burnett, of the artillery of Maury's division, and two of the pieces captured from the enemy added to it, opened upon the enemy in Corinth, and at short range and with good effect cannonaded the place for near two hours before light. The guns of the other divisions did not open. At daylight I withdrew my guns and prepared to assault the town. My line, Moore's and Phiffer's brigades, with Cabell's in reserve, was formed close to the Mobile and Ohio railroad, just on the outskirts of Corinth, and concealed from view of the enemy by the timber which then covered the bottom along the creek. The orders given me were to charge the town as soon as I could observe the fire of the Missourians, who were on my left, change from picket firing to rolling fire of musketry.

"For hours we listened and awaited our signal. Half-past ten o'clock had come before the signal to advance was given. I have never understood the reason for so much delay; but as soon as we be-

Yours Truly

R. J. Williams

gan to hear the rolling fire of musketry on the left, Maury's division broke through the screen of timber and into the town, and into the enemy's works.   We broke his center; the Missourians moved in line with us.   Gates' brigade of Missourians took all of the enemy's artillery to our left, and all along in front of Price's corps the enemy was driven from his guns, and the guns were captured by us.   Within about twenty minutes from the time we began our movement our colors were planted in triumph upon the ramparts of Corinth.   But it was a brief triumph, and won at a bloody cost.   No charge in the history of the war was more daring or more bloody.   From the first moment after leaving the timber, the troops were exposed to a most deadly cross-fire; they fell by hundreds, but the line moved on— never faltered for one moment until our colors were placed upon the works.   Every State of the Confederacy had representatives in this charge, and well did they illustrate the valor of the Confederate troops.   From general to drummer-boy, no one faltered.   A color-bearer of an Arkansas regiment was shot down; young Robert Sloan, a boy of the same regiment, scarce eighteen years old, seized the colors and sprang upon the ramparts, waving them over it, and fell pierced with balls while cheering on his comrades.   Field officers fell by scores; more than three thousand of the rank and file were killed, wounded and captured during this fierce assault.

"The whole of Price's corps penetrated to the center of the town of Corinth, and was in position to swing around and take the enemy's left wing in flank and rear, for we were twelve hundred yards in rear of the lines on College Hill, which formed the enemy's left wing, and against which our right wing south of the Memphis and Charleston railroad had been arrayed.   But since ten A. M. of the previous morning our right wing had made no decided advance or attack upon the enemy in its front, and when Rosecranz found his center broken by our charge, believing the demonstration of our right wing merely a 'feint,' he withdrew General Stanley with a heavy force from his left, and threw him against us.

"Disarrayed and torn as our lines were, with more than one-third of our men down, and with many of our best regimental officers killed and wounded, the troops were not ready to meet and repel the fresh troops that now, in fine array, came upon our right flank from the left of the enemy's works on College Hill and swept us out of the place.   Our men fell back in disorder, but sullenly.   I saw no man running, but all attempts to rally and reform them, under the heavy fire of the enemy, now in possession again of their artillery, were vain.   They marched on towards the timber in a walk, each man taking his own route and obstinately refusing to make any effort to renew the attack; and it was only after we had fallen back beyond the range of the enemy's fire that any of our organizations were reformed.

"When we returned from the town we found General VanDorn had ordered Villipigne's brigade from his right, south of the railroad, to cover our retreat from the town, and it was drawn up in line about one thousand strong, facing the enemy, and about one thousand yards from his works. These troops were in fine order. They had done no fighting. We moved on towards Chewalla again, re-organizing our forces as best we could while we marched along. Our right wing had borne no great part in the fighting, and it was in good order and served now to present a good front towards the enemy. I do not think the enemy was in a condition to pursue and attack us. He had suffered heavily, and had been greatly impressed by the attack of Price's corps, and it was not until next day that he moved in force to follow us.

"By sunset we were again bivouaced at Chewalla, and busily occupied in reforming our organizations. The flower of our men and officers lay in the environs of Corinth, never more to rejoin their comrades. We had been bloodily repulsed, but Price's corps had made an honest fight, and lost no honor in the battle. General Van-Dorn seemed to feel he had deserved the victory. In a manly spirit he assumed all responsibility for his failure, like General Lee at Gettysburg, he reproached nobody. During the whole battle he was close to his troops about the center of his lines, where the fighting was most active and constant, and not a movement was made without his knowledge and direction, except the capture by General Moore of the entrenched camp of the enemy south of the railroad, which was one of those events of battle that give no time for reference to higher authority, and which illustrate the true genius for war of the executive commander, who, as Moore did, seizes the opportunity they offer.

"It is generally believed that the battle was lost by the inaction of our right wing, which, after the first advance on the morning of the third, made no decided attempt upon the lines in its front. So notable was this inertness that the enemy seems to have considered the attack of that wing merely a feint, which justified him in detaching a large force from his left to reinforce his center, which had been broken and was in great peril. It is altogether probable that had the attack with the right wing been pressed as it was pressed by the center and left, VanDorn would have captured Corinth and the enemy's army. The troops which made the assault were chiefly Missourians, Arkansans, Texans, Mississippians, Alabamians and Louisianians.

"Soon after daylight, on the 4th, a battery on the railroad, known as Battery Robinet, which was immediately on my right flank, opened an enfilading fire upon my line, then drawn up near and parallel to the Mobile and Ohio railroad, and ready to begin the assault. I ordered General Moore to place the Second Texas sharpshooters, one of the finest regiments I have ever seen, under the brow of a ridge which ran perpendicular to my line and about two hundred yards from that battery. They reduced its fire very much in a few minutes and when the order was given to charge, they naturally charged that battery, which was right in their front, though upon our right flank. Colonel W. P. Rodgers and Major Mullen, of this regiment, fell in this work.

"The commanders of divisions and brigades who went into Corinth with the troops, were General Dabney H. Maury, of Virginia, commanding First division; General Martin E. Green, of Missouri, commanding Second division; General John C. Moore, of Tennessee, commanding first brigade of Maury's division; General Wm. S. Cabell, of Virginia, commanding second brigade of Maury's division; General Charles Phiffer, of Mississippi, commanding third brigade of Maury's division; Colonel Elijah Gates, of Missouri, commanding First Missouri Brigade, Green's division; Colonel Cockrell, commanding Second Brigade, Green's division; Colonel Moore, of Mississippi, commanding third brigade, Green's division.

"When, after all was over and the whole of the Army of the West, now reduced to about six thousand men, came out of the town and into the woods through which we had so confidently charged an hour before, generals, colonels, and staff officers in vain endeavored to rally the men. They plodded doggedly along toward the road by which we had marched on the day before, and it was not in any man's power then to form them into line. We found Generals VanDorn and Price within a few hundred yards of the place, sitting on their horses near each other. VanDorn looked upon the thousands of men streaming past him with a mingled expression of sorrow and pity. Old General Price looked on the disorder of his darling troops with unmitigated anguish. The big tears coursed down the old man's bronzed face, and I have never witnessed such a picture of mute despair and grief as his countenance wore when he looked upon the utter defeat of those magnificent troops. He had never before known them to fail, and they never had failed to carry the lines of any enemy in their front; nor did they ever to the close of their noble career at Blakely, on the ninth of April, 1865, fail to defeat the troops before them. I mean no disparagement to any troops of the Southern Confederacy when I say the *Missouri troops of the Army of the West were not surpassed by any troops in the wor l*

"In the month of November, 1862, a court of inquiry was convened at Abbeville, Miss., to examine into certain allegations made by General John S. Bowen, about the conduct of General VanDorn during the expedition against Corinth. General VanDorn was fully acquitted. A very intelligent battery commander, Captain Thomas F. Tobin, now the proprietor of a cotton-press in Memphis, was an important witness on this trial, and we quote from his testimony to show how complete was the first success of the assault on Corinth, and had it been supported, how great and complete would have been the victory.

"Question by the defendant.—First. 'After you were taken prisoner, state if you know if any portion of our army carried the interior works around Corinth. Second. And what troops, if you know them. Third. And also state whether they entered the town. Fourth. And how far they penetrated into it.'

"Answer.—First. 'Yes. Second. General Maury's division, nearly all of it, I think, and the First Missouri Brigade of General Green's division, commanded by Colonel Gates, carried everything before them. Third. And came into Corinth driving everything before them across the high bridge over the Memphis and Charleston railroad and beyond General Polk's old headquarters, which was outside the town. The artillery of the enemy went out as far as General Price's old headquarters. Fourth. Our troops penetrated to the Corinth House and the Tishomingo Hotel, and to the square in front of General Bragg's old headquarters, and into the yard of General Rosecranz's headquarters.'

"Question by defendant.—'State, if you know, any fact tending to show that the enemy anticipated a defeat on the morning of the 4th.'

"Answer.—'I judge that they expected a defeat, from their having sent all their wagons to the rear, some of which did not get back until Wednesday. They had no ordnance whatever except what they had in the limbers and caissons of their pieces, so I was told; and I was ordered to report at the Tennessee River. I was taken prisoner on Saturday, October 4th, about four A. M., on the road that leads between Forts Williams and Robinet. I was ordered by General Stanley to report at some landing on the Tennessee River, I think it was Hemiling Landing—to General Rosecranz at sunset that evening.'

"Colonel Wm. E. Barry, Thirty-fifth Mississippi regiment, of Columbus, was detailed by me to report to General VanDorn, as commander of the burial party, which was detailed and left by General VanDorn to discharge this solemn duty. General Rosecranz declined to receive Colonel Barry's command within his lines, but with a rare courtesy explained to General VanDorn that he was forced to do this by considerations of a proper character, and assured General VanDorn that 'every becoming respect should be shown to his dead and wounded.' It is due to General Rosecranz to say that he made good his promise as to the dead and wounded, of whom we left many hundreds on the field. He had the grave of Colonel Rodgers, who led the Second Texas Sharpshooters, enclosed and marked with a slab, in respect to the gallantry of his charge. Rodgers fell long before Gates called on me to reinforce him, and was buried where he fell, on the edge of the ditch of Battery Robinet.

"Colonel Barry remained near Chewalla, and had an opportunity of counting the force with which Rosecranz pursued us, and he reported it to me at twenty-two thousand men, from which I concluded the force in Corinth must have been about thirty thousand men when we attacked the place on the 4th of October. The combined effective forces of VanDorn and Price, including all arms, numbered on the morning of the 2d of October about eighteen thousand six hundred men. Jackson's cavalry was detached towards Bolivar; it numbered about one thousand effectives. Whitfield's (Texas) Legion was left to guard Davis' bridge, and numbered about five hundred effectives. Wirt Adams' brigade, one thousand effectives, was also detached, to guard the approaches from Bolivar. Bledsoe's battery was detached, with six guns and about one hundred and twenty men. The force which actually assaulted Corinth on October 4th (*Price's corps only*) did not exceed nine thousand effectives.

"I think this battle illustrated the superior *elan* of Confederate troops.

"The outer defences of Corinth had, in the spring of 1872, held Halleck's great army before them for six weeks; and although the Confederate army holding those works was not half so strong as the Federal army under Halleck, he never dared to attack us.

"In October, 1862, we found these conditions all reversed. Those same works were then held by a Federal army, which we believed to equal or exceed ours in number; yet we did not hesitate to attack them, and with no more delay than was necessary to form our line of battle. We marched upon those entrenchments without check or hesitation, and carried them in just the time necessary for us to traverse, at quick step, the space which divided our opposing lines.

"I have been careful to state correctly the force with which we made this attack, because of the gross misrepresentations which have so often been made of the opposing Confederate and Federal armies during the late war. The school histories of the United States are replete with this sort of disparagement of the Confederate armies. In one of their histories I have recently seen a statement of VanDorn's army at Corinth, at the exaggerated number of forty thousand effectives. As you know, it very rarely happened to any Confederate

general to lead so many of our troops against the enemy; and had
VanDorn led half so many against the inner works of Corinth, and
made them all fight as Price's corps did, we would have captured
Rosecranz's army.

"No commander of the Federal armies evinced more tenacity and
skill than did General Rosecranz during this battle. He was one of
the ablest of the Union generals, and his moderation and humanity
in the conduct of war kept pace with his courage and skill. Our
dead received from him all the care due brave men who fell in manly
warfare, and our wounded and prisoners who fell into his hands
attest his soldierly courtesy."

It would be proper to state that where General Maury
speaks of being in front of Gen. Grant approaching on the
Burnsville road, that General Price had his whole force of
infantry formed in line of battle upon that road awaiting General Grant's attack. This force consisted of two divisions commanded by Generals Maury and Little, and their line of battle
was about three miles west of town. This line the whole force
held till about 4 P. M. on the evening of the 19th, when the
order came for Hebert's Brigade of Little's division to be sent
at once to meet the force approaching from the south, under
Gen. Rosecranz, on the Jacinto road. To do this, they were
compelled to pass back through Iuka, and then turn square to
the right. They were drawn off rapidly and marched the three
miles on quick-time and met the enemy one mile from town.
The distance, therefore, between the divisions of the two
armies was four miles. Hebert's brigade was formed into line
at once and ordered to charge.

In the meantime, an order had been sent for the remainder
of Gen. Little's division to go double-quick to the help of
Hebert. The First and Second Brigades of Missouri troops
went double-quick the four miles, closing up with a run.
When they reached the battle field, they found Gen. Hebert's
men hotly engaged. They came up with a cheer and a yell,
formed line and charged. Gen. Hebert's men had acquitted
themselves nobly. The enemy had massed together nine
pieces of artillery and around these the battle raged furiously.
The gunners stood to their posts till every one was killed but
three, and these were taken prisoners. Around that battery,
men, horses and caissons lay in a tangled mass. None save
those who viewed the field can have a conception of the fearful

carnage and the desperateness of the struggle. When the Missourians came up, the battle was raging around this battery.
Hebert's men and the enemy had met hand to hand. The battery men aided by the infantry force were fighting with their
swords and sticks; the infantry had clubbed their guns or were
using the bayonet. It was a fight to the death. The Missourians wheeling into line came rushing up to the help of their
comrades, and the united force drove the enemy back and captured the battery. Upon one acre of ground were hundreds
slain, and the acre was washed in blood; men lay in heaps
dead, wounded and dying.

From the time the battle commenced, for two mortal hours
it raged without a lull or halt, and only ended when darkness
hovered in its shrouded blackness over the scene. That night
the Confederate line of battle was among the Federal, wounded
and dead. And a dreadful night it was, the groans of the
dying, the pitiful cries of the wounded, the pleading for the
suffering for one drop of water, to be moved a little, for some
one to hear from them one last word, to just look upon a face
once more. And the wounded artillery horses mingled their
calls and groans with the suffering. The scene was heart-
rending, and those who saw it never want it repeated. The
lines were so close together, that a movement upon one side
brought the fire of the other. But, notwithstanding the danger, many a "Rebel" risked his life that night to carry comfort
and blessing to a wounded, suffering, or dying "*Yank.*" When
we stand face to face with death, all hatred and animosity is
buried and the hand that gave the wound or the death shot is
raised in blessing. But over this dark and bloody spot we will
drop the curtain now with a hope that its sufferings and woes
may never be repeated.

At the battle of Corinth, the day of October 3rd was spent
in driving the enemy from his outer works, which was handsomely done; the Confederates capturing several pieces of
artillery, tents and a quantity of camp equipage. About
3 P. M., the First Brigade, commanded by Col. Gates, was
brought up to the support of the Second, commanded by General Green, which had become hotly engaged with the enemy.
But General Green's brigade drove him steadily before them
into their inner line of works.

The writer will never forget the appearance of General Green as he rode, smiling, along the rear of the First Brigade, that evening, just after the desperate charge of his men had driven the enemy flying to their entrenchments. He had a revolver in each hand, and his hands and face were black with powder, showing that he had, indeed, been in the battle. He had actually led the charge of his brigade.

At night General Maury's division and the Second Brigade of Gen. Green's division occupied a line fronting the town of Corinth, while the First Missouri Brigade and Col. Moore's brigade of Mississippians occupied a line to the left and rear of the town.

The enemy's works in front of these two last named brigades were crescent shaped, the two brigades facing the inside of the crescent. It will be seen at once that when they advance within this half circle, they are not only subject to a fire from front, but from each wing of the crescent.

Something of the magnitude of the undertaking of this little army of the Confederacy may be imagined when we take into consideration the fact that the Confederate forces are now preparing to storm the works of their own building and that Gen. Beauregard, with a force of forty thousand had held, and in which he had defied a force of ninety thousand under Gen. Halleck. Now these same works are held by a force of thirty thousand, while a force of eighteen thousand propose to storm them. And I will add, would successfully have done so had it not been for the inexcusable and unwarrantable inactivity of General Lovell commanding the right wing of General Van-Dorn's army.

The writer of this history must ask the pardon of the reader for referring to himself while he relates the history of this charge, which will never die from his memory. He can assure the reader that he does so with no spirit of egotism or wish to set forth his courage above that of his brave companions. He could not give a just conception of the awful grandeur and fearful sublimity of the scene without it. To him the picture was so vivid; the scene so grand, and the onset so real, that now, though thirty long years have passed and his head is frosted over with the frosts of many winters, his heart thrills with the same emotions, and his soul burns with the same martial fire that filled it upon that bloody field.

His position in line was in front of the apex of the crescent above described. This apex was upon the summit of a hill that overlooked all the town, and from which one had a view of the whole line of battle reaching away over the town and on to College Hill, on the extreme right. Here was placed the famous "Battery Robinet," the ten guns of which swept the whole center of the circle.

On the morning of the 4th, when the order was given to move forward, the line arose from their concealment behind the embankment of the railroad and sprang forward to the work. On emerging from the timber into the open field, the whole Federal line opened a fearful fire; the cannon belched forth a perfect storm of grape and canister. The Confederates met this with a yell, and the cry rang out down the line, "On to the battery! Capture the battery!" In front the ground was bare and dusty. The writer's attention was called to the balls striking the ground around him like great rain-drops in an April shower; balls from the left and balls mixed with grape and canister from the front. The carnage was fearful, men falling all around, and for once the writer felt that he stood face to face with eternity. But, notwithstanding the awfulness of the death scene, he caught a glimpse of the charging squadrons as they rushed on all along the line and away over to the right. The scene was gloriously sublime, and for a time he was lost in the enchanting scenes around him. The roar of cannon, the rattle of musketry, the clash of bayonets, and the shrill shout of the charging brigades, while great pillars of smoke rolled up along that line for more than a mile in extent, constituted a scene never to be pictured by mortal pen. How long the writer was held in this scene of grandeur he does not know. A shout of "Hello!" roused him from his reverie, and he and a mess-mate, G. N. Ratliff, were clasped in each other's arms. But here came the battle flag of the regiment proudly floating out to the breeze and with a rush and a yell the men poured over the works, and the battery and all the crescent line, and still reaching on to the town and beyond were in the hands of the Confederates.

General Maury has told you how the field was lost and

here we let the curtain drop over the bloody scene. But it covers a field of dead, many a brave will hear the shock of battle no more. It is true, nobody ran from that field of battle; it was a stubborn, a sullen retreat, and many a soldier wept bitter tears. Many a comrade parted that day to meet no more till time shall close this mortal life.

On the evening after the battle of Corinth, the Confederate force fell back about eight miles and rested for the night. Next morning a detail was sent back to bury the dead, and the army took up the line of retreat in the direction of Pocahontas. But they were now startled by the sound of cannon in front of them. A detachment of the enemy, of cavalry and infantry, about 1500 strong, had secured the bridge on the Hatchie river and perfectly blocked the way. The Confederates thus found themselves between two fires. There was heavy skirmishing all day. The Confederates filed off to the left and by constructing a temporary bridge on a dam across the river, succeeded in crossing during the night, and by the next morning had all the enemy in the rear.

The army continued to retreat until the 9th, when they took up camp at Holly Springs. Here it remained until the 4th of November, when orders were given to move. The command reached Abbeville, on the Mississippi Central R. R., some twelve miles from the former camp, and three miles from the Tallahatchee River. On the 16th, the First Brigade was ordered to move about six miles further down on the river where they threw up strong fortifications. From this position the army fell back, passing through Oxford, the 30th, and reached Grenada on Friday, November the 5th. The enemy were following and on the 6th, Gen. Lovell, setting an ambush, captured 500 prisoners and six or seven hundred head of horses.

CHAPTER XI.

THE MAIL CARRIER.

We must now turn our attention to our mail-carrier. It was late in August when he left the Confederate camp for his destination in Missouri. It is now the first of November, and surely time for his return.

He met with very little difficulty in reaching the Federal lines and passing on to St. Louis. It was after reaching the State that his real trouble began. Missouri had the misfortune of being somewhat divided in sentiment, though by far, the larger portion of the people were in hearty sympathy with the South. While Missouri was a slave State, yet but a small portion of her people were slave owners. The sympathy of the people of the State with the South, was not prompted by any selfish motive; they contended for a principle. But there is, in every community, a restless, discontented class; these, generally, illiterate and inclined to indolence, are always possessed of a spirit of jealousy and envy toward their more fortunate neighbors. Not because of the evils of slavery, if it be an evil, but that spirit of dissatisfaction with the state of things that gives one man pre-eminence over another. There are those who are not content to labor for the reward that labor brings, but instead would see those who have enjoyed the blessings of their labors brought down upon a level with themselves; men who have no ambition to aspire to a life of intelligence, and the comfort that the reward of industry secures, but would bring those who are thus fortunate down to a lower strata of life. Not that in all cases he would appropriate the fruits of that labor to himself, but he would see his fortunate neighbor dispossessed of his wealth. Hence, so often the torch is applied to fine mansions and wealth wantonly consumed. This class of people was, as a rule, the one that took sides with the Federal Government; that is, so far as Missouri was concerned. True, an occasional slave owner himself, took sides with the Government, but if he did, it was as one said to another: "I am Union and the Government will not take my negroes, but they will confiscate yours." The State being in the hands of the Federal army, it gave this class of people every opportunity to put their purpose of humbling, as they termed it, their fortunate neighbor into practice. Every device was resorted to, and every pretext invented, to bring the envied neighbor into disrepute before the powers that be. Men with whom you had been on the best of terms before, and who had even been fed at your bounty, and had shared your hospitality, suddenly became your enemy and, betraying confidence or inventing a pretext, became an informant to prefer charges against you, and that often under cover, so that it often happened that good men were thrown into prison, who knew not why or what were the reasons for it. If one had a little grudge at his neighbor, all that was necessary for him to be revenged of his supposed wrong, was for him to ride to the nearest Federal post, and inform the commandant that his neighbor was a "Rebel," or that he fed "Bush-whackers," and he would soon have his whole plantation laid waste; and if his house was not burned, soldiers were quartered upon him till he had nothing left. Under this condition of things, every man looked with suspicion upon every other man.

The writer does not wish to be understood as casting odium upon all who, in Missouri, took sides with the Federal Government; there were honorable and noble exceptions; men who fought for principle, and who dealt justly and honorably with even an enemy. He simply speaks of them as a class. Nor does he wish his remarks to be applied any further than to Missouri, or to those States in a similar condition. But he speaks of the larger class in this State who acted with the Federal Government. Nor can we call these people naturally murderers and robbers. They would, doubtless, have scorned to appropriate a neighbor's property to their own use. But those who did rob and plunder, were led to take sides, one way or the other, and most generally with the party in power. To understand the terrors of internal war, it is necessary to record all these facts.

While this spirit of jealousy and animosity actuated the

citizens known to each other a stranger fared worse; he was regarded with double suspicion and was set down by each party as a spy upon their actions. It often happened that one came to you in disguise, pretending to be a friend when only seeking your destruction. Nor was this confined to one party only. The country was infested with marauders and robbers professing to be fighting for one side or the other, and hundreds of men were murdered or robbed under a pretext of devotion to the North or the South.

Such Captain Grimes found to be the condition of things when he reached Missouri. He therefore had a thousand dangers to encounter which he had not anticipated. Another misfortune under which he labored, his plans under the condition of things were not well chosen. The men living in different parts of the State, were instructed to have their mail sent to different post-offices, supposing that by this means, the collection of a great quantity of mail at any one place would be avoided, and thus suspicion be kept down. He then expected to visit these posts and gather up the letters and put them in packages for transportation. True, he had had them directed to the care of parties who were to call for them and keep them until his arrival, but he subjected himself to great and continued danger in passing from one of these posts to another, as well as subjecting his friend, who was to assist him, to capture and imprisonment, if not to death. Men with the best of intentions cannot always keep secrets, nor can they know in whom to confide. The captain thus soon found that he had a dark and rugged road to travel.

At Springfield, Mo., some one had confided to some other one the name of the man to receive the letters and also the fact that a man would, in a short time, call for them. This news was conveyed to the Federal authorities and the result was that a watch was set upon the man; his every movement was noted and he was set down as a friend to the Rebellion. Of course the Post-master was a "Union man," as such were called, and all the letters coming to that man were marked and chronicled. Thus the evidence against him was made conclusive before the captain arrived.

Captain Grimes had taken the precaution to send each package of letters, as he collected them by express, to a friend in St. Louis, so that should he be captured, none of them would be found in his possession. But on reaching Springfield, he met with an unexpected difficulty as described above. Unknown to him he was looked for, and from the time he left the stage his footsteps were watched. To him there was no suspicion of trouble. True, there were Federal officers standing around the corridor of the hotel, but in that careless, indifferent way that created no suspicion. The friend with the letters had been notified to meet him at the hotel where they were to be turned over to him and arranged for express. But who can picture his surprise, when in the very act of receiving the letters from his good friend, they are both seized by a guard of Federal soldiers and cast into prison. The capture of the letters was conclusive proof against them that they were acting the part of spies, and after a court-martial had been summoned and a brief trial had, they were found to be guilty and sentenced to be shot.

The captain's friend was of a despondent nature, and at once gave up to the darkest forebodings and the deepest despair. They were confined in different parts of the prison, so that they could not possibly communicate with each other. But the mettle of the captain was far different to that of his friend; he knew no failures, and never gave up to defeat. He had seen too much of life and was too well acquainted with the nature of men to surrender without an effort. He had traveled a great deal and had friends in every part of the country, and then he so understood human nature that he made friends of even his enemies. While his friend, who had received his letters, was not with him, yet he had a room-mate, and though a stranger, they soon became warm and devoted friends. Through this room-mate, who was a citizen of that part of the country and well known in the town, he soon opened up a communication with the outside. Good and faithful ones were soon enlisted in his behalf and any facility for escape was awarded them that this outside could give. The jail was not a very secure one, being an old, confiscated hotel improvised for the occasion and purpose. The design was to make it secure by a sufficient guard in and around it, a kind of cordon of bayonets. It is often forgotten that these guards are men, and that having no personal interest in the matter and feeling that there is no special principle involved, or no great demand for patriotism, only the life of some poor man·at stake, they are willing for "a consideration" to lend a helping hand. Besides this, there is a feeling of sympathy for the unfortunate in the human breast which makes mankind akin. And especially is this true when our humanity is appealed to in that generous, loving way that shows our kinship. Captain Grimes happened to this good luck. There was a line of pickets surrounding the jail, while there was one guard on constant duty in the hall, besides the officer who inspected the different rooms or cells, as they were termed, once a day.

The prison was a frame building with a hall running its full length through the center. In this hall was a stairway leading to a cellar below, where fruits and vegetables had once been stored for the use of the hotel. This cellar was upon the opposite side of the hall from that in which the captain was confined. It was resolved to raise a plank or parts of plank in the floor of their room, and then dig a way to the cellar, and from there come up into the hall. The means to do this were conveyed to them by friends outside, through the help of the friendly guard. The plank taken up was so arranged, that it could be replaced in a moment if an alarm was given and all suspicion kept down. Besides, the floor was found to be at least six inches above ground, so that but little dirt was to be removed till they reached the cellar wall, and that being of brick, was not difficult to remove. The work, therefore, of clearing a passage went on very rapidly.

All things being ready, they waited until the friendly guard came on duty in the hall. Thus the inside of the prison was really at their disposal. The captain had not only determined to make his own escape, but to rescue his friend also. He was not the man to leave a friend in distress; they had been engaged in the same thing, were thrown into prison for the same offense and condemned to the same death, and the captain determined to link his life with that of his friend. He had heard of his deep despondency, but had never communicated to him a word of his own intentions; this friend, therefore, was in profound ignorance of the fact that deliverance was so near.

A friend on the outside, had managed during the day to

hide in the cellar two Federal overcoats, and one captain's uniform, with sword and belt. This for a double purpose; one, that the guard could have the excuse that he took them to be Federal soldiers, as they often visited the cellar for their games, going early in the evening before the night watch came on and staying till late at night. The other purpose was to furnish a disguise in the escape and to enable the captain to help his friend.

When the appointed hour came, the two men emerged from their confinement, donned their uniform, and marched up the stairway with the password or countersign. The cell in which the captain's friend was confined was in another part of the building and kept by a strange guard. But nothing daunted, the captain, with his Federal armor, marched up to the guard, and showing his uniform and having the password, convinced him in a moment that the authority was good. Sometimes the best and most convincing argument is the bold audacity with which it is presented. He informed the guard that he had been sent for the prisoner, calling his name, to take him to headquarters preparatory to his execution. Without a word the guard gave him up and they walked unmolested beyond all the outposts. But the poor fellow whom the captain was liberating, was all unconscious of the friendly hand that was guiding him and supposed that he was being taken to his death.

Oh, how many sleepless hours he had spent in his prison cell, waiting and yet dreading this fearful moment, and how he had trembled at the thought of death. Not so much that he dreaded death itself, as the breaking of that tie of love that bound him to earth and linked his life with that of others. Oh! how his heart now beat with fearful emotions when he was called by the captain, and with what bewildering thoughts did he go forth to, as he supposed, his death. He had a dear, good wife and some sweet little children from whom he had been suddenly snatched, and whose smile he had not seen or sweet voices heard for several days. Oh, would he be permitted to say the last good-by and if he did how could he say it and leave them in a cold, heartless world. Home had been so sweet and the prattle of those voices so dear, and the poor, trusting, confiding good wife, God bless her! All these

Respectfully
F. L. Pitts

thoughts rushed rapidly through his mind as they hurriedly passed on, and so lost was he in his own distress and forebodings, that he had taken no note of their steps; he had simply walked on mechanically, knowing not where or how.

On they hurried, the captain preserving a perfect silence until they were at least two miles beyond the limits of the town and had entered a broken, woody country. Suddenly the captain stopped, and turning round facing his friend and lifting his cap so that he could give a full view of his face, he said: "Friend, do you know *me?*" The man for a moment looked dazed and bewildered, strange emotions filled his heart, and his thoughts so overcame him, that, exclaiming, "Bless God," he sank to the ground unconscious. The captain seized him by the hand as he fell and called to him, "Friend, rouse up, you are safe. Rouse yourself, for you must fly for safety." But there was no reply, save a groan, and the stars looking down in their brightness revealed a face, as it were pale in death. "Is it possible," said the captain, "that I have taken the life I have labored so hard to save?" "Friend, friend," he cried in his agony, "speak to me, I have saved you from your enemies." But a death stillness settled around and the night wind only sighed through the forest trees. He ran to the little brook close by, and gathering a handful of water, bathed the unconscious man's face, and after a few moments he was happy in seeing him revive. The man raising up, threw his arms around the captain, but he could only say, "God bless you."

But no time was to be wasted in sentiment or congratulations. The night was far spent and there would be commotion in camp when the morning came and it was discovered that the prisoners were gone. The captain spoke a few words of cheer, apprised his friend of their danger and told him in a hurried way where to go and how to keep himself concealed, and then, after speaking an affectionate and hurried farewell, was off for liberty.

There was a sign by which many Southern people knew each other. Captain Grimes had the knowledge of this and by it was helped out of many difficulties. This was greatly to his purpose now. When daylight came, he was some distance from Springfield, and being well acquainted with the geography of the country, was in an unfrequented part of it. Cautiously

approaching a farm house, he waited patiently till the owner
appeared to attend to his stock. The farmer was gray-headed,
with a long, white beard, and had the appearance of a good
Christian man. When the captain first saw him he was
favorably impressed. We sometimes read the lives and hearts
of men at first glance. The captain had felt that he was taking
a great risk, but risks must be taken; he was very tired and
hungry, besides, he had spent a sleepless, weary night.

Although the captain was so favorably impressed, yet he
approached the presence of the man cautiously. When the
farmer discovered him, the captain saw at once that he was
not only surprised, but afraid. This to him was a good omen
and confirmed his good impression. "For," he argued to himself, "if he were a Union man he would not be afraid of a Federal officer." He gave him the sign of a Southern man, which
the farmer recognized, and after some hesitancy, answered.
It sometimes happened that the enemy got possession of these
signs and passwords and it proved evidence against a Southerner. Therefore it was by no means conclusive evidence that
one was a Southern man because he was in possession of these
signs and passwords. To the farmer here was a very suspicious
character indeed, dressed as he was in full uniform with
sword and all the paraphernalia of an officer of rank. But
the more the farmer showed his fear, the better was the captain convinced that he was a true man. By degrees he came
near to him, and being so thoroughly convinced of the farmer's
politics, the captain fully and freely unbosomed himself and
revealed his true condition. The farmer soon became earnestly enlisted in his behalf, and took him to a place of secure
hiding for a day or two, and furnished him with the best
rations his larder could afford, which, by the way, were not
mean, and which the captain relished and enjoyed. A bon-fire
was made of his Federal uniform, the sword was buried and
the captain was left in full citizen dress.

In a few nights a good fleet horse had been secured and
the captain mounted, and with a good, faithful guide was conveyed far from Springfield in the direction of the Missouri
River.

At one of the inland towns by the way, he received a
package of letters which he was compelled to take with him

until he could reach an express office at some railroad station. For this purpose and to meet other engagements, he determined to cross the river at a little town called Arrow Rock, and thence to make his way to what was then called the North Missouri railroad in Randolph county. The evening before reaching Arrow Rock, he fell in with a Colonel Peecher, a Southern recruiting officer, and four others also moving toward the river at the same point, with a design of crossing. It was not the wish of Captain Grimes to travel with a squad of men, nor did he now think it the best policy, but he was well acquainted with Col. Peecher, and knew him to be a jolly, good fellow. Besides, it was not supposed, as this was a little place and off from any railroad, that they would meet with any difficulty in crossing the river. He, therefore, concluded they would all go together till the river was crossed, at least. Another reason why he thought it best to go on, was, that there were but few places on the river where ferry boats could be found, and he did not wish to risk swimming his horse by a skiff across that ugly stream.

But the hope that the ferry at Arrow Rock was not guarded proved delusive. When the colonel and his men came in sight, it was discovered that there was a company of militia stationed there. When this discovery was made, a consultation was had as to the best course to pursue. It was argued that as it was near night, the ferry-boat, which was a flat boat to be paddled over, was on the side of the river next to the town. It was, therefore, determined to dash down into the town, and if the ferry man would not instantly obey, the men would take possession and row the boat over before the people or the militia could recover from their surprise, or understand what was going on. Had the condition of things have been as they had hoped, their scheme would have worked nicely. But who can describe their consternation and surprise when they found that the boat was on the other side of the river? The only possibility of escape now lay in a hasty retreat. But when after their surprise and chagrin had somewhat passed away, they turned around to face the inevitable they saw the way was blocked by a line of bayonets. The militia knowing the men were surrounded, and as they thought all hope of escape cut off, supposed they would surrender. They little knew the spirit of the men they had to contend with. Surrender was not in their vocabulary, and as long as a possibility of escape was before them, they determined to avail themselves of that possibility. A militia-man ran up and seized Col. Peecher's horse by the bridle and ordered him to dismount. But no sooner was this done than one of the men dashed up and with the butt of his pistol knocked the man down. The design was to save every load possible for the emergency. The men then made a dash to break through the lines. The militia were taken so by surprise at the boldness of the undertaking, and so mixed up were they with each other, that though they began firing, it was a very wild fire. Pistols cracked and muskets rattled in quick succession. Captain Grimes had his horse shot from under him at almost the first fire; but he ran rapidly down to the edge of the water and took down the river under cover of the bank, and so engaged were the Federal soldiers with the other five, that they did not seem to notice him till he was gone, having received a flesh wound in his arm. The other five men made their escape, but each of them wounded more or less severely. Nor had the militia escaped; several of them were badly wounded. But the strange coincidence of all of it was, that though in the escape they all became scattered, no two going the same way, yet they all met at the same point of the river below that night, and were carried over in a skiff, under cover of the darkness, and were cared for in their hiding place, in the hills, till they were able to travel.

"Ah," said the Captain, "there is a
Hand that shapes our ends, a
Presence that points our way."

After the captain had recovered from his wound, which was not a severe one, he made his way to the points to be visited in North Missouri, collected his mail, took the cars for St. Louis, and gathering it all together, shipped it to Memphis, Tenn., and taking a boat, soon reached that place himself. Here he dressed himself as an old citizen and succeeded in making his way through the country to Grenada, Miss., which place he reached on the morning of the 6th of November, just the day after the army reached that place.

CHAPTER XII.

ELLA HERBERT.

It was a glad and happy day to many of the old soldiers when Captain Grimes came into camp loaded with messages from the dear ones at home. True, some were disappointed; some of the letters had been captured and some had failed to write; but altogether, it was a happy day. Many of the men had heard from their people and those who had received no letters joyfully listened to the news from others, and so all were happy. The captain was congratulated upon his success, and encouraged to undertake again.

But the captain had learned by experience that his undertaking was too much for one, and he must have some help. He and George Tracy were great friends and often in each other's confidence. They both understood the condition of things in Missouri, and were acquainted with many of the people. He therefore sought George's tent and laid his plans before him. He said that he had many friends in St. Louis, and that he had determined to have all the mail sent to that place; that it could be addressed to different names and all be collected into one place, and save the trouble and danger of going over the country and collecting it up. "But," he added, "I must have help, and the best help I can have, will be a brave, discreet, trusty young woman—to her will be attached less suspicion and her ingenuity can contrive to get the mail to Memphis better than I can. I must have a lady of calmness under trying circumstances; one that can face danger, knowing it to be danger, and yet face it without flinching; one whose lips can remain sealed under any necessity, and yet one of ready wit, and who can give an answer when that answer can do good."

In an instant the last words of Ella Herbert flashed over George's mind: "Remember, if I am needed, for you, your comrades, or our country, I shall not be found wanting"; and he replied, "I know one in Missouri who fills your measure to perfection."

"But," said the captain, *"will she fill it?* Can you vouch for her assistance in case I call for it? I must know this before a move is made."

"If you call upon her she *will* fill the place," was the emphatic reply, "and in everything, you can rely upon her with the most implicit confidence."

"Well, then," said the captain, "the question as to who it shall be that is to help in this matter is settled. I do not believe you would send me upon an uncertain mission in so important a matter. It now remains for you to give me her name and address, and for you to send to her a letter of introduction, and to inform her of the part she is expected to act."

"But," said Tracy, "Captain, I do not know that in this case my own skirts would be clear."

The truth is, Tracy had been talking from impulse and enthusiasm, in the success of the plan. Now that it was about to be adopted, he began to hesitate, and as the danger presented itself more and more, he began to regret what he had said. May be there was a degree of selfishness about it; but whether there was or not, he knew that Ella would be exposed to great danger and may be lose her life. Therefore, he continued:

"That woman, captain, is to me what no other can be, and while I know she will not falter in this undertaking, yet how dare I ask it at her hands. Should misfortune befall her, will I not stand condemned as her murderer? And can I murder her whose life is sweet to me as my own? Oh the bitterness of such an hour! And how dark the world would be with its brightest light blotted out, and that by my own hand. Will she not reproach me as ungrateful in asking her to risk so much; and would she not in the hour of a fearful death, should it ever come to that, curse me and the hour in which I was born?"

"Remember," said the captain, "that while you, doubtless, have the strongest affection for her, yet you have an obligation to your fellow-men, and if she be the woman I take her to be, she will be glad of that opportunity that is thus afforded of bringing blessings to so many homes and hearts. And she will but honor you the more for that trust you have reposed in her. Nor will she attach blame to you, or think your love the less, should she meet even with death, for, doubtless, when this struggle began, she encouraged you to go forward in defense of the right, yet knowing you might never return."

"True, captain, it may be so, but the thought that if she die that death will lay at my own door to haunt me through life, how could I endure it?"

"But some one must, and if success crown our efforts, think of the thousand blessings thus conferred and how sweet the recollections of them will be in the after years, when the storm of battle has passed away."

"Well," said Tracy, "I will give you her address and name, and I will send her a message as to your coming; but, captain, I must acquaint her of all the dangers and difficulties that will attend the undertaking and ask her forgiveness for calling upon her to fill so dangerous a place."

The captain replied that that was all perfectly right. "Let her know the undertaking and knowing, if she undertake, she will succeed."

It was, therefore, arranged that each one writing home, or to friends, should inform them how to answer. St. Louis was to be headquarters for the mail, and the different regiments were given different names, so that, in collecting the letters, suspicion would not attach too much to one person.

These names all meant the same person, and Capt. Grimes kept a list of them so that it could be known whose name to use in calling for letters.

Having made these arrangements and having acquainted the soldiers of what was expected of them, Tracy sat down and wrote the following letter to Miss Ella Herbert:

DEAR ELLA.—When you read this, you will doubtless regard me as both unfaithful and ungrateful. But I assure you that I have been prompted to it by the highest considerations of manhood and womanhood. It is not a thing that is in any sense dishonorable, or that will bring discredit upon any one. The disgrace that may attach to it, if there be any, lies in its failure. With success there is a crown of honor and a blessed reward. But even failure cannot attach odium to an act of charity and a messenger of love and mercy.

But as my space is limited, I must hasten to inform you of the part you are asked to play in this awful drama.

It has been determined to establish a mail line between the Missourians east of the Mississippi River, who are in the Confederate army, and their friends in Missouri. Captain Grimes has made one trip that was in great part successful. But he cannot attend to it alone. He has found it absolutely necessary that answers may be sent, collected and safely delivered, that some one help him. I remembered your parting words and I thought that providence might bring us together some day. Pardon this selfish thought of mine, for it was prompted by the highest consideration of your welfare, and from the deep interest I felt for you, and the longing to see you once more in these dark and dreary days. I also felt that you would take pleasure in such an act of kindness. For I can assure you that these letters do bring great blessings to the weary soldier. And I knew you was capable of the great undertaking. I, therefore, suggested your name, and you were readily accepted.

The captain has your address and will either write or call upon you—most likely call, and will inform you of the part you are to perform. You will find him a man of perfect honor, and one in whom you can safely confide.

But, my dear, you must understand that the undertaking is a hazardous one. If you are captured, you will be treated as a spy, and the rules of war are such, that if found guilty, you will be shot. Oh! I shudder at the mere mention of the word.

But somehow, I feel that you will succeed, and then thousands of blessings will fall upon your head. Remember, the work in which you will be engaged will be one of love and mercy, and I believe that the God of mercy will guard and keep you. Remember, you believe He cares for all, and marks the course of every dart, and watches the missiles as they fly. But I want you to keep in mind that if you are ever in need of a friend, and you can get word to me, I will come to your help at the risk of all. Do not fail to trust me.

And now may that God in whom you believe, and by whose mercy alone I am preserved, and who gives us all needed blessings, preserve you and be your sufficiency, and bring us both to the blessed home of peace in the near future. Farewell.

GEORGE TRACY.

There were a few more busy days in camp preparing the messages for the home circle and again Captain Grimes took his leave of the command and was off for Missouri.

CHAPTER XIII.

GRAND GULF AND PORT GIBSON.

On reaching Grenada, Gen. Price's corps occupied the left, the First Missouri Brigade the extreme left—Gen. VanDorn's corps the right. Gen. Pemberton, having assumed full command, occupied the center. Fortifications were thrown up all along the Yellow Bushy River, in front of the army and preparations were made for defense.

On the 14th, the army received the news of Lee's victory at Petersburg, and also that President Davis and Gen. Joseph E. Johnston were on their way to pay the army a visit. They arrived the 24th of December, and reviewed the whole army. As the president passed along down the line in review, the First and Second Brigades were requested to give the Missouri yell, which they did with a will. The president acknowledged the compliment by raising his hat. Then three cheers were given for Gen. Joseph E. Johnston. After the president and his escort had passed down the line, the whole army passed in review before him.

Everything remained quiet in camp till the 28th of January, when the whole command fell back to Jackson, the capitol of Mississippi. On the 2d of February, a gun-boat passed the batteries at Vicksburg. On the 7th, the camp of the Missourians was moved to within fifteen miles of Vicksburg, and on the 15th, another gun-boat ran past the batteries at that place. The roar of cannon was distinctly heard in camp.

While in this camp Gen. Price took leave of his command and went to Richmond. The purpose of his mission was to ask to be transferred to the Trans-Mississippi department. Permission being given him, his command in Gen. Pemberton's army ended here.

General John S. Bowen was placed in command of that division of the army known as the First and Second Brigade of

Missouri troops. He having been transferred with his (the First) regiment of Missouri troops from Gen. Lovell's command. These two brigades were now composed of the following regiments. The First Brigade was composed of the First, Second, Third, Fourth, Fifth and Sixth Regiments of Missouri Infantry, and was placed under the command of Col. F. M. Cockrell. This was the first time he took command of that brigade that afterwards became known as Cockrell's Brigade.

The Second Brigade was composed of the First and Third Missouri cavalry (dismounted) and the Fourteenth, Fifteenth, Sixteenth and Seventeenth Arkansas Regiments of Infantry. It is proper and just to say that both before and after this, these Arkansas regiments fought side by side with the Missouri troops, and whatever of valor, endurance, hardships or devotion was attached to the one of right belongs to the other. Gen. Lovell was removed from command by order of the President, and Genral VanDorn was placed in command of the cavalry.

General Grant had become satisfied that he could not successfully move upon Vicksburg with his base of supplies at Memphis, which was to be kept open by railroad. He, therefore, withdrew his whole force to the west bank of the Mississippi River and sat down in front of Vicksburg. To his land force was added the immense gun-boat, mortar and naval fleet of Admiral Porter. From the very condition of things, it was evident that Gen. Grant intended to swing around and attempt the capture of the place, either from above or below.

To watch and guard the approach of the enemy from below, Gen. Bowen, with the First and Second Brigades, organized as above, was ordered on the 9th of March, to move down the river to Grand Gulf, and to occupy and strengthen the fortifications at that place. The march to this place was through a beautiful part of the State of Mississippi, and that too, in the spring time when nature had put on her most beautiful garments. It was also through the wealthy and cultured part of the State. For once the soldiers of these brigades could truly say that their pathway was strewn with flowers. Not only by nature's lavish hand, but the generous, noble-hearted people lined the way, and every soldier carried a bouquet, fashioned by some fair hand, a marked contrast between this and some of the dark and bloody days. Besides all this, the men were passing over historic ground. A part of the way they marched over the road cut out in 1815 by the troops under "Old Hickory Jackson," as he marched to the historic fields of New Orleans. Leaving Camp Pritchard on the Big Black River, after a three days' march, the troops reached the neighborhood of Grand Gulf, and pitched their tents March the 12th, 1863.

Grand Gulf is very properly named; not alone from the beautiful body of water, but in connection with this, Nature's hand has painted it with a beautiful landscape of variegated form and colors. At the confluence of the Black River with the Mississippi is formed a beautiful sheet of water forming the gulf, and at this junction is formed high promontories of land rising some three or four hundred feet above the water, and at this point reaching down to the water's edge, gradually receding as the line extends down the Mississippi, forming a narrow valley in which was once situated a beautiful city—now laid waste. At this point and somewhat under the bluff was situated what was known as the upper battery, while down below, about a quarter of a mile, were the lower batteries. Between these two batteries and running along at the port of the bluff was a line of entrenchments occupied by the infantry.

Standing upon the top of this promontory, one had a grand view of the river, reaching up above almost directly in front, as the river made a great bend, to Hard Times, some five or six miles away, and below almost as far as the eye could reach, while away over and beyond this grand river was the beautiful lake, St. Joseph, twenty-five miles in length, whose banks were dotted with the finest farms in the State of Louisiana.

Passing up from the river a mile away from these hills, was a beautiful table land, of the finest quality of soil, and dotted over with the finest farms in the State. The camp of the Missourians upon this table-land was both healthy and pleasant. And to add to their comfort, they were in the midst of cultured and refined civilization. Every soldier found at each fireside a home, and received a welcome that stamped upon his memory the good hospitality of the people of that part of the State. The soldier will never forget the kindness shown him by these generous, whole-souled people.

While in camp at this place, General Price took his leave

of the army and crossed the river to join the forces in the Trans-Mississippi department. This was very trying to the Missouri veterans. They had been promised that their stay in the Mississippi department should be brief, and they had long and patiently waited for the order to cross over. And now the order had come for their loved Chieftain to leave them and to take command of their brothers in the other department. But in this trying hour they proved themselves men, as they were; duty rose above selfish desires or selfish ambition, and, with a devotion and a heroism that only brave men know, they bowed submissively to the command of their superiors. General Price went with the blessings of all his men.

Governor Reynolds took leave at the same time and several others, not members of the two brigades, crossed over to the Trans-Mississippi department.

From the 12th of March, to the 31st, were the most pleasant days the two brigades ever spent in camp. There was nothing took place to disturb the peace and quiet of camp; rations of the best quality had been supplied in abundance; the camp duties had not been arduous, and the gentleness and kindness which the soldiers had received from the people had made their stay exceedingly pleasant. Besides all this, the hand of nature had spread its bounty and beauty all around them. The Missourian had dreamed of the "Sunny South," the land of flowers and the twining evergreens; now, for once in his life, he beheld them in their reality. Not only the beautiful flowers, but the air was fragrant with their perfume. What a contrast with the rugged days of battle and the toils of conflict. One goes back to these glad hours and would linger on that blessed spot, and, if possible, shut out the darkness of battle forever.

But time moves on, nor asks to stay, and fate in its inexorable decree, suddenly drops the blackness of night over the brightest days and adds its remorseless sting to the pleasures of life. On the 31st of March, the command is awakened to the reality of things; to a knowledge that the war is not over and that in the midst of sunshine the storm is gathering in the distance. Word came to camp that the war ship, Hartford, and two gunboats, which had passed up the river on the 14th, were on their way down. They anchored up the river till night-fall, and then came down and passed the batteries very rapidly, firing as they passed. The sight was a very beautiful one. The boats whirling down the river with the light burning brilliantly in all the rigging, firing broadside after broadside, sending the burning shells as so many meteors plying land-ward, while all the river batteries answered back with bursting shot that presented a weird scene, beautiful and charming.

After this momentary flash of battle, things moved on quietly till the evening of the 4th. Gen. Bowen had learned that the enemy was advancing down the river on the Louisiana side, and he determined to send a force across to intercept and watch their movements. This fell to the lot of the First, Second, Third and Fifth Missouri Infantry, with no artillery and no cavalry except Major Harrison's Louisiana battalion, which was already on that side. The troops were put on board a transport and conveyed up the river to a little station called "Hard Times." From there they marched along Lake St. Joseph, a distance of twenty-five miles, at the head of which and fronting the river was Col. Perkins' dwelling. He had had a beautiful residence, in front of which was a large grove of live oaks running out to the river a distance of near a half mile. In this beautiful grove the army camped. Col. Perkins, on the approach of the Federal boats some months before that, had burned his own residence rather than give his enemies that pleasure. Here, in this grove, the army rested quietly for several days.

Since hostilities had commenced, the levee on the river had been cut in several places, besides, it had broken in others and no repairs being made, it was in a very bad condition to resist a flood. The spring rains above had raised all the streams flowing into this great river, and the flood was coming pouring down, breaking through the gaps in the levee and flooding all the low country in Louisiana. The high ground along the river bank and around the borders of Lake St. Joseph were all that was left uncovered by the water. The skiffs and little boats on the lake were gathered up and a considerable fleet was organized and manned under the command of Capt. Patrick Caniff, of the fifth regiment with his company, and a company under Capt. F. B. Wilson, of the Second regiment.

This command formed the skirmish line, or line of pickets. On the night of the 14th, Col. Cockrell, with the First and Second Infantry, having waded through swamps and water that averaged waist deep, for about six hours, surprised and completely routed a body of cavalry, capturing many of them together with their commissary stores and camp equipage. About the time of the capture of these, which was after midnight, heavy cannonading was heard above, indicating an engagement with the gunboats and river batteries, and on the morning of the 17th, Col. Cockrell received information that a fleet of gunboats had passed Vicksburg and was on its way down the river to cut off his retreat. The command was busy cooking breakfast, when the cry was heard, "a gunboat! a gunboat!" At the same time an orderly dashed up with orders, from Gen. Bowen, to retreat with all possible speed. The order was, to be ready to march in ten minutes.

"Ah, then and there was hurrying to and fro."

The Missourian had faced the enemy in many ways and under many adverse circumstances, but this was a new feature in war. He had never raced with gunboats. The day was one of those oppressively hot ones; not a solitary cloud to hide the sun even for a moment; and a march of twenty-five miles to make and a fleet of gunboats puffing and steaming in the rear. Breakfast was thrown into the haver-sacks half cooked, and in ten minutes the army was on the march. Not a soldier broke ranks, not one lagged behind; at quick step they started and at quick step finished the day's march. The march from camp to Hard Times, a distance of twenty-five miles, was made in seven hours. When the command reached Hard Times, the gunboats were in sight above and the boat to convey them from there to the gulf was hid up in the mouth of Black River, afraid to come out. The soldier dropped exhausted upon the river bank feeling that all his effort had been in vain. But it sometimes happens that an enemy does not know the advantages it has. Such was the case this time; for after coming around the bend of the river, but a few miles away, and in full view of the works at Grand Gulf, the fleet withdrew out of sight and the transport ventured over to the relief of the troops, and soon after dark the whole command was safe in the fortifications at Grand Gulf.

On the night of the 22d, heavy cannonading was heard in the direction of Vicksburg, and it was learned that more gun-boats had passed with several transports. By the 28th, there were gathered at Hard Times, on the Louisiana side, and five miles from the gulf, seven gunboats and five transports.

On the morning of the 29th, the gunboats above formed in line with the evident intention of making an attack upon the Confederate works. From the high promontory above, where one had a view of the whole scene, the advance of the fleet was watched with the deepest interest. It was a sight never to be forgotten. Those seven black monsters formed in line one above another, while from mast-head and rear streamed out a hundred banners, partially obscured by the black columns of smoke that rolled up from each chimney. There was never an emblem of war more striking. These boats were steaming down from the west, and the sun's bright rays from the east upon those immense columns of smoke, and its reflection through them upon the fiery stars and stripes, made one feel that all the pent-up wrath of ten thousand furies were moving down upon him. They moved slowly, majestically, grandly, frowning as they came. A kind of dread silence hovered over the whole scene, such as settles upon nature before the burst-ing storm.

When within about a mile of the works, three white puffs of smoke from the front of the foremost boat, followed by the shrieking noise of shell, announced the battle opened. The foremost boat followed by two others, passed the upper battery firing broad-side after broad-side as they came and took posi-tion in front of the lower battery. The others took up their position in front of the upper battery. And then "Thunder answers thunder's muttering sound of sullen wrath " The waters quivered, the earth shook, and the air seemed filled with the missiles of death. Broad-side came after broad-side in quick succession.

One gunboat was disabled early in the action and floated below. Another came up under the guns of the upper battery so close, that the guns of the battery could not be depressed so as to touch it, and was doing terrible damage to the works, when a company of sharp-shooters was detailed to open fire upon it. The fire into the port-holes was so destructive, that they soon had to be closed and the boat shoved off. The bombardment lasted five hours. It was estimated that the enemy threw ten shots a minute, or 600 shots an hour, or during the five hours, 3,000 shots. Col. Wade was killed at the lower battery, and thus the Confederates lost a loved, brave and honored artillery officer. Eleven men of the third Missouri, which was in the ditches, were kill ed and wounded by the bursting of a shell.

About one o'clock the fleet drew off up to Hard Times, and each gunboat lashed a transport to the opposite side of it from the Confederate batteries, and just after dark pass by and anchored below. Gen. Grant transferred his troops by land to a point on the river below, opposite a little station called Bruinsburg, and just below the mouth of Bayou Pierre, and by five o'clock the next evening was ready to begin the work of transferring his men over.

Mrs. R. M. White.

CHAPTER XIV

BATTLES OF PORT GIBSON AND BAKER'S CREEK.

It has not been the part of this history to criticise the actions of the commanding general. Still there are some things connected with these movements that the historian cannot pass over without some comment. The writer cannot indulge, for a moment, the thought, that some historians have charged, and that many seemed to believe at the time, that General Pemberton sold Vicksburg. The result shows that if such a thing had been true, that it not only reflected upon the character of Gen. Pemberton, but also upon that of Gen. Grant. If such a thing could have been true, it was sold at the cost of thousands of lives, and the entailing of untold hardships upon two armies. It could not be that Gen. Grant would be a party to the purchase of military glory at such a cost, or that Gen. Pemberton's manhood would be so low as to so traffic in human suffering. But it must be conceded that he was incapacitated for so great a work. There is, also, another question that reaches above and beyond this, that certainly shows at least a blunder in some one else. The question naturally arises, why was Gen. Pemberton ever given command of so important a post? He was a man untried and entirely unknown to military fame, was a perfect stranger to this part of the army, and had on no occasion been given in command of an important point. When, then, the position was so important, why was not some one given in charge of known ability? It was not because the South did not have such men. The question is, who were most to blame, Gen. Pemberton for his incapacity, or those who put him there.

Notwithstanding that the movements of Gen. Grant were plain to be seen, and it did seem his object so clear, it would seem that Gen. Pemberton could not wake up to his danger.

To a very casual observer, there could have been but one purpose in running the transports by the batteries at Vicksburg,
and then by Grand Gulf. Besides all of this, from the high
bluff at Grand Gulf, Grant's whole infantry force could be seen
marching down the river on the opposite side. Gen. Bowen
sent courier after courier to Gen. Pemberton notifying him of
this fact, and that he must have reinforcements, or all was lost.
Still Gen. Pemberton hesitated—still he delayed.

On the evening of the 30th of April, Gen. Grant began the
work of crossing his infantry over the river and landing them
at Bruinsburg. To meet this advance, Gen. Bowen had the
First Missouri Brigade, commanded by Col. Cockrell, and the
Second Missouri which had just arrived from Edward's Station,
commanded by Gen. Martin E. Green. With this little force
it will be seen that Gen. Bowen was powerless to meet the
advance of Grant's army. It will also be seen, that had Gen.
Pemberton have thrown all his available force from Vicksburg
to this point, he might have beaten Gen. Grant's force by
detail. True, he was crossing his troops over under cover of
his gunboats. But these were in such condition as not to be
the dangerous things imagined. The river had fallen till they
were down in the banks, so they could not rake the ground
with grape and canister, but would be compelled to fire at an
elevation. So that, after the men had passed a certain line,
the fire passed over their heads. But we would throw the
mantle of charity over the failures of men. Man in adversity
is always to be blamed, however well his plans may be, and
sometimes he receives great praise for his success in spite of
his plans.

On learning of the movements of Gen. Grant below, Gen.
Bowen dispatched Gen. Green with his brigade to meet him.
Gen. Grant was pouring his men over under cover of night.
Notwithstanding, Gen. Green attacked him with a force of
fifteen hundred men, and kept up a fire upon his men all night,
Gen. Pemberton had been induced, after repeated entreaty, to
send two brigades. But they were sent too late. These were
commanded by Gens. Tracy and Baldwin, and arrived next
morning, worn down and exhausted, in the very midst of the
battle. Gen. Green disposed of his little command as best he
could, to meet such overwhelming numbers. He so disposed

of his men as to make the enemy believe his force was very large and to compel him to move with great caution. The battle began in earnest at sun up, and the brave Alabamian, Gen. Tracy, was killed, leading his men. Gen. Green fell back slowly to a range of hills about three miles from Port Gibson, where he was met by Gen. Bowen who now directed the battle.

Port Gibson was a beautiful inland town, and had been to the Missourians, who were far away from the associations of home, truly, an asylum. The people were of the noble, generous type of Americanism, and their doors were open to the soldier, private or officer. His coarse, rough uniform made no difference. It was seen that within those uniforms was a noble, cultured, refined manhood, and a spirit of chivalry and devotion to the principles of right, and a deportment worthy the knight of honor. For the people that had received them with open arms and cheering words the soldier was ready to do and die. The sick who could carry a gun, poured out of the hospitals; the convalescent in camp, shouldered his musket, and every soldier reported for duty. They knew they were but a few, and that they must meet eight or ten times their number, but that thought but nerved them to action. Their patriotic blood was stirred to its depths, and they fought for these homes and firesides. I quote from R. S. Bevier's History. Page 178-182.

"The right wing of the Confederates was composed of Green's command, and lay with its right on the bayou, striving to protect the bridge, which was the only means of escape. The left wing was composed of Cockrell's command, and there was only a single battery of artillery to occupy, at first, the space between the two. The army had *no center*—it was all *wings*, and the artillery was gradually massed at an advantageous point to serve as a center. Generals Bowen and Green deceived the enemy as to our weakness by marching bodies of troops near the park of artillery, in full view, then withdrawing them out of sight, double-quicking to the right, and attacking with all the vigor of fresh troops.

"Soon the overwhelming force of the enemy began to push the right wing back to the bridge. That attained by them we would all be lost. It seemed necessary to sacrifice a part of the army to save the rest. The Third and Fifth Infantry were selected to make a desperate charge on what was supposed to be the extreme right of the Federal army, and create such a diversion as would call a halt of their left, which was so sorely pushing our right. Generals Bowen and

Cockrell in person conducted the two devoted regiments a mile and a half to their left, formed them in line on the summit of a hill, opposite which, on the sister hill, was planted two Federal batteries, and in the ravine were drawn up three brigades of their infantry, whilst a steep hill, two ditches and a dense canebrake intervened.

"The commanding officers, Colonels Bevier and Gause, gave the word, and the men sprang forward with their wonted impetuosity and the regular Missouri yell, but keeping step and preserving their alignment as perfectly as if only on parade. They soon came to a gully twenty feet in width and twelve in depth, which they must necessarily cross. It was too late to go round, and the men sprang in, clambered up the opposite side, coolly halted till the line was re-arranged, and again moved forward until stopped by another ravine, which was raked by the galling fire of a whole brigade, and could no more be crossed than a bridge of fire. Falling back a few steps to the first gully, and sheltering themselves in the canebrake they fought for over an hour with the desperation of brave men anticipating death or capture.

"At length the tardy order to retreat was given, and they fell back as best they could over the hill, and rallied on the farther side. A most terrible fire, of both artillery and small arms, had been concentrated upon them all this time. They had routed one brigade and maintained their ground until ordered back, and the greatest wonder is that out of the six hundred engaged in the gallant and reckless charge only one hundred and twenty men were killed, wounded and missing. The brave and efficient Adjutant Greenwood, of the Fifth, fell in the beginning of the fight. Says Captain Covell:[*]

"When we began the charge, the enemy's infantry, perceiving us, raised a shout, came down towards us from the crest of the ridge on which they were posted, and stopped at its foot, close to the ravine. At the same time their cavalry moved to their right, to prevent a flank movement on our part. Their artillery opened on us with great rapidity, and as soon as we got within range the infantry poured the Minie balls into our ranks as thick and as fast as hailstones from a thunder cloud or rain drops in an April shower. The storm of leaden rain and iron hail which was flying through the air was almost sufficient to obscure the sunlight.

"In its results the charge was a success, the left wing of the Federal army was suddenly halted and drawn back, their right was heavily reinforced and moved by the flank, supposing that General Loring's corps had arrived from Vicksburg and was gaining their rear.

---

[*] Diary, p. 192.

"General Bowen soon galloped up to the point where the banners of the two regiments had been planted as a rallying point, and complimented the men most highly for the manner in which they had performed their duty, and expressed himself gratified that they had lost so few. 'For,' he added, as the tears filled his eyes, 'I did not expect that *any* of you would get away, but the charge *had* to be made, or my little army was lost.'

"In the meantime General Bowen had led on the assault from that part of the field covered by General Green's forces, in which the Sixth Missouri Infantry and the First and Third Missouri Cavalry and Baldwin's brigade participated. Col. Eugene Erwin, who commanded the Sixth, supposing that Baldwin's men were advancing with him, rushed onward until he found his regiment far ahead of all support, just under the crest of a high ridge, on the opposite side of which, and not thirty paces distant, four regiments of Yankee infantry were waiting to receive the assault. Each hostile commander gave the order to "fix bayonets," which the other heard and with stern resolution each determined, should a charge be made, to repulse the other or die in the attempt. For two mortal hours the gallant Sixth remained there, shouting fierce defiance, but the Federals, ignorant of their numbers, refused to charge. The whole army had been withdrawn before Colonel Erwin could extricate himself. This he did by giving the command in a loud voice: 'Charge bayonets, march!' quickly adding, however, in a low tone, 'by the left flank!'

"The *ruse* succeeded, he slipped away unperceived until too late, by the enraged Federal brigade commander. Generals Bowen and Green were overjoyed to see Erwin coming back at the head of his men, supposing that they had all long since been captured.

"In this final charge General Green drove the enemy back nearly a mile, giving Bowen's whole army ample time to withdraw quietly from the field, through the town and across the stubbornly defended bridge, which was all done before dark, unmolested by the enemy. The last regiment to leave the field of battle and to cross the bridge was the Sixth, which had done such noble work during the day.

"The little army bivouaced on the north side of the bayou, and with the soft loamy soil were soon strongly entrenched and prepared for another assault.

"The day's work had made General Bowen's division famous. With an insignificant force of five thousand men he had held in check for a night and a day a thoroughly equipped army of fifty thousand men, inflicting severe losses upon them with but comparatively slight damage to himself, and had succeeded in removing all his stores and supplies except the siege guns, which were spiked. Colonel Cockrell thought, and he was unquestionably correct, that with ten thousand more men, who could easily have been spared by General Pemberton, we could either have driven Grant back into the river or have checked his march to such an extent as to have disarranged and nullified all his plans.

"The most reliable statistics (at least so appearing) of the losses in this battle, I find in H. C. Clark's 'Diary of the War.' He estimates the Confederate loss at six hundred and seventy, and the Federal loss at nine hundred and thirty. This I think is possibly exaggerated, although he includes all the causalties of the retreat and up to the battle of Baker's Creek.

"On the morning of the 2d the Yankees, from across the bayou, opened a heavy cannonade on the improvised entrenchments, doing but little harm. General Bowen sent a flag of truce asking twenty-four hours' armistice to bury the dead. The refusal to accede to this request was accompanied by a demand for our surrender. Of course this was promptly declined, but during the night the entrenchments were evacuated, the fortifications at Grand Gulf dismantled, and the army commenced a retreat towards Bovina station.

"General Grant had found an upper ford across the bayou, by way of which a heavy force marched to gain Bowen's rear, and came very near doing so. A lively race ensued for the upper ferry on the Big Black. The skirmish companies (Wilson's of the Second Caniff's of the Fifth infantry), moved cautiously but rapidly on the right flank, striking and driving back a Federal cavalry regiment, but at Rocky Spring running in upon the enemy's main column. Landis' battery was hardly in position before the enemy appeared in force, in a large field that lay in our front. They advanced several times into it from the woods beyond, but were driven back to shelter by the well-directed fire of Landis' guns. The rapid and skillful management of this battery, and the style in which the boys handled their pieces, were certainly splendid. Covered with black stains of powder, and almost enveloped in smoke, they worked in a manner and with a will that indicated plainly they were in their element, and their hearts in the work they were doing. The appearence of the enemy in the edge of the field, about five hundred yards distant, was invariably the signal for cheers from the boys, when thundering away with their twenty-four pounders, the men who fought each piece seemed to vie with the others in driving him back as quickly as possible to the cover of the woods.

"Without further resistance, Bowen effected a junction with General Loring's division and with General Pemberton at Hankerson's ferry on the Big Black, and arrived at Bovina about midnight on the 4th of May, with his men completely exhausted by hunger and fatigue."

The First Brigade Missouri troops was still under the command of Col. F. M. Cockrell. The Second under the command of Col. Gates, and the division under the command of Gen. Martin E. Green. Gen. John S. Bowen commanded one wing of Pemberton's army. These two brigades, including the Arkansas and Texas troops as enumerated before, numbered about 8,000 men for active duty.

On the evening of the 15th, the army marched out by Edwards' Station, across Baker's Creek, and formed line of battle. The line was in the shape of a half moon with its base on the above-named creek. At 8:20, on the morning of the 16th, the first gun was fired, and from that hour to 12 o'clock, there was considerable skirmishing and maneuvering, both sides seemingly seeking the vantage ground. In the crescent line above described, Gen. Green's division C. S. A. troops occupied a position some distance to the right of the center. About 12 o'clock heavy firing was heard in the direction of the extreme left, and soon a courier was seen dashing up with orders for the First Missouri Brigade.

It sometimes happens that an army gets into such a condition that a sacrifice has to be made in order to extricate it from its environments. Such was now the condition of Pemberton's army. Without one desperate effort it must meet with utter destruction, and what was done had to be done quickly. The order was to march double-quick. The men who had been lying down supporting Landis' battery for nearly two hours, sprang to their feet, and with a yell and a bound were away. A few minutes' run brought them to the front of the enemy. Grant's forces had charged the Confederate line and had broken through it, and, flushed with victory, were pushing their way into the very heart of the Confederate camp. The Confederate forces were flying, broken, confused and panic-stricken from the field, while the Federal forces poured in unbroken column through the gap. With their friends dashing through their ranks and the enemy pouring in a destructive fire, they were ordered to form line of battle. Nothing but cool, undaunted bravery could accomplish such a feat under such circumstances. Looking at that gallant handful of men coming on with a shout, colors flying, and defiance in every face, whirling on "left into line," while confusion and death reigned all around, who would not feel proud that he was a Missourian. Before the last man had hardly reached his place in line, Col. Cockrell dashed up and gave the order to "Charge." There were, then, clearly to be seen in front, three distinct lines of battle one behind the other. These lines had halted, either to look at the sublimity of the scene before them, or in amazement at the bold audacity of the undertaking.

At the command, "Charge," a blaze of fire lit up the whole line, and so well ordered had it been, that the front line of the enemy almost melted away. The remainder, in confusion, broke back to the second. The Confederates, with a yell peculiar to the Missourians, thronged into the gap thus made, and like a whirlwind pounced upon the second line. For hours together the battle raged. By the time the second line of the enemy had been routed, the Second Brigade of Missouri troops joined the First, and the roll of musketry was fearful. There was no surging back and forth, but a continual push forward. Never, from the word "Charge," did the Missourians halt till the whole of the enemy's forces were swept from the front. The enemy brought up line after line of fresh troops, but the fresh volley never staggered the onward march of the Confederate forces. The men, in their advance, availed themselves of every protection which the hills and trees afforded and pressed on, never over thirty yards from the foe, and sometimes hand to hand. The enemy slowly and stubbornly gave way, leaving the ground literally covered with the dead and the dying. Thus the Confederates pressed on for one mile into the Federal ranks. The continuous and terrible fire lasted for three hours and a half without a lull in the storm. The slaughter was fearful. The entire enemy was driven from the Confederate front, and the ordnance train of Gen. Grant was in their possession with fifteen pieces of artillery. But the ground was so rough and so covered with timber, that they could not be brought away. The advance of Grant's army had been checked, Pemberton had extricated his command and by the loss of many a brave man the Missouri Brigades succeeded in getting from the field.

So completely had the enemy been driven from the Confederate front, and so far was the main line of Grant's army in their rear, that they could have gone on and joined Gen. Joe

Johnston better than to have undertaken to retreat back to Pemberton's forces. Grant's lines had so nearly closed in the rear, that, after retreating nearly a mile, they were subject to a terrible cross-fire where they lost most of their men, and had not Landis' battery with its gallant men have come to the rescue, they could not have escaped. Here Gen. Tiglman, a gallant officer was killed, and many a brave man fell to fight no more.

As it finally proved, it was unfortunate that these two brigades did not press on to Jackson instead of falling back to Vicksburg. But good soldiers only know to obey orders, though the General giving them may have blundered. After the battle, it was learned that the two brigades of 8,000 had met and defeated Logan's corps of 30,000. This was one of the most desperate and bloody battles of the war, according to the number engaged in it. Did history record the facts as they were, no conflict was maintained so long nor against such overwhelming odds as was that held and maintained by these two brigades of Confederate troops on that bloody field. History has never done them justice in this battle. It was said that an officer inquired of Gen. Pemberton, "How goes the battle?" He replied, "Whipped, except the Missourians, and they are rushing to death." (We must not forget to state that the 12th, Louisiana regiment fought with the Missourians, and acted grandly that day).

The two brigades were finally extricated from their perilous condition and succeeded in re-crossing Baker's Creek, when they found that the whole Confederate army was in full retreat toward Big Black and Vicksburg. They reached the works at Big Black about 9 o'clock at night and a part of the army took position in the entrenchments.

There was a great bend in the river at this point circling to the west; the works were crescent-shaped circling to the east, and situated in the bottom land on the east side of the river. When it is remembered that upon the west side of the river, and reaching down to its very banks were high bluffs, upon which artillery could be placed and the bridge and fords thoroughly protected, it is strange, and has forever remained unexplained, why the men were put in the low ground and on the side next to the enemy. Should the enemy succeed in driving

the men from the works, there was only two ways of crossing
the stream; one by the railroad bridge, which was very high
with long trestle works, and under such circumstances would
be impossible to cross; and the other by a pontoon formed by
turning a steamboat lengthwise across the river.   The men
fully understood the situation and feared the consequences.
Gen. Pemberton had all the artillery horses sent over on the
west side, thus making it impossible to extricate the guns in
case of retreat under fire.   In this line of circular works, reaching from the point of the elbow in the river above to the point
of the elbow below, the army took position in the following
order: The First Missouri Brigade occupied the space to the
right of the railroad; the Second, under Col. Gates, that of the
left, while Gen. Vaughn's Brigade of Tennesseeians and Mississippians occupied the center; Gen. Green commanding the
division.   Stevenson's division occupied the bluffs across the
river with Landis' battery as support.   All the rest of the
artillery of Bowen's division of eighteen guns were in the works
occupied by the first named troops.

Before the men had dispatched an early breakfast, on the
morning of the 17th, the enemy opened upon them with parrot
guns which were replied to from the Confederate batteries and
a brisk cannonade was kept up till about 9 o'clock when the
enemy advanced in force upon the Confederate left and center.
The center gave way and the enemy pouring into the gap succeeded in cutting off a great part of Gates' brigade from the
crossing.   A part of it cut through, a part swam the river, and
a portion of it was captured.   Among the captured was Col.
Gates, but he, with several of his men, succeeded in making
their escape that night, and the next day joined the command.
The First Brigade and Vaughn's command all succeeded in
crossing safely, but the eighteen pieces of artillery fell into the
hands of the enemy.   Landis' battery opened upon the enemy
from the bluffs and rendered great assistance to the retreating
Confederates.   There was but little loss of life on either side in
this contest, as the race for the bridge took up more time than
loading and shooting.

Gen. Pemberton now continued his retreat toward Vicksburg, which place he reached about sundown that evening.
Early on the morning of the 18th, the Confederate forces began

filing into line and taking position in the trenches. The enemy advanced rapidly and at a little past 3 o'clock in the evening the first gun was fired in the rear of Vicksburg. Sharp-shooting was kept up till night. Next day Gen. Grant continued to bring up his forces and take position in front of the works, coiling his line from the bluffs of the Yazoo River above to the Mississippi below. About 4 o'clock he made an attack upon the Confederate left and was repulsed with great slaughter. This attempt was repeated with the same result. The repulse of these two attacks gave the men great confidence in their ability to hold the place, and taught Gen. Grant the lesson that he had no easy task before him. The next few days Gen. Grant occupied in getting all his army well up to the works and his artillery in position so as to make a determined attack all along the line.

CHAPTER XV.

THE SIEGE OF VICKSBURG.

The 22d day of May, 1863, is one never to be forgotten by the Confederate soldier who was inside the fortifications around Vicksburg. From the time of the bombardment of Grand Gulf, April the 29th, to the falling back to within the fortifications of Vicksburg, the little army of General Pemberton had met with nothing but misfortunes and reverses. Defeat after defeat had followed in rapid succession. Port Gibson had fallen; Grand Gulf, with all its munitions of war, was in the possession of the enemy; at Baker's Creek the Confederate forces, after a bloody battle, had been beaten, and at the battle of Big Black, if battle it may be called, they had been considerably demoralized. True, they had done all that brave men could do, but however brave men may be, they cannot accomplish the impossible. In all of these battles they contended against overwhelming numbers. The only wonder is that the little army of defense was not completely annihilated.

This little army of twenty-three thousand men was fully conscious of the great odds against them. And now they fully realized their condition. With the great Mississippi River rolling in their rear, lined with gunboats above and below, thus cutting off all possibility of retreat, and a cordian of frowning cannon and bristling bayonets supported by five times their number, completely girdling their front, forming a wall impregnable to any assault they might make, the soldier knows that if relief cannot come from the outside that the surrender of the place is only a question of time. With all these discouragements before him, it took a brave man to fight.

It is evident that Gen. Grant fully understood the nature of things, and it was reasonable for him to conclude that a dispirited and discouraged soldiery would be easily beaten by an assault upon their works. The more would he reach that conclusion when he considered the great disparity of numbers and that his own men, flushed with victory after victory, were confident of success. There was just this one mistake; he had underrated Southern valor and endurance.

But with the conviction that victory would be easy, on the morning of May the 22d, that grand army of invasion, having closed up all its ranks with immense supports at every point, forming a solid phalanx of column after column of glistening steel and frowning guns, prepared for the assault.

As the calm that precedes the fearful cyclone so the stillness of that little band crouching behind the breast-works around Vicksburg. Not a sound was heard save the heavy breathing of the men, or a whispered word of encouragement to comrades, as they watched the forming lines around the girdled city, and the frowning cannon upon every available hill or mound that overlooked the battlements. Yet the stern face, the set teeth and the firm grip upon the tried musket told that there was a fixed determination to do or die. Had the eye of General Grant have glanced along that line of determined faces at this moment, he would have seen that his task was no small one, and that many a man full of life and vigor, now, would lie cold in death before the sun went down. But now,

> "The dreadful burst of cannon rends the skies,
> And all the thunders of the battle rise."

The earth trembles beneath the roar of the monster guns. From every hilltop around the whole circle of works rolls up the black smoke of war; while from above and below those black monsters of the water are pouring their maddened fury into the city. All around are shooting up flames of fire, followed by the thundering roar of guns. The very air is pregnant with a million missiles of death; yea, death rides upon the wings of the wind and dances in wild delight around the shelter of the little army.

For one solid hour nothing is heard but this incessant roar of monster guns and the hissing sound of shot and shell. But it is silenced now, and as the smoke clears away from the river above, circling to the river below, is one solid, compact line of bristling bayonets and flashing swords moving with martial tread to the assault.

During all this roar of guns and dashing sound of shot and shell, the little army had remained under cover; not a word spoken, not a shot fired. But now, as the advancing avalanche comes on, the cannoneer stepped quickly to his gun; the infantry man grasped his rifle and moved to the front, and with bated breath all awaited the coming tempest. On it swept confident of victory, its colors flying and its drums beating. When that girdling line had reached within thirty yards of the works, suddenly, by a signal given, there burst forth a flame of fire from the Confederate line. There were many pieces of artillery concealed behind those works, double-charged with grape and canister. These hurled at once their missiles of death into the face of the advancing foe, and to these were joined the rattle of twenty thousand rifles. That advancing column seemed to almost melt away. It halted, staggered and for the moment dismay and bewilderment seemed to seize hold upon it. But in this supreme moment another column came rushing up to the rescue and now shot answered shot, arm met arm, and bayonet crossed bayonet. Here the surging mass in its irresistible force crossed over the works, and the stars and stripes took the place of the stars and bars, but again it was hurled back, and the stars and bars, torn and tattered, waved proud defiance at the foe. And thus, for more than an hour, the battle raged, and the savage roll of guns and the harsh grating of bayonets mingled with the yells of the victor and the groans of the dying.

But that little band of living valor could not be vanquished. The Federal forces began to give way, and soon in broken column and confused rout, they flew to the cover of the woods and hills beyond. But the Confederate soldier had not long to watch the flying foe or to look over the field of desolation all around him, nor even to administer a cup of cold water to a wounded friend, or to listen to the last words of a dying brother. From these hills beyond, frowning with artillery, came again the cannon's thundering roar, and, as if maddened by defeat, it came more savage than before. This was followed by another charge, and thus the battle raged from early morning till the sun was low in the west.

It was 4 o'clock in the evening before the assaulting columns were entirely withdrawn, and the hope of capturing Vicksburg by assault was entirely given up. Then the hush of death hung heavy over all the field and the grim-visaged soldier, with powder-burned face and blackened hands, turned his attention to the cries of the wounded and suffering. Here lay a brother cold in death, and a friend mangled and torn, begging piteously for a little help. One glance at the dead brother's face and then a word of comfort to the dying and a drop of water to the suffering. Oh! to look over that bloody field, now, one shudders at the horrors of war. Death all around, while all in front of the works between the two lines the ground is covered with the dead, dying and wounded, who are out of the reach of help. Stout frames and noble forms that but a few hours ago were filled with vigor and manhood, are now cold in death; the friend and the foe lay peacefully together, resting in that last sleep that knows no waking, while the soul has gone to Him who rules over all battles.

CHAPTER XVI.

THE MAIL ARRIVES IN VICKSBURG.

Where Tracy fought the battle had raged with fearful fury, and he was found among the "badly wounded." He was, gently, by loving hands borne to the rear and placed in an ambulance and sent to the city hospital. For several days he seemed to linger between life and death, and then there came a change for the better.

It was Sunday morning, June the 7th, that the attending physician came in very early, and, after feeling his pulse and passing his hand over his brow, said: "You are better now. You have had a serious wound and I feared the worst, but I think now that you will pull through."

"Thank you, doctor, thank you," said Tracy; "it all seems like a dream to me. O that fearful day of carnage! It seems to me that I have lived those hours over and over again, with all the scenes of death. But the sun shines brighter now, and last night I had a sweet dream of home; and I sat before the old hearth-stone, and with father, mother and all the loved circle of better days, sang the evening hymn and heard the prayer of intercession go up from father's aged and trembling lips, and we all talked of the better home in the fadeless land. And, doctor, when you came in, I had just awakened from that sweet dream and was wondering why I could not have slept and dreamed on. And then I asked, would I ever realize the sweetness of that dream."

"Ah, well," replied the doctor, "You are better now, sleep once more, maybe you will dream again."

"Yes, doctor, but I shall wake for my dreams to mock me."

"Your pleasant dreams will do you good. And I shall expect to find you much better when I return in the evening. You need quiet and rest," were the words of the doctor.

Yours Very Truly,
J. W. Finks

He then bade him good-by with a pleasant, assuring smile, and hastened on to give instructions to the nurse and to attend to other patients occupying other rooms of the hospital.

The bunk on which Tracy lay was in the third story of the large brick building and near a window, looking out from which one could see the great Mississippi River, whose murky waters, coming down from above, were flowing on southward to the Gulf of Mexico. The June morning was beautiful and balmy; the turbid waters glistened in the sunlight and he thought he caught the fragrance of sunny flowers. In the glance and the glow he had almost forgotten his surroundings.

Speaking to the nurse he said, "Move me a little nearer the window that I may catch a little of the refreshing breeze. Thank you! Now pillow my head a little higher that I may have a better view of the grand old river. There, that will do now, let me rest, and do not disturb me for a while."

And then looking away up the river and around the great bend, he saw the Federal fleet with their savage guns and black sides, and the mortar boats from which the enemy had been throwing shells into the city, and the whole truth flashed upon his mind. "Here we are," he mused, "shut in from all the world; a little world within itself; imprisoned within this little space of ground and a host of savage foes standing guard." True, nothing was heard now save an occasional sharp-shooter's rifle at some misguided one who might show himself from behind some parapet or above the skirmish pit, but up yonder are all the evidences of war. But his mind soon wandered away from all this, and his eyes resting upon these waters followed the river line as it wound up the valley far beyond the Federal fleet till it was lost in the thread-like maze away up in the distance. And then he followed on in his mind until he saw those waters rolling and tossing in their billowy waves through his own native State Missouri. Missouri! the word was sweeter to him this morning than it had ever been before. "Missouri!" he repeated; "O, for one hour of the better days." More than one long, dreary year had passed since he trod her broad prairies, or looked over her vine-clad hills. Nor was this all; those days had been a long and terrible silence. He knew that a cruel band had been laid upon her fair fields and that sorrow and suffering was the part of her heritage. But what of the dear old home? Was it in ashes, and the dear ones gone, or were they victims of some merciless hand, or did they languish in some loathesome prison uncared for; or were they still peacefully resting in the old homestead. When Captain Grimes came with the letters, George Tracy was one of the unfortunate ones that got no message. So, as he wandered back, the long and dreary days lengthened out before him. "Ella; where is she? It has now been over six months since Captain Grimes started for Missouri with the mail, and still not a word. Had he been captured and robbed of his treasure, or had he reached his distination; and had Ella Herbert been found out as an accomplice and captured and imprisoned, and the penalty of a spy meted out to her?" The thought of it made him shudder. "How long this siege will last, who knows but until that is over there is no hope of a solitary word from the old home. But," he impatiently said, "I am helpless here," and with an effort threw off these foreboding thoughts and began to picture a happy meeting in the after years when wars are all over and he should find a home in the glowing prairies, with love's own blessings crowned, and peace and good will its portion.

In this revery he fell asleep and slept a sweet, peaceful sleep, while the soft wind from off the waters of the flowing river fanned his glowing cheeks. The nurse tripped softly across the floor, and each inquiring friend was told that the patient slept and was better. The sun had mounted up toward the meridian till the hands of the clock pointed to the hour of ten. The nurse heard several voices approaching up the stairway, and he hastened to the door and with his hand upon his lips motioned silence.

There were three or four men in the company, one a handsome, well built man, in citizen's dress and apparently about thirty-five years of age, the others were Tracy's messmates. They inquired how the soldier was.

"He is better," said the nurse. "He has been near death's door, and, in fact, he is not far from it now, but he rests and the doctor says he is better."

The men held a whispered conversation and then with a pleased look they all piled into the doctor's office. They were not gone long until they returned with a permit from him to enter the sick room. They came in very quietly and took their seats near the wounded sleeper, determined to wait his awakening. Nor had they long to wait, for somehow, mind effects mind, and even in our sleep we are made conscious of a strange presence.

The wounded soldier opened his eyes as half sleeping, half waking, and in a kind of a dazed way looked at his three companions sitting near him. Then becoming fully conscious, he expressed his pleasure at seeing them, asking them of how they did, and about their comrades in the line of battle.

The men replied that the "Yanks" are not disturbing us much now, and we obtained permission to come and see how you were getting on. We are so glad you are as well as you are, "for," said one of them, "I never expected to see you again when we took you off the field that dreadful day. But the doctor says you are doing well, and we are so glad to see it; besides, we have good news for you."

Just then the man in citizen's dress, who had been seated at the head of the cot out of sight of the wounded, stepped to the front, extending his hand, saying, "Glad to see you, old friend."

A shade of bewilderment passed over the pale face, a look of deep surprise, but it soon changed to a sparkling eye and a glad smile as he lifted his feeble hand and, placing it in that of the other, exclaimed, "Captain Grimes." And then as if he felt it all to be a dream, he said: "Is this true, or do I sleep? How came you here, how *could* you come, and what of home and Ella, where is she?"

"Stop, stop!" said the captain, laughing; "I cannot answer so much at once. You are not dreaming, I can tell you that. I am here, that is a solid truth. As to how I came you shall know after a while. I will say all is well."

"Yes, yes," said the messmates, "Captain Grimes came in last night and this morning we all had news from home. Some had bad news, but most of the boys are happy, even if the news were sad, they heard from home and know that there are still loved ones watching and waiting their return, and that is something good."

"You succeeded well then?" said Tracy.

The captain replied that nothing could have been better.

"Miss Herbert is a jewel, and did her part faithfully and well. But how it all happened, you shall hear from her own self."

So saying, he laid before the soldier a package of letters, telling him to read them at his leisure, and he would know as far as they had gone. "Some evening I will drop in and tell you how I got into Vicksburg."

The soldiers rising, told him that they were glad to bring him the good news, and now they must return to the command. Wishing him a good day, they all departed and left him alone with his letters.

The soldier was very feeble, and the unexpected news almost overcame him; he laughed and cried by turns. One arm had been made helpless by a wound in the shoulder, and the bursting of a shell had cut great furrows in his flesh, and the subsiding fever had left him very weak. But he had the nurse to undo the package of letters and taking them up one by one as he recognized the hand-write, he kissed them again and again. Rejoiced as he was to receive them, yet he hesitated to have them opened. "What secret did they contain? In the unfolding of the last dark year, what sorrows would they record, and what clouds reveal, and what sufferings had been endured?"

The nurse seeing his hesitancy and knowing his feebleness, said: "Shall I read them for you?"

"Not now, not now, wait a little while. It all seems so strange, so unreal. I feel like I was about to look into a great unfathomed darkness; into a shadowy unknown. And while I dread, yet I long to turn those dark leaves over. But wait a while, I cannot now. I feel tired, let me rest, I shall feel better after a while."

The nurse understood and retired, leaving him alone with his treasure.

And then the soldier prayed; "Oh, Thou all seeing One; Thou ever present help, Thou hast been my stay and strength through all the dark years, and in the secret trials Thou hast been my sufficiency. Thou hast heard my prayer, and Thou hast answered. O, now, let me be reconciled to Thy will, for Thou doest all things well. Prepare me for this hour, and whatever of revelation these letters may make to me, let me say, 'Thy will be done.' I know Thou hast watched over me, and no enemy may harm except Thou wilt. O blessed Father, be near me now and give Thy blessing.''

And a sweet, calm spread over his face, and a holy resignation came over him, and he said, "Blessed Father, how sweet is Thy presence, and how abundant Thy mercy." Thus he lay for some moments with his eyes closed, holding sweet communion with the All Seeing One.

After a little time the nurse returned, and seeing the calm composedness of the wounded soldier and noting the look of perfect resignation, he approached the side of the cot.

"Here," said Tracy, "sit down beside me now and read to me these letters. Were it so I could, I would rather read them myself, that my eyes might catch the gleam of home love, and my own sense of hearing be greeted first by those sacred thoughts. But it cannot be, and you know how precious they are to me and will bear with my weakness." Pointing out one, he said, "This is from the dear old home. It is sister's hand and she will tell of all that has passed in all these long, dark days."

The nurse took the letter and opened it. A few tokens of love dropped out of its folds; a withered leaf; a faded flower; a sprig of casia, and a rose bud. He laid these treasures on the soldier's bosom, and to him they were, indeed, love's own jewels, and were "more precious than gold; yea, than much fine gold, sweeter also than honey and the honeycomb."

The letter told of the stormy days, of the weary hours, of the many trials and hardships. But it said that through them all a Gentle Hand had led them; an All Seeing Eye had watched over, and a God had provided. No harm had come to the home. True, Father's head was whitening, his eyes growing dim, his steps tottering, but the Lord was holding him up. Mother's health was failing and the light of her eyes was fading, but still she was cheerful and hopeful. And all, father, mother and sisters, joined in one great bundle of love to the brother far away, and concluded with a prayer that God would watch over and bring him safely home.

When the last line was read, the soldier said: "Thank you! That was done so well and it is all so good. Let me rest now; I have just lived life over in the old home, I have been a boy again on mother's knees, I have felt her sweet kiss once more upon my brow, and have listened to the precious words of counsel and encouragement drop from her own dear lips. I have heard father's prayer for a blessing, and have had a sister take my hand and together we have walked the flowery fields. Let me be quiet now and maybe I shall sleep once more in the sweet shade of home."

After the noon hour the nurse came in with new bandages, dressed the wound, washed the face and gave some refreshments. The soldier then seemed stronger and rested in quiet, until the sun's slanting rays from the west, peering in through the open window, lit up all the room with a mellow glow of golden light, and the gentle breeze from the southwest fanned the fevered brow with its soft touch. So rest the weary, and so sleep the tired soul, whose heart has been touched by the tender power of unfading love. By him lay that large roll, with its seal unbroken, upon which was the impress of a gentle hand, the touch of tender fingers, while he dreamed of its hidden mysteries, of its assuring words and its token of love. He had heard that she was safe, noble and true, and here he would fondly dream of the pictured scenes that its opening would unfold. Ah, he even fancied she was near him now and was about to confide to his keeping her devotion, her sacrifice, and her triumph.

When the doctor came in upon his rounds that evening, he looked pleased upon the pictured scene. "Let him sleep," he said, "for this has been a strange, glad day and he is overcome with his crowding thoughts that cannot find utterance. Tomorrow he will be stronger."

In breaking the seal of those folded leaves, we shall not intrude upon the pages of sacred love; these are for his eyes alone, and these words to rest in his own bosom. There, let them remain unspoken, save by his own lips, forever. But as the mail agent, her history is for other eyes as well.

She says: "Captain Grimes reached me safely and delivered your message. Be assured that whatever befalls me I shall lay no blame to your charge. I only feel too grateful that I should be deemed worthy of such confidence, and to be trusted with such a work. In those long, dark days I have longed to lend a helping hand, to find some way to lighten the burdens of the soldier, and to administer some comfort to him in his dark and dreary hours. And what better than this? To carry some message from the home circle, some token of love, some balm of consolation, some promise of hope, some thought of blessing. O, to be, as it were, an angel of mercy to the exiled.

"While I fully realize the danger, and while my sense of honor and my devotion to my Master would forbid anything wrong, yet I know that upon such an act the Master smiles and stamps the seal of His approbation with the 'Lo, I am with you.' He only is my keeper, my guide, my all and in all. To Him I confide my life, my all, and in Him is my everlasting portion. And 'though He slay me, yet will I trust in Him.'

"I took your letter, and, as one of old, I went to the mercy seat and spread it out before the Lord; and I said, 'Dear Lord, I am Thy hand-maid and Thy servant; my times are in Thy hand. Thou knowest that I am but a poor, weak woman, a feeble worm; Thou knowest that I am too weak for this great task. But Oh, Thou who buildest up kingdoms and over-throwest armies, who keepest Thy promises and faithfulness through all generations, must I undertake this, and wilt Thou, O merciful Father, wilt Thou undertake for me? Wilt Thou bless my humble effort? I am ready to die if need be in Thy service. And then there came into my soul such a holy calm, such a blessed assurance, such exquisite sweetness, I almost heard the words repeated over, "I will be with you."'

"Feeling so sure that the Father holds my hand, and knowing that in Him alone I trust, whatever may be the result, my whole soul is in this matter. I know I am not acting the spy, but only a messenger of mercy. But I have had such a taste of war, that I know all of this will be overlooked, and that if I am captured, I shall pay the penalty with my life. Be it so, God's will be done.

"The captain said that he met with but little difficulty on his way up, and that after he was well within the Federal lines he mailed the letters at different places so as not to create suspicion by too large bunches being posted at one place. By the time he reached me he had given them all out. He stopped at St. Louis and arranged rooms with a trusty lady of his acquaintance, where I was to go and gather up the letters. I was to go at once, so as not to allow too many letters to accumulate in post-office, thereby creating suspicion. So you may know that there was a confusion and a stir in my getting ready. I could not think of going alone, so I asked father to let me take our boy Sam. He is, as you know, a little fellow and young, only sixteen, but he is so devoted to me, and I know I can trust him. Only people who know the negro know how to confide in him.

"Sam was so delighted, he fairly danced for joy. 'Is I sho' nuff goin' wid my good miss?'

"'Yes, Sam, you are to go with me. But we have some dangers before us. You know these are war times and the Yankees may get us, and you may be taken from me.'

"'O, no, miss, de Yankees can't git you for sho', dey can't, I'll tell 'em you good.'

"'But, Sam,' I said, 'they will not listen to you. All I want is for you to tell nothing to anybody only as I direct; this I think you will faithfully observe.'

"Sam replied, 'Dat I will, miss, dat I will, 'cept I'll tell 'em you's a lady. My mamma says she wishes dem Yanks would let us niggers alone. She says she specs we is better off dan lots of dem Yanks are now; good homes, good mars and miss, and a plenty to eat and war. Law sakes, I spec's lots of dem Yanks would like to have all dat.' Sam was really growing eloquent in defense of the South. But I stopped him in the midst of his grand effort by telling him he must hurry up and have his mamma get him ready, for we must start in a few days, and away he danced to his mamma's cabin.

"So soon as matters could be arranged, I and Sam were off for St. Louis. We found that very nice, comfortable quarters had been arranged for us, and we had a hearty reception.

"Sam proved a great help to me, going to the post-office and collecting the mail. They poured in on us very rapidly for a while, and then they began to drop off. But it took us some time to perfect our arrangements and to get our letters in shape for safe conveyance through so many guards.

"It was arranged that I should carry the mail as far as Memphis, Tenn., and then Captain Grimes would take charge of it and convey to your lines. With the assistance of Sam, I tacked the letters all to my under skirts, making them look more like a crazy quilt than anything else. But you would have been surprised to have seen how snugly they were hidden away and how well I looked dressed up in so much wisdom. I laughed a big laugh at myself.

"The captain took boat a few days ahead of us, so as to reach Memphis in time to make arrangements for us when we should reach there. Having everything secure, as far as could be, I and Sam took boat and started down the river. There did not appear to be a particle of suspicion attached to us, as not a question was asked till we reached Memphis, and then an officer only asked our destination. Finding it was that place he said no more. The captain had everything arranged for our convenience, only I put up at a hotel instead of a private boarding house. I thought a private house would have been better, but our hotel accommodations are very good and we are doing well. But among so many strangers we attract attention and have to be continually on our guard. There were so many curious eyes and enquiring faces that one always felt a degree of uneasiness. But I suppose that this was more from our fears and the business we were in than anything else, so more imaginary than real. At any rate, everything passed off well.

"I made for the captain a kind of round-about or jacket, with double lining and the letters were distributed evenly around it and tacked so they would remain stationary or to prevent their collecting into bunches. He dressed himself up like some old farmer citizen, got himself an old plug of a horse and mounted for his journey. No one would have known him as Captain Grimes, so complete was his disguise.

"So far, my task is done. If he reaches you he will tell you the remainder of the history. I feel very lonely now that he is going away, and I being so near. How I wish I could accompany him to your camp. But it seems that it is not best, and so I shall be left here in a strange city and among strange people. I am to remain here till he returns, or I hear from him. O the anxiety of those waiting moments. One would rather be facing the danger than to remain housed up somewhere imagining dangers that never come. But such is life, and I have here with me that Ever Present Guide that has been my unfailing Friend through all these dark days, and I shall try to be satisfied with my lot. O, how hard it is with our impatient nature to say, 'Thy will be done.'

"I have it in mind next time to go through the lines and to see you all in the soldier's camp. God bless you and all the old friends. I still have an abiding faith that we shall meet again. I need not say to you to put your trust in the Omnipotent Arm, for that I know you will do, and rest assured that any service I can render at any time, I will do all that is in my power to do. Again, God bless you. Farewell."

ELLA HERBERT.

CHAPTER XVII.

THE PERILOUS JOURNEY.

Captain Grimes had learned before leaving Memphis that Vicksburg had been invested by Grant's army, but he could not ascertain what portion of the army was inclosed within the fortifications. He understood that Gen. Joe Johnston was at Jackson, Miss., with a considerable force and he did not know but that the Missourians were with him. But whether this or not, he thought it best to report to Johnston. For if the Missouri troops were in Vicksburg, he determined to make an effort to reach them, and he thought he might be of some service to Gen. Johnston by carrying any message he might wish to send to Gen. Pemberton. He reasoned that if he could run the blockade with the mail he could do so with his dispatches.

Traveling by various ways and meanderings, he reached Jackson, Miss., on the morning of the 1st of June, and reported at once to Gen. Johnston. He presented to the General his papers and acquainted him with his mission in all its details. Learning from him that the siege would last an indefinite length of time, he determined at once to make the effort of reaching the garrison. Of this he acquainted Johnston and proposed to take any message he might wish to send.

The General thanked him for his offer and informed him that he greatly desired to communicate with Gen. Pemberton. He especially wished to know his condition and how long he could hold the place; the state of the defending army and all the information concerning the army of Gen. Grant, and should an effort be made for his (Pemberton's) relief, where would be the most available point of attack.

After all arrangements had been made, Captain Grimes informed the General that it was his purpose to strike the Mississippi River at some point above Vicksburg, and by some kind of a raft float past the enemy's gunboats under cover of darkness, and he asked information as to the nearest point he could reach unmolested. Gen. Johnston informed him that his scouts went as far as to Yazoo City, on the Yazoo River, and that he could furnish him with a safe and rapid conduct to that point. Accepting this offer and thanking the General for his kindness as quickly as possible, he was off for the Yazoo.

Taking a circuitous route they experienced but little difficulty in evading the pickets of Gen. Grant's army and reaching the Yazoo.

The Yazoo River empties into the Mississippi some twelve or fifteen miles above Vicksburg, and as Yazoo City was some distance above the mouth of that river, it was too far for the captain to undertake to float down from that point to Vicksburg in one night. And as the whole country was full of scouts and spies from Grant's army, it would not do for him to be seen floating in day time. Taking two of his guides for protection, he wound his way among swamps and cane-brakes until he reached a point near the mouth of the Yazoo. Here fortune seemed to favor him, for right upon the banks of the river lay a cottonwood log, having lodged there by being washed from some saw-mill above. It was at least three feet across the face end, and from fifteen to sixteen feet long. With the help of the scouts it was soon put afloat in the river. Dismissing the guides, the captain waited the going down of the sun before he pushed out into the stream.

The night itself was propitious. For as the sun went down a white fog began to rise upon the water, marking the whole river line. Under cover of this he mounted his log, which lay about half submerged in the water and with a long pole for a guide, pushed off into the stream.

That was a lone, strange ride. The fog soon became so dense, that it was impossible for him to distinguish either shore, or to discern a single object save himself and the log upon which he stood. Smoothly, softly and noiselessly he glided on, not knowing what was before him. But it was not long before he became conscious from the roar of the waters and the rush of the waves that he had entered the grand "Old Father of Waters," and was being borne rapidly toward Vicksburg.

His craft was a very unwieldy one, and he had only a

long pole and a short paddle with which to steer it, and these could only move it slowly. Besides, it would be necessary in passing through the Federal fleet for him to lie down upon the log and as much as possible become a part of it. The difficulty was to steer his craft so as not to come in contact with a gunboat. The fog had become so dense, that even a light could be seen but a short distance ahead. The whereabouts of the boats or the number of them he knew not, but a kind of consciousness came over him that he was nearing the danger line. Peering into the darkness he can distinguish just in front of him a glimmer of light and he begins to make an effort to go round it. But he is nearer to it than he had supposed. He had scarcely time to drop flat upon the log after giving a few strokes with the paddle before the lights of the boat flashed full upon him and he was under its bow. Glancing up, he saw the sentinel standing at his post, the soldiers passing to and fro, and each watch staring out into the waters.

The few strokes he had given with his paddle had turned his craft a little in the right direction and the water parting at the boat's bow gave it a turn that sent it sweeping along the boat's side, but so near as to almost rub it as he passed. But this proved to his advantage. For he is now under the shelving sides and thus hidden from the view of the guards. He can reach out his hand and touch the sides of the great monster, and he fancies he can hear the tread of the sentinel on board. As he approaches the stern of the boat, he sees a flash of light upon the waters below and he knows that in a few moments more he will be in full view of those on board. His heart almost leaps up into his throat as he shoots out from his hiding place as it were into full view, as he supposes, of the guard. He had not taken into consideration the fact that one looking back at the light, could see objects much plainer than those looking from the light could see them. While the light shone with a kind of halo upon the dense fog and waters below, yet so dense was the fog, that it gave only an indistinct outline of objects upon the water.

The pushing of the waters sent his unwieldy craft with a bound out into the light below. Glancing back, he can clearly see the great guns all around and the sentinel on his beat. Just above and not ten feet from him is a guard looking over the stern of the boat and, he imagines, peering down right upon him as he sweeps along. The sight almost froze the blood in his veins and he looked away, listening every moment to hear the crack of a rifle ring out over the waters. But whether the sentinel saw or not, he never knew. The dread suspense was only for a moment, and he felt conscious he had passed safely out into the darkness. Looking across the river each way from the boat he had passed, he could see a line of lights, indicating the position of the blockading fleet, and he felt that he had passed in safety.

The next point for him to consider, was the landing at the right point. Could he see the lights on shore. But here the river came again to his help. It makes a great bend in passing Vicksburg throwing the current close under the batteries on the heights. Upon these heights were lights of the greatest magnitude, arranged so as to throw the greatest light possible across the river. Knowing that the city was at his left hand, he brought his craft as near the left bank as possible. His joy can hardly be pictured when he finds himself under the very guns of Vicksburg, and sees the sentinel upon the shore. He called to the guard who was surprised to hear a voice coming to him apparently out of the waters. Bringing his gun to a ready he shouted, "Who comes there?"

"A friend," said the captain, "I have run the blockade to reach you all here and you will please step down quickly and help me land and anchor my craft."

The log drifted into a little eddy and by the help of the guard the captain was soon ashore, and the log made fast.

"Now," said the captain, "I am your prisoner, call the sergeant and let him take charge of me."

The stream of light darting up in the east showed the captain that he had reached his destination none too soon. The thick fog hung over the river only and a little way from the water's edge, and he was standing in the light of the morning. By the time the sergeant had reached him and he had been conducted to guard headquarters, the sun was up and he could see all around him the work of the great siege.

"Captain," he said, addressing himself to the captain of the guard, "I am a prisoner of war, so far as you are concerned, but I have valuable papers for Gen. Pemberton and I wish to be conducted at once to his headquarters."

"Your request shall be granted," said the guard officer, and calling up two soldiers, he sent them as an escort to Gen. Pemberton.

This is the Sunday morning of the 7th of June, when so many hearts of the Missouri soldiery are made glad by messages from home.

Captain Grimes spent a week among the men, and in gathering up the mail for a return, besides the messages from Gen. Pemberton to Gen. Johnston. Selecting another night when the fog rested heavy on the river, he once more boarded his unsightly craft and by the help of some Confederate soldiers launched out upon a hazardous journey down the river, designing to once more float through the fleet which was anchored below the city, and having passed it, to land at the most available point and make his way to Gen. Johnston, and thence back into Missouri with his precious mail.

Many were the good words spoken and the tokens of love for the dear ones at home whom th e captain might meet with by the way, as his craft drifted off upon the bosom of the great waters, and many eyes peered out through the darkness, watching the moving craft until it was lost in the solitude and they knew that he was gone upon his perilous journey.

CHAPTER XVIII

CAPTAIN GRIMES RETURNS SAFE TO MEMPHIS.

During Captain Grimes' stay in Vicksburg, he had noted the movements and position of the fleet below and the passage was easily effected. He determined to stick to his craft until he passed the mouth of Big Black River, and to land at or near Grand Gulf. This river runs twelve miles in the rear of Vicksburg, and empties into the Mississippi about twenty miles below. Gen. Grant's lines are all between the two rivers. True, he keeps watch by means of scouts and spies upon the movements of Gen. Johnston's army stationed at Jackson, but aside from these there are no Federal forces beyond Big Black River.

It being late at night when Capt. Grimes set out he did not reach the mouth of the Big Black till daylight overtook him. Not being willing to risk himself on his unwieldy craft when there was danger of gun-boats overtaking him, he drew to land and spent the day in the cane-brakes near the water. When night again came on, and a clear, starlight night it was, he mounted his log and pushed out into the broad waters.

It was very easy to distinguish Grand Gulf from the broad expanse of waters. Just below these are the high bluffs rising up from the very water's edge. Upon these hills had once been the Confederate batteries of defense, but here, where a few weeks ago such a great land and navel battle had been fought, all was now silent and still as the grave. At the upper battery the works had been demolished and the old guns, too heavy to be removed by land, lay dismantled; and what was called the lower battery was but a heap of ruins. Not a sentinel kept guard, nor a single soldier wandered through the once strong ramparts of defense. Here captain Grimes pulled his unsightly craft ashore. There was no enemy to meet him

Yours truly

W. H. Kennan.

4

nor friend to extend a hand of greeting. Walking among these ruins he was alone in the solitude, the stars only looked down upon him and smiled; not a sound save the low murmur of the waters of the great river as they rolled on in their hurried march to the gulf at the foot of these grand old hills. Here and there he marked the grave of some fallen veteran—the little house where rest the brave, safe from the sound of war, sleeping in the solitude. These scenes brought to him strange reflections of the past, and solemn memories of the present. In the past he saw men, brave men, strong men, in the very bloom of life, battling for home and country, but now they are sleeping the last sleep. Doubtless many of them far from home, where no familiar feet ever tread, where no gentle hand ever wreathes a single bunch of flowers, no voice ever pronounces a God bless you, and no greetings are spoken. Amid these lone hills he wandered, around these hallowed spots he lingered, not heeding the rapid march of time until the morning star followed by the quick dawn, told him that another day had begun.

Breaking off from his reverie, he took the road direct for Jackson, Miss. Meeting with some friends by the way and obtaining help, by night he found himself at Gen. Johnston's headquarters delivering his papers from Gen. Pemberton, containing the news and progress of the siege.

Having discharged his obligations to Generals Johnston and Pemberton, he set out early next morning for Memphis, Tenn. Gen. Grant having drawn all his available force around Vicksburg, he had no difficulty in making his way. Gen. Johnston sent an escort with him far beyond the Yazoo River, and, assuming his disguise, he had no difficulty in entering the Federal lines.

From the time that Captain Grimes left Miss Ella Herbert the last of May, in Memphis, till his return the last of June, was, to her, a long, weary month of watching and waiting. She was here all alone among strangers and in a strange city, and to her, under strange and peculiar circumstances, with strange scenes transpiring all around her. Nor had she made many acquaintances. Being of rather a secluded turn of mind, diffident and timid in her nature, and withall, dreading inquiry into her objects and the cause of her stay in the city, she deemed it best to keep herself as much as possible to herself. Her faithful servant, Sam, had secured quarters near the river with a motherly old colored women where he spent each night, but ready to meet his mistress each morning, and to attend to all her wants. He accompanied her upon her walks, or to the levee to look at the boats and little crafts that ply upon the waters, or maybe to take a ride in a skiff some calm evenings.

How she loved to play upon these waters. They washed the shores of her own loved State, and to her they seemed to be the connecting link between her own lone heart and the dear old home. She would gaze upon that great stream and almost picture herself floating up its current until the broad prairies of old Missouri opened up to her view, and memory carried her to the scenes of her childhood.

But she would then break off from these reveries to the mission of Captain Grimes. She read every day of the siege of Vicksburg and had learned that the Missouri troops were inside the fortifications. Had he reached them, or had he been captured? And if he had reached them, how had he found them? Who were among the slain? Or what the news? In the still hours of the evening she could hear the roar of the great guns in the distance as it was borne upon the bosom of the mighty waters and she could but wish herself inside those works if only for a day. Oh, to be so far away and yet so near. In such moments as these, the dread suspense was unbearable and she would say to herself, "How long must this dread unknowing and unknown continue? What if Captain Grimes is now a prisoner, or, more dreadful still, if he has met his death? How shall I know, and when shall I know?" But she had this thought, that the capture of so important a personage would be chronicled in the papers. She, therefore, scanned every paper that came to the hotel for the least possible tidings of him. Sometimes she walked with Sam to his new home and to have some talk with his other grandma as he called her. And, indeed, she was a model of motherly love and Christian devotion.

"La, chile," she would say, "de good Lord will take care of you; He cares for po' ole nigger like me, an' ef He do dat, He care for white folks. Dese am skeery times, an' I dunno what de worl' am comin' to, but we jes hab to trus' in de Lord; He know all about how to take care of us."

Ella found much comfort in this plain, simple faith. Only trusting and so sweetly trusting. Happy such an old age.

"Yas, miss," the old negro would say, "you young, you has many troubles before you, if you lib to be as old as I is. You dunno what dis wa may bring to you yit, but you'll fine de good Lord de bes' frien'. I is ole, jis on de ribber brink, and many is de trials Ise passed froo, but de Lord has nebber lef' me. Ole marse is gone and ole miss is gone; an' I doan know what fur, but I is here yet. But I'll cross ober fo' long."

And thus Ella spent many pleasant moments upon the banks of the river, in the cool shade listening to these comforting words of the good old darkey, who had learned such precious lessons of grace. "There is," she said to herself, "a reality in the religion of Jesus." As never before, she understood that the blind see, the deaf hear, and the poor have the Gospel. How the highway was made plain and the wayfaring should not err therein. Here was a simple child-like faith, a true and blessed reliance, and a hope which was indeed an anchor to the soul.

In her dread, dreary and long waiting, Ella had not forgotten the house of prayer. She was a regular attendant at the Sunday service, morning and night. Though strictly on the reserve, yet as a strange visitant she came and went, apparently wrapped in the solitude of her own thoughts. Little did she dream of the many inquiries made of the strange visitant, and that she was doing the very thing she was striving not to do. While not creating any suspicion of the real role she was playing, yet she was making of herself a specially marked character. She had come, a stranger among strangers, and that strange character was still maintained. Her reserve, her dignity, her noble bearing, and her devotion, all spoke for her of the Christian woman that she was. But the question on many lips was, Who is she? Where is she from? and why is she here?

People were generally acquainted with the circumstances of war, and while this strange being, who, nevertheless, carried something of sunshine in her walk, moved among them so unknown, yet the conclusion was that she was some refugee from Missouri who had been banished, or had fled the horrors of guerrilla warfare, and had sought obscurity to wait till the war was over.

Sunday, June the 28th, was a long, lone and weary day to Ella Herbert. True, she had attended church, and the congregation had seemed to enjoy the service: for all she knew it was good. She had heard nothing, had seen nothing. She was living away from herself, she was an abstract of something she knew not what. This terrible suspense, this dark uncertainty, this awful dread of she knows not what; this great anxiety for the future, and yet the dread of its revelation; what weal or woe hangs upon the uncertain hour? What the unfolding of these dark and dreary days? The suspense was becoming unbearable.

The shades of night were settling down and the heavy clouds hung like a death-shroud over the city and the sighing night wind only answered the throbbing of the lonely heart. Ella retired early to her room, unable to look out upon the dark world that seemed to mock her constant effort to unveil the future. Lighting the lamp and taking up her Bible, she tried to find some word of promise, some gleam of hope, some ray of light, some sweet spot of sunshine, but all seemed a dark and dreary blank. O, could she but lock the wheels of thought, could she but shut the doors of her mind, it would have been a sweet relief. But mind would not stop, thought crowded upon thought till she felt overwhelmed in the depths of its mysterious workings. Laying the book aside, she folded her face in her hands and found relief in tears. And they brought a sweet relief. And then she prayed, "Father, help Thy child; here she is alone, poor, weak and weary thing, tossed upon life's billowy waves in this strange place, knowing nothing and yet dreading all. Father, be to me the Friend Thou art, my light, my strength, my all." A sweet calm came over her, and taking up her Bible again, her eyes fell upon the 23rd Psalm, and to her it was like a ray of light from the glory world. She read: "The Lord is my Shepherd, I shall not want"; and the whole truth of it seemed sealed to her heart. "Yes," she said, "He *is* my Shepherd, and on this promise I will rely. And here she realized the promise of God spoken of in Isaiah lxv: 24. "And it shall come to pass, that before they call I will answer, and while they are yet speaking I will hear." For just as she had finished reading the Psalm, and while she was yet drinking in the sweetness of it, she heard excited voices approaching the door and she recognized one as the voice of Sam, her faithful servant. He seemed to be in perfect raptures of delight. She heard him say, "She's been mighty sad all day, didn't say nuthin' and 'peared away off. But how dem bright eyes 'el sparkle now."

Divining what it all meant, she did not wait to hear a knock at the door, but hastened to open it; and there, sure enough, stood Captain Grimes.

"Bless God," said Sam, "he's come," and the boy was almost wild with joy. Not so much for himself, but his mistress had looked so sad, it had troubled him.

"Yes, Sam," replied Ella, "bless God he has come," and she felt that the dark cord of uncertainty had been broken, that whatever the news he brought whether of life or death, the chain of vague, dark, doubtful nothingness had been severed, and the spell that had bound her, growing darker and darker each day and hour had been torn off and a something, whatever it might be, of life or death, tangible, was before her. Anything she would say, but this lone enclosure, this prison house with one's self, this living shut out, and shut up from all material things, and dwelling alone in one's solitary thoughts.

-"Captain," she said, "you know not what I have suffered during these lone and dark days." And when she had heard his report she said: "A thousand times would I have passed through all these perils rather than to have suffered in this dread solitude."

"Then," said the captain, "You do not propose to be shut up in this place any more."

"No, indeed," was the reply; "I shall go through the lines. I feel that I might have been some benefit this time, but as our forces are shut up in Vicksburg, it may have been as well that I remained here. But when we return, if we cannot go through together, I am sure I can reach the Confederate lines. Besides, it would be my delight to see the Confederate camps."

And so it was determined that both would go through on the return trip, the details of which could be arranged after they had collected the mail.

They immediately began to arrange for the return to Missouri, and the distribution of the mail the captain had collected and brought that far upon his journey. It was divided
into two parts, Miss Ella taking one, after leaving St. Louis and
going up the North Missouri railroad, distributed it at the dif
ferent offices.   The captain took the Missouri Pacific to
Sedalia, and from thence by stage, to Kansas City.

This arrangement was carried out with but little difficulty,
and in one week more, Ella Herbert found herself in the old
home circle surrounded by her many friends to whom she
brought tokens of love from the far-away scenes of conflict,
and to whom she revealed, with thrilling interest, her many
adventures.

While in St. Louis, the captain arranged with some friend
for the collecting of the mail so that it was not necessary for
either of them to return to that place till all was ready.

CHAPTER XIX.

SURRENDER OF VICKSBURG.

We must now return to Vicksburg and its gallant defenders. The siege continued with its varying changes, sometimes a comparative quiet and then a bursting storm. The men had been living on reduced rations from the time the siege began. And now it was very apparent that, with all this precaution, the rations could not last much longer. The bread supply was exhausted by the 15th of June, but some ingenious brain had originated the idea of making bread of what was known as Cow Peas. These peas were raised in great abundance throughout the cotton States, and when stewed with a little pork, or seasoned with butter and cream, were very palatable. The soldier sometimes had a little pork or beef, but to him butter and cream was an unknown quantity. But to take these peas and grind them like corn or wheat, and make them into dough with a little clear water and bake them into bread was a very different thing. True, hunger will give an appetite for almost anything that will appease its gnawings, but not many incomiums were ever passed upon the inventor of "*pea bread.*" While the bread supply had been exhausted, yet the meat supply lasted until about the first of July and then "pea bread" was all there was left. In this extremity, a mule that had unguardedly come within the range of the enemies' guns was killed by a stray shot and some of the men concluded they would see how it would do as a substitute for beef. To their surprise it was a good substitute. The appetite being so quickened by hunger may have had something to do with this. But, however that may be, the result of the experiment soon spread through camp, and then began the slaughter of mules. The meat was taken from the bone and cut into thin strips or slices, and hung over the fire to roast or dry. This was called "jerked mule," or "mule beef."

But even the supply of mule could not last long, and it was evident that the garrison could not hold out much longer. There was no apparent prospect of relief from without. Gen. Johnston was at Jackson, Miss., with all the available force that the South could give him, but this was insufficient to make a successful attack upon the great army of Gen. Grant. While Vicksburg was a very strong place and ordinarily impregnable to assault as had already been proven, yet Gen. Grant's position was also impregnable. He had the Big Black River in his rear with its frowning bluffs and all the intervening country a succession of hills, and these hills strongly fortified. Johnston, therefore, to make an attack, must cross the river in the face of this opposition and then force his way through this range of fortified hills for a distance of twelve miles. This, with his small force, was out of the question. All he could hope to do, would be to make an attack, so as to draw Grant's attention, and by drawing off some of his force enable Gen. Pemberton to cut his way out of Vicksburg. This course might have been practicable at one time, but at this date it was utterly impossible. The soldiers had lain in the ditches from the 18th of May to the first of July, with but little exercise and living on quarter rations, and these of a poor kind. Under this condition of things it would have been impossible for Pemberton's men to have marched more than twelve miles in a day had they have had no enemy to contend with. The question of relief, therefore, was out of the question.

To add to all these difficulties, the Fourth of July was approaching. And, whether true or untrue, the word had gone out that on that day, General Grant's forces would make a desperate assault upon the works. The two lines were in easy speaking distance of each other and it was the taunt of the Federal that he would celebrate the Fourth in Vicksburg. This belief had obtained throughout Pemberton's army. The soldier could but look upon such a thing with dread. The lines were so close, that almost in an instant, and without warning, the Federal army could be pouring over the fortifications, and men stood aghast at the mere thought of the carnage that would follow.

Whatever may be said of the blunders that brought General Pemberton's army into Vicksburg or caused it to be thus shut up in the fortifications, there can no blame attach to the surrender. Far better to surrender upon honorable terms than the dreadful carnage that must follow an assault upon the works.

After General Pemberton had held a consultation with his leading officers, among whom was Gen. John S. Bowen, commander of one division of the army, it was determined to send out a flag of truce to know of Gen. Grant the terms upon which he would accept a surrender. The time in reaching Gen. Grant's headquarters and of the conference, lasted from about ten in the morning to three in the evening. During this time, hostilities were suspended, and the soldiers of the two contending armies extended courtesies over the works. Standing upon the top of the works, each could touch the guns of the other. To men unused to the ways of war and the soldier's life it looked strange to see those who but an hour ago were engaged in mortal combat, seeking every opportunity to take each other's life, now in friendly conversation and even relating some of the amusing incidents of the siege.

On the return of the flag of truce in the evening, hostilities were resumed and from then until night-fall, it seemed to be with renewed vigor upon the part of the Confederates Especially was this true upon the river front. The Confederate commander of the heavy guns on the river front felt that he had not enough to do, having been compelled to save his ammunition for an attack of the gun-boats. This inactivity had enabled the Federal forces to erect a line of batteries in the low ground on the opposite side of the river, unmolested. The Confederate battery commander understanding that a surrender was on the tapis determined to show his "friends" across the river how dexterously he could handle his guns. Turning them directly upon the enemy's batteries, he poured such a storm of shell and shot, plunging down into their midst where they had but little protection, as soon dismantled most of their guns and swept the whole bottom beyond of a single foe. In the language of Capt. Lowry of the Third Regiment Missouri troops, who was watching the battle, "You could see brass flying in the air for half an hour after the firing was over."

The closing of the day ended the struggle. The Confederate forces knew they must surrender and the Federal troops firmly believed they would. With this impression the two armies lay down to rest and to sleep. One to dream of the sad hours of to-morrow, the other of its glorious victories. Such is the life of man. That which is life to one is often death to another, that which brings sorrow and weeping to one heart, brings joy and smiles to another.

The terms of surrender were as reasonable as could have been expected. The Confederates were to lay down their arms and all the munitions of war were to be turned over to the Federal authorities. But the Confederate troops were to be paroled and allowed three days' rations, and to march into their own country where they were not to take up arms until duly exchanged. The sick and the wounded were to be sent by boat to Mobile, Ala., and delivered to the Confederate authorities.

During the night it was determined to accept these terms, and early next morning a flag of truce was dispatched to Gen. Grant, asking for a conference between him and Gen. Pemberton. The place of meeting was soon arranged, and Gen. Grant, with a few of his officers, met Generals Pemberton and Bowen, and the conditions of surrender were signed.

Gen. Pemberton then informed Gen. Grant that he had no rations for his men and asked him to furnish them until the terms of surrender could be complied with, and his men could reach a place where they could be supplied by their own country-men. To this Gen. Grant very generously acceded, and from this on the garrison was fed from Gen. Grant's commissary stores, while they remained in the city and then were given three days' supply for the march.

The morning of the Fourth of July was clear and beautiful, but to the poor Confederate soldier the sun had lost much of its lustre, and the Fourth of July all its charms. Whatever the circumstances that forced the surrender, and however impossible it was to hold out longer, it was very mortifying to the true soldier to lay down the old battle-worn flag that he had carried on so many battle fields, and that had waved defiantly so long over their heads as an ensign of valor. And the "old musket" that had been their trusted friend, and had sent death into the enemies' ranks and had driven back so many assaults; to lay it down was no easy task. And then there was that, overreaching it all, principle for which they fought. Many sacred memories cluster around those consecrated hills. Besides the deeds of valor due every defender, here slept many a friend the long sleep that knows no waking till the trumpet shall sound the end of the last great battle and the beginning of an endless peace. Among the slain was none more lamented then Gen. Martin E. Green, commander of the Missouri troops. He was killed by a sharpshooter on the 28th of June.

It was a solemn line of men that formed that morning and took up their guns for the last time and marched outside of the works with a trailing flag. But their captors were generous. There were no signs of exultation, no shouts of rejoicing, no taunts or jeers. The Federal officers stood with heads uncovered and swords at salute, while the privates, in a long line upon either side, stood at a "present arms." The guns were "stacked," the flags were folded and the Confederate line marched back to their camps amid a silence and stillness befitting their feelings. They even felt grateful to their fortunate enemy. Thus Vicksburg, the key to the Mississippi River, had fallen and a free access was given the Federal fleet to the Gulf of Mexico.

So soon as all the requirements of the conditions of surrender, such as giving parole could be complied with all that part of the army not disabled by wound or sickness, marched out of Vicksburg, and by easy stages continued the march to Demopolis, Ala., on the Tombigbee River, where they went into "parole camp" to await an exchange.

But we must not forget to look after our wounded soldier, George Tracy, in the hospital. His wound had indeed proven to be a serious one, but with all the annoyance, his careful nursing, with the blessings of the Power Above, he was enabled to conquer, and each day, from the time Capt. Grimes left him till the surrender, found him stronger. He was among those who were not able to march out with the men and must be sent by flag of truce to Mobile. In fact, he could walk but little when the surrender took place. It was the 30th of July before arrangements were completed, and a boat was ready to set out for "New Orleans," and then two boats were necessary to convey all the sick and wounded.

The boats arrived at New Orleans on Saturday, August the first, about 3 P. M. Orders were immediately issued, forbidding any one going ashore and refusing permission for any one to come aboard the boat and for the first time since the surrender a Federal guard was placed over the prisoners. The news soon spread over town, of the arrival of the Confederate prisoners from Vicksburg, and the women of the place began to gather from every quarter, bringing all the delicacies the place could afford or that could tempt the appetite of a hungry soldier. For a while these provisions were permitted to be sent aboard the boats, but it was soon apparent that there would not be boats enough to contain all that was being brought. The women came in swarms, not by the hundred, but thousands lined the shore up and down the levee, and by night a perfect sea of faces reached back from the wharf some distance, each woman with a parcel showing her devotion to the Southern cause. Despite the efforts of the guard, which had been doubled, some of these ladies forced their way into the boat to shake hands with the defenders of their homes. When night came on, all disappeared quietly. But next morning, by the time it was light, there began such a stream of women pouring in from every direction as was apparent would treble the demonstration of the day before. There were old women with gray hairs, middle-aged women with their children and charming young maidens with their fascinating curls and wavy hair all eager to show their devotion to the Southern soldiery. They were quiet and orderly. But thousands and thousands jammed all the available space up and down the wharf and clear back to the houses and even the tops of many of these were covered with women and children eager to catch a glimpse of a "gray coat." These pressed down to the very edge of the boat. Orders to disperse did no good. The fact is, there was no need for such an order, as all was quiet. But this was "Ben. Butler's rule." The guard was doubled and trebled until a cordon of soldiers with fixed bayonets, girdled the prisoner's boat. About 8 o'clock a regiment of infantry pressed its way to the boat and with fixed bayonets began pushing the vast throng back. At the same time, a squadron of cavalry came dashing down among the women and children, and a six gun battery was brought down under whip and formed on the wharf. Some few of the people were run over, and all were sent frightened and screaming back to the houses and pavement. Here a Federal officer, mounted on horseback, came dashing up the pavement in front of the houses, but in making a short turn his horse fell, and he was sent whirling to the ground; whether killed or not the writer never knew, but a yell went up from that great throng which was joined by the rebel prisoners on the boats. This so incensed the authorities, that the Confederates were forced into close quarters and threatened with punishment were such demonstrations repeated.

About twelve o'clock, the Confederate prisoners were transferred to the gulf steamer, "Gen. Banks," and were off for Mobile. After some delay, Mobile was reached, on the 7th of August, where Tracy spent a few days and then took boat for Montgomery and thence through Columbus, Ga., to Union Springs, Ala., where he spent several weeks recruiting and gaining strength. On the 11th of September, he started to join the command at Demopolis, at which place he arrived on the 16th.

During the stay in camp, arrangements were made to consolidate the two brigades into one, and at the same time to consolidate regiments and companies. The Second and Sixth, the Third and Fifth, and the First and Fourth were consolidated in the order named.

Gen. Bowen, who had formerly been the commander of the division, soon after the surrender of Vicksburg, was taken sick and was never able to go with the command further than Raymond, Miss., where he died the 20th of July. Col. F. M. Cockrell, the former commander of the Sixth Regiment was promoted to Brigadier-General and placed in command of the brigade thus consolidated.

The whole of the command that surrendered at Vicksburg, having been exchanged by the 15th of September, 1863, they were ready to join the army under Gen. Leonidus Polk.

CHAPTER XX.

SHERMAN'S ADVANCE INTO MISSISSIPPI AND THE GEORGIA CAMPAIGN.

The command broke parole camp the 19th of October, and took train for Meridian, Miss., at which place they arrived on the 20th and went into camp for a month.

It now seemed to be the purpose of the Federal authorities to invade the Southern States from the West, and to take Mobile, Ala., by attacking it in the rear. To this end Gen. Sherman marched out of Vicksburg on the morning of February the 1st, 1864, at the head of a column thirty thousand strong, marching in the direction of Meridian, Miss. At the same time, Gens. Grierson and Smith left Memphis, Tenn., at the head of a force of ten thousand cavalry and mounted infantry. The purpose was to overrun, as much as possible, the State of Mississippi, destroying supplies and cutting off communications by tearing up the railroad. The two columns to form a junction at Meridian, and then, with the combined force, to move on to Mobile.

Gen. Polk was in command of the Mississippi department, but not with sufficient force to meet the advancing column under Gen. Sherman. But he at once put his column of about twenty thousand, in motion to meet the advance under Gen. Sherman, while he sent Gen. Forest to watch, and as much as possible retard the progress of Gens. Grierson and Smith. Gen. Polk fell back slowly before the advance of Sherman, saving all his baggage and provisions, to Demopolis, Ala.

In giving an account of the work done by Gen. Forest on this campaign, I quote from "The Civil War," by Mrs. Snyder:

"In contending with the other column, General Forest added new laurels to his fame as a cavalry officer. With only a force of less than twenty-five hundred men, it was imperatively necessary for him to crush this magnificently equipped cavalry of the enemy, nearly

142

thrice his own number. Near West Point this undaunted Tennesseean made a stand, and having posted his men irregularly in the bushes, he waited the rush and onslaught of the enemy. As the Federals rode to the attack, the Confederate rifles began to crack and with these whip-like reports, the enemy were seen to fall in such alarming rapidity as to produce confusion and to check their advance. However, they reformed and charged again, but the empty saddles continued to increase to such an extent as to spread a contagious terror among them and they gave up the contest and fled.

"Again, at Okalona, on the evening of February the 21st, the Federals made a disastrous attempt to crush Forest's small force. In this conflict, the rout of the enemy was more complete than in the first, and they turned and fled precipitately in the direction of Memphis, with Gen. Gholson pursuing with only six hundred men."

Gen. Sherman had depended upon this column of cavalry and mounted infantry to gather supplies for his army of invasion, but now, not only was this swept away, but the indomitable Forest had swooped down like a swift eagle with most of his forces upon his column of infantry. Gen. Polk gives this account of the results of this campaign:

"The concentration of our cavalry on the enemy's column of cavalry from West Tennessee formed the turning point of the campaign. That concentration broke down his only means of subsisting his infantry. His column was defeated and routed, and his whole force compelled to make a hasty retreat. Never did a grand campaign inaugurated with such pretentions, terminate more ingloriously. With a force three times that which was opposed to its advance, they have been defeated and forced to leave the field with a loss of men, small arms and artillery."

The campaign from Vicksburg and Memphis having proved such a disastrous failure, General Sherman transferred all his force except a - few guards along the river to Chattanooga, Tenn. Here he collected a force of ninety-eight thousand men which was divided into three divisions under Generals Thomas, Schofield and McPherson.

General Joseph E. Johnston was placed in command of the Confederate forces, numbering not over forty thousand men. Leaving Gen. Forest to protect the borders of Mississippi and Alabama with his cavalry, General Polk, with all his force was ordered to join Gen. Johnston. Heretofore the armies had been divided into comparatively small portions, scattered from Arkansas, west of the Mississippi River, through Tennessee to

Virginia. Now they were concentrated into two grand divisions. One under Gen. U. S. Grant, whose objective point was Richmond, Va.; the other under Gen. W. T. Sherman, whose purpose was to penetrate the South by way of Savannah, Ga., where again recruiting his army and getting supplies he was to form a junction with Gen. Grant in Virginia.

General Cockrell's brigade, now a part of Gen. French's division, had moved up to Tuscaloosa, Ala., where it remained in camp a few days, but on the morning of the 16th of May, it had orders to move with all speed by way of Rome, Ga., and join the forces under Gen. Johnston at Kingston.

By a rapid march of sixty miles in two days, the brigade reached Rome where a small force of Confederates were being hard pressed by a force of the enemy. The two days' march were telling ones upon the men. Foot-sore and weary they reached Rome about an hour by sun, and were at once put aboard the cars. After a short run, they reached Kingston and next morning were assigned their position in line, being attached to Gen. Polk's corps.

General Johnston had now received all the reinforcements that it was possible to give him and it seems he determined to give the enemy battle. He had been falling back stubbornly and slowly before the advance of Sherman, contesting every inch of ground from Chattanooga to Kingston, and here, on the morning of May the 18th, he issued his battle order, stating that the army would retreat no longer, but give the enemy battle. The Confederate army had unbounded confidence in their commander, and when he declared that he would turn and fight they believed that he felt able to meet the force that was against him. The proclamation, therefore, was received with shouts of joy by the devoted soldiery. But it was a matter of great surprise to them when, after waiting all day for the order to advance, they received orders at night to fall back across the Etawa River.

The failure to fight at this point was a mistake. Gen. Johnston himself admits it. Gen. Sherman had, the evening before, divided his force, sending a large portion of it to cross the river at Rome, Ga., and had directed them to move down the south bank so as to strike Johnston's rear. That portion of Gen. Sherman's army was, on the morning of the 18th of

H. A. Ricketts

May, twenty-five miles away and across the river. Had General Johnston have thrown his whole force against the enemy in his front, he had the chance of overthrowing it before this flanking party could be called back to its assistance.

Gen. Johnston assigns as the reason that he did not fight, that after having formed his line of battle early in the morning and when he was just in the act of ordering an advance along the whole line he received word from Gen. Polk, commanding the left wing, that the enemy was moving in force upon his flank. This necessitated a change of his line of battle. But by the time that this change was effected, it was discovered to be a mistake as to the enemy advancing, and by the time General Polk had returned to the position which he had held in the morning, it was 2 o'clock in the evening. To begin a movement that late in the day, even though successful for a time, it could not be rapidly followed up, and the enemy, seeing the intention, would have an opportunity during the night to call together his force and retrieve such loss as he might sustain in so short an engagement. To await and give battle next day, gave the part of Sherman's army marching down to Johnston's rear too much of an advantage provided the attack in front was not successful. General Johnston, therefore, determined to fall back and await another opportunity.

General Sherman instead, as Johnston had hoped, of following the Confederate army to the Etawa River, moved his whole force across the river at Rome, thus uniting the two divisions. The division that had already crossed was halted until all were joined together. General Johnston having brought all his army safely across the river on the 23rd, again put it in motion to meet the advance of Sherman's column. On the evening of the 25th, the two columns met and the Divisions of Generals Claborne and Stewart had a heavy engagement lasting until darkness put an end to the battle, the Confederate forces occupying the battle ground. On the morning of the 26th, Polk's corps took position at Elsworth Mountain which position it occupied until night, when it was moved to the right and took position at New Hope church, a position formerly occupied by some Alabama troops. Here the Missourians found themselves in close proximity to the Federal lines. Next morning sharpshooting opened furiously and continued during their stay in that position.

On the night of June the first, the army was again put in motion, falling back through rain and mud in the direction of Lost Mountain. The enemy did not follow closely and the mountain was reached on the morning of the 6th of June. On the evening of the 7th, Gen. French's Division was moved about four miles to the right and placed on reserve. On the 8th they were moved a mile further to the right and still held in reserve. On the 9th, they were put in position at Latamore's farm, where they remained until the night of the 18th.

Some very hard fighting took place on this line and French's Division suffered considerable loss. But the worst loss to the division was that of their corps commander, Gen. Polk. He was killed on Pine Mountain the 14th of June, 1864. Gen. Stewart was placed in command of his corps.

From this place the army fell back on the night of the 18th, to Kennesaw Mountain, and began to fortify. The enemy followed closely and by 10 o'clock were throwing shell over the mountain. The men never did enjoy throwing up breast-works and when they reached this place, weary and tired, they argued that the enemy could not reach them with shell. The summit of the mountain was covered over with rock, so that breast-works were very difficult of construction. Under these circumstances they went to work very reluctantly. From their high position they could see all the movements of the enemy, they watched them move up within a mile of the mountain, take up their position and plant their batteries. With the impression that the enemy could not reach them with their guns, one can imagine their surprise when the first shell thrown went whizzing far above the summit of the highest peak. It was not a question of doubt any more, and the men forgot their weariness in the endeavor to throw up protection. Picks flew and shovels were brought into quick requisition, and in a few hours there was a line of works the whole length of the mountain.

About 3 o'clock in the evening the enemy opened fire upon the mountain with about thirty-six pieces of artillery and to one at a distance it looked impossible for one to live in such a position.

From the top of the mountain there was a fine view of all the valley below and one could see all the movements of Sherman's army for a great distance.

On the morning of the 27th of June, the enemy was seen massing his forces in front of the mountain, evidently with the intention of attacking the Confederate position. From the Confederate standpoint this was a most daring and even reckless undertaking. And considering Gen. Sherman's usual cautiousness was a great surprise. Yet there were some good reasons for it. Gen. Johnston had extended his lines further than usual, and it was natural for Gen. Sherman to suppose that the mountain being naturally strong, Johnston had but little force upon top of it. To add to this impression, there was never more than a mere picket line in the works, just enough to keep watch while the great body of the army lay over on the opposite side for protection. They had cut narrow, angling trenches across the summit through which they could rapidly pass and in a few moments fill the trenches. Gen. Sherman, therefore, concluded that the skirmish line, as it were, was all the infantry force that occupied this position.

Notwithstanding the fact that Gen. Sherman's army numbered ninety thousand and that there was probably not over six or eight thousand men upon the mountain, yet they felt able to hold it against the whole force of ninety thousand. The mountain, from its highest point, ran in a southerly direction a distance of a mile or more. This highest peak formed the apex of the ridge; it was from this in the other direction almost due east inclining north of east a succession of hills forming a kind of mountain range. It was upon that wing running south that the Federal forces were preparing to make an assault. Around the extreme south end flowed a beautiful stream of water in a southwesterly course. All along upon the banks of this stream was a thick cluster of undergrowth lining the banks, put, at intervals, behind this undergrowth and out of view of the enemy were thirty or forty pieces of artillery, so arranged as to sweep the whole face of the mountain fronting the enemy. Coming down from the highest point was a canyon or cave. In this was concealed six or eight pieces of cannon, so that opening fire from the batteries along the creek and those in the canyon would subject the advancing enemy to a terrible cross-fire. Beginning at the base of the mountain and running back near a half mile was an open field through which the charging column had to pass; that was also in full range of all the Confederate guns.

With a knowledge of the condition of things it was not a question with the Confederates whether they could repulse the enemy or not. The only question with them was as to how many of the enemy would ever return to tell of the desperate undertaking.

In the woods beyond the field described, the enemy massed his force and prepared for the assault. The height of the mountain permitted the enemy's guns to play upon the Confederate works over the head of the advancing column till it was well up its sides and near the works. When the enemy was ready to advance, they opened a terrific cannonade upon the Confederate works.

The advance of those columns was a grand sight, as they came out of the woods into the open field with swords glistening in the sunlight and colors flying, and bayonets sparkling, and the martial tread of trained heroes. Here they came pouring on in column, in line, in mass, filling all the plain below and still pouring out of the timber in the rear. Despite the fact that the enemy's guns were doing havoc with the Confederate works, pouring in one constant stream of shell and shot, filling the air with the missiles of death, the Confederate soldier caught the inspiration of the hour. That line of men moving so grandly, and the thought of its awful fate thrilled his every nerve; he mounted the works, took off his cap and waving it over his head, gave cheer after cheer to the advancing host. Several of Cockrell's men lost their lives while standing upon the works, cheering the foe. The order was passed down the line not to fire until the gun on the highest peak of the mountain gave the signal. On swept the advancing enemy, and up the side of the mountain until their artillery ceases its firing and leaves the infantry to finish its work. The moment before the firing of that signal gun was one of fearful import; the firing of that gun means death to thousands. An awful stillness hovers over the Confederate line, the soldier is crouching as the lion behind the works, ready for the spring upon its prey. Breathlessly they grasp their guns as they listen to the heavy tread of the advancing column. That column understood the stillness, and a kind of fearful dread took hold of it as it contemplated the bursting storm. Upon the extreme left the enemy has actually reached the works, and just in front all along the line they are within ten paces of the intrenchments. But now, above the din of the enemy's muskets and the tread of the marching hosts rings out the signal of death. Suddenly, as if the mountain had burst wide open from crest to base along the ridge, and poured forth all the pent-up fires of buried ages, a blaze shot out of the whole length of the Confederate line. Cannon belched forth as it had been streams of red hot lead rolling down and around the mountain side; the mountain was shaken from summit to base by the roaring thunder, as flame after flame of leaden fire shot out and around it. The enemy did not reel or stagger, they were literally swept down the mountain side, and fled across the open field through which they had just passed in such grandeur. The flight was in wild disorder and utter ruin.

Never was destruction so swift or a grand charge so disastrous. Fifteen minutes from the time the signal gun was fired, the battle was over and the Federal forces were beyond the reach of the Confederate guns, leaving all the mountain side and the field beyond, covered with the slain. "A few more such charges as this would have left Gen. Sherman without an army." The loss of the Missouri Brigade was about seventy.

On the night of the second of July, Johnston's forces fell back to what was known as Sand Hill or Bushy Ridge; on the night of the 4th, fell back to the Chatahooche River, a portion of the army crossing, leaving Stewart's corps, formerly Polk, on the north bank, till the night of the 10th, when they crossed over. Both armies seemed weary with the long watching and fighting, and stopped to rest, which was enjoyed by the men for several days.

The Confederate forces had now fallen back to within six miles of Atlanta, one of the objective points of the Federal army. The enemy having crossed the river above on the morning of the 19th, the Confederate troops took up the line of battle east of the railroad, the line running northwest and southeast, and began to throw up breast-works.

The whole army was startled this morning by the news that General Joseph E. Johnston had been removed and Gen. J. B. Hood placed in command. Gen. Johnston was not only loved, but idolized by his men, and the men were not only amazed, but indignant. The expression could be heard on every hand,

General Johnston removed! and for what! His retreat before
so great an army had been a masterly one. He left nothing to
fall into the hands of the enemy and there was never a
moment that he was not ready for battle. When his army fell
back, every division went direct to its place, and the line was
formed at once and ready for the reception of the enemy.
Never did a man handle his men with more ability. True,
Atlanta might have fallen, but in every move he was drawing
Sherman farther from his supplies, giving him a longer line to
defend and with only one road by which to receive his supplies,
making his condition more critical; his forces were being
weakened every day one way and another. The question may
well be asked, Why his removal? But it was all too true, and
the only reason an incensed army could give, was that he did
not suit the President.

It was now evident that a different policy would be pursued, and it occasioned no surprise when it was announced on
the morning of the 20th, that the army would prepare for
action in front. The battle which was fought that evening,
was called the battle of "Peach-tree Creek," in which but little
was gained to the Confederates. The troops engaged were
Hardee's Corps against Gen. Thomas, of Sherman's army.
The troops fought well, but the enemy was prepared for them
and held their own.

On the night of the 21st, the Confederate forces fell back to
the works around Atlanta. Gen. Hardee occupied the right,
Lee the centre and Stewart the left. On the morning of the
22d, Gen. Hardee moved out from his position and attacked
the enemy in flank and rear, routing him and capturing sixteen
pieces of artillery and 3,000 prisoners. Had not his men began that detestable practice of plunder, the victory might
have been carried to success.

Now began a series of engagements which resulted in but
little advantage to the Confederates; the same monotonous
scenes were re-enacted here that had been repeated over and
over during the whole line of march, shelling and sharp-
shooting.

On the 18th of August, Gen. Sherman withdrew his force
from the front of Atlanta, and swinging around Gen. Hood's
left, marched with the greater portion of his army toward

Macon, Ga. Gen. Hardee was sent with his corps to meet this flank movement, and on the 30th, he met Sherman's advance column near Jonesboro, and at once attacked it in force, but the Confederates were repulsed with considerable loss. Gen. Hood being outflanked and all his means of supplies cut off, evacuated Atlanta and joined Gen. Hardee at Jonesboro.

CHAPTER XXI.

GATHERING THE MAIL. THE CAPTAIN AND MISS HERBERT IN TROUBLE.

Leaving General Sherman in quiet possession of Atlanta, and the Confederate army resting after a hard campaign of over three months' duration at Lovejoy, we will now look after the "Confederate Mail Carrier."

When Captain Grimes and Ella Herbert separated, the first of July, it was their expectation to return to St. Louis by the first of August and to make their journey to the Confederate army and back again to Missouri before the winter closed in upon them. "But the best laid schemes o' mice and men gang oft aglee." Not long after Ella returned home, the scarlet fever broke out in the neighborhood and her brother and two sisters were stricken with the disease. After weeks of weary watching and waiting, she saw her little brother and one sister laid in the cold grave. Soon after, she too, was stricken down and brought very near to death's door.

O, the darkness of those sad hours. The tramp of war upon every hand, the dreaded robber, or marauding bands as they were called, prowling through the country; every day bringing the sad news of some good citizen being taken from his peaceful home and shot down like a dog; no feeling of safety anywhere. And then the angel of death taking from home some of its sweetest jewels. Ella Herbert never realized till now how hard it was to say: "Thy will be done." But then when she read of the mansions on high, of the bright home in the fadeless skies, where life is ever glorious, and then knew that these sweet ones had gone from the dark trials here; and still more, when she had a realization of God's sweet presence and care over her, with firm conviction she could lay hold upon God's promise and rest calmly upon His Word. In such moments as these, she felt ashamed of her own faithlessness.

In this dark hour, how sweet to her were the words of the blessed Lord, "Let not your heart be troubled; ye believe in God, believe also in *Me*." "Yes," she would say, "I believe in God, not only that there is a God, but a great God; a God of power and of purpose, and a purpose concerning the least of the works of His hands; and I believe that that purpose will be fulfilled. He who knows the end from the beginning, knows best what is for good, and He will not, He cannot do wrong. The loved ones are gone from the sorrows of this life, and now I shall only think of them as in heaven. Jesus, the good Master, who has provided for them, is more dear to me than ever before. It may be, for aught I know, that some day God will turn it all for my good. Yes, all things work together for good to them that love Him, and who knows but this may be my comfort and blessing some dark day, or God may use it to strengthen me for some trial that awaits me. I see and know so little of to-morrow, but the eyes of God reach all the beyond of my life and He knows how to provide for all its trials.

"In my Father's house are many mansions, and I go to prepare a place for you." "O, I can but wonder sometimes if I shall ever realize this promise. Mansions for *me*, in the blessed beyond? And then the promise 'I will, come for you.' What for *me? Me*, a poor, worthless worm, the Master come for *me?* Yes, that is the promise: O, sweet, blessed words. I will sing, 'Thy will be done.'"

And Captain Grimes, too, had met with misfortunes. It was a time when suspicion rested upon every one, and every man's hand was against his neighbor. The fall of 1863, and the winter of '63–'64 were indeed dark periods in the history of Missouri. The whole country was infested with bands of marauders, professing to represent one side or the other, but who, in reality, were nothing more than land pirates seeking to rob and plunder. And the "Home Guard," or State militia took many privileges and did much plundering unjustified by the rules of war and entirely unknown to a civilized people.

Captain Grimes fell into the hands of one of these companies of militia and was thrown into prison. It often happened that a man languished for weeks and months in one of these prisons with no specific charge against him, only that he was a suspicious character. Sometimes these mere suspicions cost a man his life. Capt. Grimes escaped narrowly with his.

After laying in prison at Macon City for a number of weeks, closely guarded, he induced one of the guards to accompany him to a spring in the outskirts of the city for a little exercise and a cool drink of water.

During his confinement, he had induced the guard to purchase for him a quantity of pulverized red pepper, ostensibly for the purpose of seasoning his victuals, but really to aid him in making his escape, if opportunity ever offered. Before starting to the spring, he filled his pocket well with this strange fire. When they reached the spring, they were a short distance outside of the picket line. But there was but one sentinel in sight. It was only a mile from the spring to the hills and brushy woods of the East Fork of the Chariton River. After taking a drink of water, the captain very quietly engaged the guard in pleasant conversation over the merits of the spring and how he enjoyed the refreshing breeze, at the same time keeping watch upon the lone picket upon his beat. When the picket had reached the farthest point from him, giving him at least 300 yards the start, he stepped carelessly in front of the guard and suddenly jerking his hand from his pocket, dashed a handful of the pepper full in the poor soldier's face. He then whirled upon his heel and made a dash for the hills. One can imagine the excruciating pain of the guard; his eyes were full and his mouth was full; he could neither see or cry out, and for some moments could do nothing but squirm in agonies. All this time the captain was flying for liberty across the open prairie. At length the guard did manage to give a kind of scream or groan that attracted the attention of the picket, who, looking up, saw the captain darting away. He raised his gun, took aim and fired. But the distance was too great; a spent ball struck the calf of the captain's leg, but instead of retarding, accelerated, if possible, his movements. Before the guard could be summoned and pursuit undertaken, the captain had gained the hills and with them comparative safety. From this on it was necessary for him to remain in hiding and to conceal his movements.

By the time that all these hindrances were overcome,

winter, with all its rigor, had set in. The winter was a very severe one, freezing the river over far below the mouth of the Ohio and rendering navigation from St. Louis to Memphis impossible. All that could be done under these circumstances, was to await patiently the breaking up of the ice in the river. Captain Grimes had secured where he could obtain it, a list of the names of correspondents to soldiers, and these he notified as far as could be of the delay, and instructed to have all answers at St. Louis by the 15th of February.

About the 15th, according to previous arrangements, Captain Grimes and Miss Ella Herbert, with her ever faithful servant, Sam, met in St. Louis. As the mail had already been collected through the agency of friends, they had little to do but arrange it for transportation to Memphis, Tenn. It was determined as before, that Miss Herbert should take charge of the mail and convey it to Memphis, while Sam took charge of the mysterious jacket. Captain Grimes was to precede them to this point, and, if thought best, they were to go on from there down the river to Vicksburg or some other point. If this was not done, then they were to proceed at once to Corinth, Miss., and to the Confederate lines, making no delay in the city of Memphis.

But they had some things to contend with upon which they had not reckoned. Some of the letters that had been formerly written by friends in Missouri, had miscarried and had gone to the dead-letter office. Some of the soldiers had written to parties that had moved away or had fled to other States as refugees and hence these letters remained uncalled for. These too found a place at headquarters in Washington. These letters not only developed the fact of an underground mail route, but that its headquarters was in St. Louis. Some of the writers had been so unthoughtful as to tell the name of the mail agent and of his coming into Vicksburg.

While the captain had anticipated some things and had provided for them, yet he could not provide against all the unforseen things that were now against him. While he felt conscious that he was being closely watched, he attributed it more to the rigors of war than to any suspicion of the real purpose of his mission. He little suspected that the United States Government had him under such close surveillance and that

his every movement was closely guarded. While it was understood that he had an accomplice, yet so careful had he been
and so guarded in his movements, that no suspicion had, as
yet, attached to Miss Ella Herbert.

Early one morning the captain informed Ella that a boat
would leave there that evening and that he would take it and
run down to Memphis. There was another to leave at nine
o'clock next morning and she was to take that. He would
thus only be in advance a few hours, but he would have time
to make all necessary arrangements for their further movements. With this understanding they separated, he telling
her he might not see her any more till they met in Memphis.
She was, therefore, not surprised when he did not return that
evening.

The next morning, at the appointed hour, she was on
board the boat. Sam had brought all the baggage, and after a
due examination of its contents by the guards, and finding
no contraband goods, they were soon sailing grandly upon the
bosom of the great Father of Waters. Miss Herbert retired to
her cabin while Sam busied himself with the hands on deck,
learning how to handle a boat, but not forgetting to look after
the necessities of his young mistress to whom he was perfectly
devoted.

Nothing of note took place to mar the pleasure of the trip
and with high spirits Miss Herbert was contemplating her
journey to "Dixie," and thinking of the surprise she would
bring to George Tracy and his companions in arms.

It was a little after 12 o'clock one day when they hove in
sight of Memphis. Ella could not refrain from going to the
railing of the boat and watching anxiously the approach to
shore. She felt that leaving Memphis would be the beginning
of new and exciting scenes in her life's history, and that that
new, strange history was soon to be begun. She felt as if just
embarking upon some new, strange sea, the waves and billows
of which had never been tried; the perils of which were, as yet,
unknown. And yet it was with a feeling of joy mingled with
one of fearful dread that she contemplated the journey. She
anticipated with a thrill of rapture that first emerging from
the perils that would surround her into the clear sunlight of
that land of flowers, and the meeting in the rugged camp of

the Southern soldiery. O, that such blissful thoughts should
be blasted in one short hour! Truly one can say:

> "How vain are all things here below,
> How false and yet how fair."

It was near 2 o'clock when the boat reached the wharf,
and the long stage planks had been run out and the passengers
for Memphis were going ashore. Ella had eagerly scanned the
face of every one on the wharf, as the boat approached the
shore, for Captain Grimes. But he was not to be seen. And
now that she was upon land and he had not made his appearance a strange bewilderment and confusion came over her.
Sam had joined her with the baggage and together they waited
for some minutes, but they were still alone. Her heart
throbbed wildly, and the whole of the future became dark.
But they could not stay here, they had already begun to attract
attention. In this state of confusion, Ella determined to go to
her former boarding place.

Here she made her first great blunder. She was all unconscious of the attention she had attracted when she was there
before. Such is our nature, that when lost in our own thoughts
and our minds fixed upon our own purposes, and feeling our
own unimportance, we forget the impressions we leave upon
others; or the importance of our own lives in connection with
that of our surroundings.

Too, the Government detectives had learned of the visit of
the strange woman, had surmised her mission and were awaiting her return.

But mistake as it was, it was very natural that she would
make it. She had not anticipated putting up in the city at all,
and the captain failing to meet her she had unawares become
bewildered, and it was more from instinct that she went to her
former boarding place than from reason. And yet there was
some reason for it. It had not entered her mind that Captain
Grimes might be a prisoner somewhere and separated from her
forever. She simply thought his boat had been delayed somewhere, and that he would soon join her and that he would know
best where to find her if she went to the old hotel.

She was readily recognized as she entered the hotel and
registered her name. She little dreamed that from that very
moment a watch was put upon her every movement, and that

from an unseen aperture in the wall her every act was discovered by unseen eyes. Retiring to her room and ordering
some refreshments, she threw herself into a chair and tried
to collect her thoughts and to consider what best to do
under the circumstances. After the refreshments had been
served, she gave Sam permission to look for his old colored
aunt down by the wharf, where he could keep a lookout for
Captain Grimes. She took the mail jacket and gave the boy
instructions to report to her at half-past seven.

She had determined to change the letters, and put them in
the jacket and send it down to the wharf in care of Sam, so that
if the Captain should have met with any misfortune, as a suspicion had begun to dawn upon her that he might have been
captured, and if such should be, and any clew given to her
whereabouts, she would have the mail out of the way. The boy
was glad of the opportunity of the visit and also as anxious to
see the Captain as was his mistress; for he, too, had pictured a
grand visit to "Dixie."

So soon as Sam was gone, Ella began the work of transferring the letters to the mail jacket. By seven o'clock the work
was completed and she laid the jacket down to await the coming of Sam. Little did she dream that curious eyes, through
that aperture in the wall, hidden by a darkened glass, had beheld all that she had done, and perfectly understood its meaning. But there are times, when we feel that we hold the life
of a fellow-being in our own hands, and when we know what the
revelation of our secrets will bring upon them, that we hesitate,
we falter, and a kind of nervous sensation creeps over us. It
is not cowardice, but a vague suspicion that our actions are not
just; that we are seeking and taking advantage of the innocent
and unsuspecting; that we are thus taking a life we cannot re-
store. In such moments one becomes confused, and his brains
grow wild, as it were. Here sat that detective, used to all
the realities of war and to following the tracks of men with a
dogged, unrelentless determination. But when he looked
through that glass and saw that innocent, timid, shrinking
form, with womanly grace and a Christian radiance in her
every movement, although he knew that the proof of her guilt
was beyond all question, he became excited to the highest degree. He knew, perfectly, what her fate would be, as martial

law knows no mercy. His head almost grew dizzy at the
thought, and he almost cursed his eyes for what they had seen.
He felt that he was acting a mean part. But he had been sent
upon that mission; he had sworn to be faithful, and he felt in
duty bound. Besides, his reputation was at stake, and maybe
the destiny of a nation hung upon his action.

While all these conflicting feelings and emotions are passing through his mind, and just as he has determined to break
in and capture the prize, making safe all her possessions as
trophies of his vigilance, he sees her drop upon her knees and
lifting her snowy-white and tender hands, clasped together,
and turning her face toward heaven, begin a silent prayer to God.
He is at once riveted to the spot. Upon one of those snowy
fingers is a ring, a pearl, a jewel, maybe the gift of a sainted
mother, or the token of a brother's love, or a dear sister's affec-
tions. Or, perhaps, the gift of one whose life is bound to her
own, given as a token of better days. And then that face of
pictured innocence, upon which the lamp shown so brightly as to
reveal all its angelic features. He can hear no words, but from
the movement of those pale, yet expressive lips, he fancies he
can hear her say, "Dear, good Father, protect your child,
and save her from the fiend that hides upon her pathway." And a tear, sparkling as a diamond in the lamp-light
trickles down her cheek. The detective feels abashed, ashamed
of himself, of his life, of all he has done, of what he has seen,
and almost curses the hour of his birth. As never before, he
felt that he was in the presence of the Eternal Judge of all, and
he trembled from head to foot. At last, in sheer madness, he
tears himself from his hiding-place. He feels that though the
innocence within that little room sees him not, yet the Being
whose eyes are over all, knows his secret purpose, and he cannot, he dare not face that innocent woman.

How little did Ella know that even then God had heard her
prayer and had, in a measure, provided deliverance. Had the
detective as was his purpose, have rushed in, he would have
captured all. But such a dagger had been sent to his own
heart, that he almost feared that God would smite him down
before such a being as this woman.

As he rushed from the room in which he was hiding, his first
impulse was to keep all that he had seen within his own bosom

and to leave the place. But then there were other officers who knew something of what was going on. He knew that his own life was at stake; it would be expected that he would report, and a failure to do so would create a suspicion, and set detectives upon his own steps. Feeling that he could not face the innocent creature in that hotel himself, he now determined to report to the officer in command of the post all of his discoveries and turn all over into his hands.

All thoughts, by the detective, about Sam had been forgotten; and really he had concluded that the lady would not leave before morning and that all that was necessary was to guard the hotel closely during the night.

But scarcely had the detective gone when Sam made his appearance. But he brought no news of Captain Grimes. Ella gathered up the mail and giving it to him told him to take it down to his old aunt's and to ask her to keep it until he called for it, giving a caution to let no one know of its whereabouts, and to keep watch for the Captain; to go to every boat that landed, night or day, and to report any information he might get. With these charges and injunctions, Sam was soon lost in the darkness outside, and wending his way with his treasure to the river.

J. L Bowen

CHAPTER XXII.

THE DETECTIVE AND THE CAPTURE.

After the detective had left the room and had gained something of his composure, he sought the commandant of the post and informed him of his discoveries. The commandant expressed surprise at his not taking possession of all at once.

"I could not," said the detective, "I dare not; that woman is an angel, a heavenly queen, and after seeing that face of innocence shining with a radiance of the heavenly world, and the tear-drops of innocence dropping down her cheek, and the earnestness of her petition to the heavenly Father, I dare not approach her."

The commandant laughed at what he called his childish timidity and taunted him with forgetting his obligation to his country and falling in love at first sight.

"There is no love about it," replied the detective, "the look at that woman in prayer made me feel my own contemptible meanness, and ashamed of the part I was acting. You may call it cowardice if you will, but I dared not break into that sacred place."

"Well, well," said the commandant, "something must be done at once, and if you are too timid to act, I shall have to send a guard."

The detective felt the sting of the reproof, but said nothing. It was a thing beyond all doubt that this lady had an accomplice, and that sooner or later he would come to her help. The commandant felt sure that some one would come for that mail jacket, and that might be at any time. His purpose at once was to take possession of all, put a secret watch at the hotel and capture the first one that called for the strange woman. Summoning a sergeant and a couple of guards, he ordered them to go to the hotel and arrest the woman and bring everything of a suspicious character found in her room to his headquarters. He especially described the mail pouch, and then turning to the detective, he said with some sarcasm in his tone, "Are you afraid to go?"

The detective was not insensible to these reproofs, but without a reply, signified his willingness to accompany the guard by a touch of his cap by way of salute, and arising to be off. He knew he was no coward, so far as facing danger was concerned; nor did he till now know that he feared anything. He could face the savage monster and grapple with the robber and feel a pride in his manhood; but for the first time in his life he stood face to face with a holy innocence and a pure womanhood. As never before, he felt his own pollution and shrank back before that pictured purity. Yet he felt that no one but an all-seeing eye knew his heart, and that men would call him coward. The commandant had only expressed the thought that all would have of him, and this thought impelled him on.

The guard was instructed not to molest the woman any further than to take posession of her property and to inform her that she was under arrest and that it would not be expected for her to leave her room without a guard. The detective went with the guard to the hotel, and with the landlord designated the room, but yet he did not feel that he could accuse that woman to her face. He stood back in the hallway while the landlord gave a gentle tap at the door.

Ella, although she had lain down upon the bed, wa not sleeping. Recovering from her first hours of bewilderment and confusion, and after her devotions, she had calmly looked over the whole field.

"It is possible," she said, "Captain Grimes has been captured; these are times when we know not whose eyes are upon us, nor can we divine what a day may bring forth. If he is captured, it may give a clew to my retreat, and for aught I know I shall be a prisoner before the morning." Little did she know that even then the guard was on its way to take posession of her. "But," she continued, "the Lord's presence has sweetened the prison house in other days, and such can be done now, and I will trust Him; He has never failed me and He never will."

A perfect calmness had taken possession of her and she

was not in the least alarmed when, after the gentle knocks, she opened the door and saw three soldiers with their muskets standing before her.

"What is your wish, gentlemen," she said in a perfectly easy way.

"Beg pardon," said the sergeant somewhat abashed at the calmness of the queenly form before him. "I—you—the commandant of the post sent us to search this room and to take possession of whatever we might find in the way of contraband." And then he apologetically said, "Very sorry to disturb you," at the same time politely touching his cap, "but we are ordered here and must obey our orders."

"O yes," she replied gently and politely, though with something of an effort at calm deliberation, for the truth was beginning to dawn upon her, and she feared, not so much for herself as for others. "Poor Sam," she said mentally to herself, "What will become of him." But this, while continuing to the soldiers, "I know you soldiers must obey orders, and I suppose I am in your power; come in, you see what is in the room."

There was only the valise and hand-basket to be seen, though every nook and corner of the room was searched. The sergeant only had orders to bring what he found to headquarters. Leaving the two soldiers stationed at the door of Ella's room, he, with the detective, reported to the commandant. The valise was opened and searched, but nothing found. The commandant was at once indignant, and indirectly charged the detective with making a false report. He said to him, "You simply lost your head before a pretty woman, and it seems that you do not know what you saw. The Government should send men into such business as this who never lose their presence of mind."

The detective felt bitterly stung by this reproof, so much so, that he determined to resort to what was to him desperate measures. He declared that he knew most positively that the letters had been transferred, that he witnessed it with his own eyes. He, therefore, demanded that two ladies be sent to search the prisoner. "She may have," he said, "the jacket on her own person." His demand was granted, and a most diligent search was made, but to no purpose, so far as the missing mail was concerned. They did find, however, a few letters on her person, especially those from George Tracy, that did convict her of being engaged in carrying the mail, and that was clear proof of her guilt, thus far confirming the report of the detective, but so far as the mail jacket was concerned, it had as thoroughly disappeared as if it had dropped out of existence; search as they would and did, there was not a trace of it to be found.

Miss Herbert, while fully realizing her condition, yet kept her perfect composure, and with it her own counsel. She said nothing and answered but few questions.

The curiosity of the detective was thoroughly aroused. Besides, the questioning of his veracity stung him to the quick. He could not possibly doubt his own eyes; it was not possible that the transfer was not made. Being so piqued by the charge of the commandant he had forgotten some of the grand impressions left upon his mind by that sweet prayer, and those lovely pictures, and only thought of how he, himself, would appear in the eyes of others. While fearing to be called a coward, yet he had been acting the part of a coward from the time he left that room and determined to reveal what he had seen. He simply feared the opinions of men. He now determined to resort to more determined and, to him, desperate measures.

While the picture he had seen before him, while Ella was transferring the mail, was one of loveliness and grace, and while that moment of prayer had been one never to be forgotten, yet he had only seen in his pictured fancy, a poor, weak, innocent Christian woman. While in part, his picture was true, yet he had never known the virtue of prayer nor the power of faith; he had never known the boldness of one whose trust was in God, and who confides all to His care. While he had seen the tear trickling down the cheek, and while his own heart beat in sympathetic unison with his pictured queen, yet he knew not, nor understood that these tears were but the fruits of the sweet breathings of the Spirit of the Most High, that they were but the results of the soul's swelling up into rapturous joy at the sealing home of the sweet promise, "Fear not, I am with you." He had but little conception of the power of those words, nor with what strength the sealing them home to the heart, gave the soul of that fair girl to meet the trials that were before her, and he knew nothing of a dependence upon an Omnipotent Arm.

With his conception of the weak and timid girl, he thought he could frighten her into a revelation of the secret.

With this feeling he summoned all the courage he was master of and marched boldly into the room. He even made an effort to be severe, but the little tremor in his voice, and the unsteady movement of the eye betrayed him. Ella, though fixed in her determination, knew the character before her. Though she understood not the cause, at that time, yet she knew that it was simply an effort at bluff.

When the stranger entered the room where Miss Ella and the two women, who had searched her, were sitting, Ella arose to meet him. The very moment that her eyes, in their bright, steady gaze met his, he felt that he had before him no ordinary person; before that piercing eye he winced, and would have turned away had it been possible. He felt that she read his thoughts, and even looked upon him with contempt. But to retreat now was impossible. His sheer desperation, in an effort to retrieve what he felt to be his standing as a detective, drove him on. He tried once more to fix a firm and defiant look upon those bright eyes, but their luster did not dim. There she was, with womanly grace and timid virtue, tinged with lovely reverence and pity, yet, so fixed, firm and steady that spoke of nerve and fixedness of purpose.

While feeling the failure of his undertaking, yet having no other subterfuge, he began:

"Madam, I shall not at all try to disguise from you the fact of who I am, and what I am, and, as filling my office, of what I have witnessed. I am a government detective, and as such have been sent here for the sole purpose of watching your movements. From my position in that room," pointing to the room adjoining, "I saw, through that glass you see there in that wall, (for the first time Ella saw it,) you take a quantity of of letters from about your person and put them in something like a roundabout or soldier's jacket. Now, understand, lady, your life is in my hands. I demand of you to tell me where those letters are."

This great speech was made in a kind of halting, unsteady way, the speaker's eyes, once in a while, rising to meet the steady gaze before him and then dropping to the floor. The last words were spoken with a great effort at boldness and authority. But stern and terrible as the detective would have them be, Miss Herbert stood fixed before him; she never moved a nerve or muscle. Nor did she turn from him the steady gaze of those searching eyes, except when directed to the other room and the glass in the wall; nay, those eyes grew brighter if possible, and a blush of animation mounted her cheek as, in her queenlike majesty, she gave answer:

"Sir, you are a detective? One appointed by the government to hunt and betray people; an informant on other people's business; a betrayer of the secrets of men; think you to make me act the part of a traitor to myself? Never! I will leave that for *detectives* to do. As to my life being in your hands, now, I should say you have no power over me. When you sat in that room secretly spying out my actions, as you say, my life might have hung upon your actions; but your story has been told, and the only thing you could do now to benefit me would be to say your story is false; for no consideration would I ask that."

There was no madness in that womanly voice, but the detective felt the sting of the withering rebuke, and before that woman, who stood as a queen enthroned before him, he faltered and betrayed his chagrin. Seeing this faltering and hesitation, she added, "If you are the detective you say you are, and if you have seen all you describe, it was your place to see more."

There was a little tinge of sarcasm about these last remarks which the detective was quick to observe, and he felt their sting. And as never before he felt the guilt of his profession. But however abashed, or however criminal he felt his actions to have been, there was a kind of pride in the success of his undertaking that mechanically urged him on. And rather imploringly than threateningly, he urged:

"Do you know, dear lady, the nature of the. crime that will attach to your actions? and do you know the proof we have of your guilt?"

Nothing faltering she replied, "Yes, sir, I perfectly understand what the rules of war are in regard to my case, and of what I may be adjudged guilty, and am fully apprised of what the result will be if so adjudged. But my mission, whatever military laws may be, is one of love and mercy; I carry messages of love and good will, and the God whom I serve, and before whom I stand, will clear me of all guilt. I stand before Him with a conscience void of offense, and no human being can lay his blood to my charge."

"Then," said the detective, "you confess your guilt?"

"I confess nothing," was the reply, "nor do I deny anything. You have those letters that speak for themselves, I shall not deny them."

"But," the detective added, "you are encouraging the enemies of the Government, and the Government must hold you to account."

"I am," was the reply, "comforting the oppressed, and if, for being faithful to my people and to the land of my birth, I must die—be it so. I am Southern born; one of my brothers fills a Southern soldier's grave; another one is in the army, and what is my life that I must not lay it upon my country's altar?"

The detective saw the futility of his efforts in the line he was persuing and, after informing Miss Herbert that she must consider herself a prisoner, he took his departure.

Ella was given the full possession and all the privileges of her room, but she understood that a guard would be placed at the door and that of a truth she was a prisoner. When the door was closed and bolted, and she found herself alone, the awfulness of her situation flashed upon her. A prisoner! All the bright hopes and cherished ends blasted in one moment of time. All her womanly nature was aroused, and she burst into a flood of tears. All was dark, O so very dark, the future had no bright pictures now.

"And poor Sam, what will become of him? What will the poor, innocent child do? He knows nothing of the dark trials of life, nor of being alone and in the hands of enemies. Where is the poor boy now? Is the mail safe? and Captain Grimes, oh, what misfortune has befallen him? Where is he, and why did he not come? Had we met him, all these misfortunes would not have overtaken us." All these questions passed rapidly through her mind, and for the moment her own condition was forgotten in the thought for others.

And then she reflected over the work of the last few hours. It was all so strange, so unexpected, so like a dream, a vision, and yet so real. She felt surprised at her own words, and yet she hardly knew how she had answered the detective. She only felt that she had been moved by some strange impulse; some power had taken hold of her, and held her, calm, fixed and unmoved. Of one thing she was perfectly conscious, she had betrayed no one; the one secret that concerned others was still locked in her own bosom and there she felt confident it would ever remain.

And then she began to think over the mistakes she had made in coming to the hotel, of her actions when she landed at the wharf, and it all flashed over her of what a mistake she had made. "Of course," she said to herself, "I was known the very moment I entered the hotel, and as no one knew my mission when here before, it is but reasonable, if anything has been discovered of what is going on, that suspicion should attach to me." And then she remembered the special caution Tracy had given her, never to repeat herself; that is, "do not put up twice at the same place."

But it had all come upon her so suddenly and so unexpectedly. She had put the most implicit confidence in Captain Grimes to make the journey safely. He had been so upon his guard, and had become so well acquainted with the enemy, their ways and movements that he could almost divine their intentions. The possibility, therefore, of his capture had never, till now, entered her mind. "O why," she cried, "did he not give me some instructions if there should be a failure of his coming? Then I would have known how to act."

But the truth was, that the captain, like herself, had too much confidence in his ability to carry out his plans. But that is all passed now, and beyond recall or remedy. Ella feels that she must now face the reality; that whatever the mistakes of the past may have been, they are the things of the past, nor is it in the power of man to undo them. "O," she said, "if we could always think of this, how different would be our walk in life. If we could always understand that we are writing a life history, the pages of which are to endure forever; that not a single letter or syllable can ever be blotted out; that all our actions are gone beyond recall, how careful we would be in the writing." She sees the futility of regrets now, and that they cannot change anything of the past; she must now face the reality of the present and the darkness of the future.

A sense of her loneliness came over her, and a realization of her weakness. No one to sympathize with her; no kind hand to lead, or arm upon which to lean; no one to counsel or cheer in these dark moments. "In a prison house!" A shiver passed over her as the words flashed through her mind. "Walls all around to shut out all care and sympathy, and as a bar to all love and friendship. A prison house!" How terrible the words now, as she awoke to all their reality. "Not only friends shut out, but enemies are those that keep guard." How could she endure it?

Her first impulse was to write to the friends at home and get some of them to come to her help. But, then, she reflected, they are in the same condemnation, that is they were regarded as "rebels," and to call upon them for assistance, would be to subject them to the same treatment as she might receive herself. Instead, therefore, of bringing her the needed relief, it would bring them into trouble. She, therefore, determined to suffer alone, and trust all to an All Wise Providence. Though earthly friends be shut out, she felt that she had one Friend that no power of earth could drive away; one Friend who cared not for prison walls or heeded the commands of a million guards; one who overleaped all heights, and held the destinies of all men in the hollow of His hand, and how sweet to her now were the words of Isaiah: "When thou passest through the waters I will be with thee; and through the rivers, they shall not overflow thee; when thou walkest through the fire, thou shalt not be burned; neither shall the flames kindle upon thee. for I am the Lord thy God, the Holy One of Israel, thy Saviour. * * Since thou art most precious in my sight, thou hast been honorable; and I have loved thee." She stopped and paused upon these words: "Precious in His sight, oh, how sweet! and to be loved of the Lord! O, He has been such a Friend to me, I know that, poor and weak as I am, and as little as I have done to merit it, yet He loves me. And He will love me in the time of trouble." The sweet words came unbidden, as if they flowed from the never-failing fountain of unspeakable love, and she lingered upon their sweetness. "Therefore, will I give men for thee, and people for thy life. Fear not, for I am with thee." "O," she said, "I do feel that He is with me, I have found Him my portion in the time of peace, and shall I fear to trust Him in the time of trouble?" And then she lifted up her hands in a fervent petition, "O, Lord," she said, "Thou knowest the secrets of all hearts; our down-sitting and our uprising, and art acquainted with all our ways. Thou art able to make the wrath of men to praise Thee, and, dear Lord, thou knowest that I am but a poor, weak woman, and that I am in the hands of enemies; that my life is in danger; Thou knowest that I am too weak to do anything for myself as of myself. Dear Lord, undertake for me. There is nothing too hard for Thee. If it be Thy will I will suffer, only let Thy name be glorified, and let me feel that in me and my sufferings Thy will is accomplished, and all is well."

She could not sleep. Sometimes she would feel perfectly calm and composed, and then again she would become confused, and her thoughts as a tangled web. Everything had become so changed in one short moment, as it were. In the early morning she was full of life and hope, looking forward to a delightful journey and a glorious meeting when she should enter the Confederate camp with good news from home. But now here she was, shut up in a little room with a Federal guard standing at the door. Shut out from the world, hearing nothing and knowing nothing. Nor could she inquire. She dare not mention the name of Capt. Grimes. And those dear love messages, those letters that were to gladden so many hearts, she could not know what had become of them, and the poor servant, the trusting child, she dare not even mention his name, and yet he was to her of all others, the object of her thoughts. How would he be treated, and what would become of the poor child among strangers. She pictured him, even now, captured and a prisoner, pleading for a word with her and wondering why she could not come to his relief.

That night to her was one of darkness and sorrow, mingled with but few sweet moments, and somehow she felt relieved when the rays of dawn, peeping through her window announced the beginning of another day. Although she knew not what it would bring forth, yet she felt that there was no change that would worst her condition. She had made her resolve, she had put her cause in God's hands and she felt sure that He would care for her, and that His grace would be sufficient.

"Yea, though I walk through the valley of the shadow of

death, I will fear no evil; for Thou art with me, Thy rod and Thy staff, they comfort me."

And she said, "Am I not walking through the valley of the shadow of death even now? and may I not trust Him to comfort me? Indeed, I do believe that the Lord will provide, and that He will not leave me comfortless."

She arose from her troubled couch and made her toilet. The night had been to her one of doubts, and yet of assurance; of human fears, and yet of faith's triumphs; of human weakness, and yet of Christian trust; of doubt's darkness, and yet of trusting light; of humanity vanquished, and yet the victory of grace; of how weak are all things earthly, and yet how strong in the Lord and the power of His might. She composed herself as best she could, and came down stairs. For the first time in her life she was conducted to the breakfast table by a guard. There were strange faces all around her, but she took but little note of them. She would rather have taken her breakfast in her room, but for the hope that she might see a familiar face. But one glance satisfied her. She was conscious that those strange eyes cast upon her a kind of sympathetic glance. So strange was her condition, and such were her emotions, that she ate but little. But with it all her face shows a sweet, sad composure, revealing a firm resolve within. She drank a cup of coffee and minced a few crackers. This constituted the meal.

While perfectly silent herself, she listened to every whisper around her, and watched every movement that she might catch any information as to Captain Grimes, poor Sam, or the precious mail. O, if she could get one glimpse of Sam, and yet she feared to see him. If he should come into her presence, he would rush to her and thus betray himself. But then she satisfied herself that poor Sam had already fallen into the hands of the Federal officers, or he would have reported to her long before this. She looked at her watch, it was now 8 o'clock in the morning; the sun had already mounted high in the heavens and the boy would not have made such a delay without just cause. "It must be," she said, "that he is a prisoner and the poor, ignorant child (that is ignorant of evil), has doubtless been frightened into a revelation of the whereabouts of the mail."

She was satisfied that he had reached the hiding place safely. For she knew that the mail had not been found when the detective had entered her room the night before. But it was now evident to her that her servant had been taken prisoner, or at least that he had been prevented from seeing her. The day wore by and she was still a prisoner in her room. She had been left all the morning entirely to her thoughts. The authorities seemed to be satisfied, that so far as she was oncerned, she was fixed in her purpose, or else they had made all the discovery that they desired to make and were deliberating on her case.

About 2 o'clock in the evening a squad of soldiers filed into the hall, and an officer announced that she should get ready for a journey. "A journey," she mentally repeated, "A journey where?" But no answer came to the soul's thoughts. With her face heavily veiled, and heedless of the curious eyes that were fixed upon her as she passed, she walked with her escort out of the hotel and turning an angle down the street she found that they were going toward the river. The officer, to all appearances, was a nice, clever gentleman. When he came into Miss Herbert's presence he took off his cap, and when they started for the journey, he very politely offered her his arm. This she very gently, and with true, womanly politeness, refused. Yet she privileged him to walk by her side. Her valise, which contained only her wearing apparel, was given in charge of one of the guards. When they had come near the river she saw a boat at the wharf with steam up, ready to start and she understood that she was to take the boat for somewhere. "Of course," she thought, "a prison; but what prison?"

"May I ask," she said, breaking the silence, "where I am going?"

The officer replied that he did not know; that he had orders to conduct her to the boat, and that there he would get further orders, and then he could, perhaps, inform her of her destination.

After reaching the boat she was given a state-room, and every convenience necessary to her comfort was furnished her. The officer, after being absent a short time, returned and told her that their destination was Fort Pillow. As to how long she was to remain there, or as to what disposition they were to make of her, he knew not.

"When we get there," he said, "you will be turned over to other hands and my task will be done. But I hope," he added sympathetically, "that you will fall into good hands." And yet his tone and manner seemed to have a suspicion of doubt.

Ella thanked him kindly for the information and his expressions of regard for her welfare.

"The soldier," he added as he left the room, "can only obey orders," as if he thought he ought to offer an apology for the part he was taking.

Ella replied that she understood some of the duties of a soldier.

When the officer was gone she looked out upon the bosom of the great waters, the boat had pushed out from shore, and was now in mid-stream, puffing and laboring against the current of the rushing waters. How different were her feelings and emotions to that of a few days ago. She was then floating down the current full of life and hope; the spires of the now fading city were glorious. But now the waters were dark, and the labored tossing of the vessel answered the sad heart-throbs of the troubled soul. "Yes," she said, as if talking to the old ship, "I am like you, laboring against tide and current. But," she continued, "such is life. Sometimes we float, we sail upon life's beautiful sea and all is glorious. But then the billows rise and we must face the tempest."

Toward sunset the hills around Fort Pillow were in sight and there was that heavy throbbing of the heart that anticipates the dread unknown, yet pictures the darkest hours. Into whose hands would she fall? and what fate awaited her? and where would she be on the morrow? All these questions passed rapidly through her mind, but those frowning hills made no answer. The place looked dark and desolate, and from these gloomy forebodings she turned away. Looking out to the West she caught a sight of the golden sunset. The heavens seemed to be lit up with a new glow; the waters of the great river sparkled with a new lustre, and the skies with a new radiance.

"Is it a mockery?" she said, and then as if catching herself charging God with injustice she said, "No, no, it is the bow of promise. To those who trust Him so fades the day of life; so sets the sun of our days here, but what glory does it picture in the great beyond. The Master has said, 'Unto you that fear

My name shall the sun of righteousness arise with healing in wings,' " and as she caught the last glow of the departing day, she thought of how glorious the rising would be on that fair morning when eternity pulls back the curtain of time and gives us a view of the bright beyond.

CHAPTER XXIII.

TROUBLES THICKEN—THE PRISON AND THE COURT MARTIAL.

It has been said that our troubles never come singly; that when trials come upon us they thicken as the days go by, and that when we would be gladdest to see the sunshine, the clouds are the darkest. When the evil one would torment us, his name is "Legion"; when he would seek our destruction he summons all his armies, he makes no halfway effort. Ella Herbert was made to realize all of this in the troubles that now surrounded her.

In her younger days there was one who had sought her hand, but there was that about him that was repulsive to her very nature. And though he was persistent in his pleading, yet she shrank from his every advance, she could not endure the thought of linking her life with his. Though with all the gentleness and kindness she knew how to command, she had told him again and again that such a thing could never be, yet he pursued her steps with a persistence that made her life miserable, and at last, with even a persecution that not only made her despise but fear him. He seemed to have no conceptions of the rights, comforts and pleasures of others, but was wrapped up in his own selfish desires. To her he had betrayed a character vile and destitute of every principle of manhood and had rendered himself entirely unworthy of confidence or trust.

But this was in days gone, and the man and the circumstances had almost dropped from view. Though he had left her in great wrath, swearing to be revenged for, as he claimed, the great wrongs done him, yet those tragic scenes had almost passed from memory, or only lingered as the expressions of a moment of frenzied passion. Little did she dream of all this coming up before her, to mock her in this sad hour.

When the boat touched the wharf and the long stage plank was run out, the officer in charge told her that they were ready to go ashore, and giving her baggage to a soldier, conducted her to land. Here they found a guard of soldiers ready to receive them. They were all negroes except the commander. The officer, who had Miss Herbert in charge, stepped up to the officer of the guard and after holding a little whispered conversation with him, the guard was dismissed and she was put in charge of the white officer only.

As they walked up into town, they met some one on horseback who, by his dress and general bearing seemed to have considerable authority. From his regalia Ella took him to be a colonel. He beckoned the officer conducting her to him and they held a private conversation together. While this was going on, Ella lifted her veil that she might get a better view of both the officer and surrounding country. When she caught a full view of that face, she recognized it. And then she thought, as a kind of tremor passed over her, it cannot be him. But another glance told her that she could not be mistaken and she was about to drop the veil when his eyes caught hers. She saw the flush mount his cheek, and she knew that she was recognized. The veil dropped and she hoped that he had not noticed that she knew him. O, how her heart ached, and she felt almost like sinking down overwhelmed by the difficulties surrounding her. She knew how he had pursued her in the days gone, but she could not divine what that flushed cheek and flashing eye meant now. She could not conceive they meant good to her. He could be a friend, but she dare not believe he would be; friendship was a term unknown to that hard nature; that was incapable of anything but hate and revenge. She remembered that he had once sworn that he would have that revenge, and of this eternal hate he was entirely capable. Now she felt that strangely she was in his hands and that he would satisfy his vengeance.

This belief was strengthened when, indeed, she was taken to a prison and put in a little narrow room with grated windows. The room was bare, save one chair and a narrow bunk. Not a picture or even a looking-glass adorned the walls. But, however, a negro woman came in in a little time and arranged things a little better. She brought in a little stand table and

other conveniences, and informed Miss Herbert that she was to be her attendant. After the little conveniences had been arranged and a light brought in, for it was growing dark, she was left for the night.

Notwithstanding all that Ella had passed through, she rested better than she had expected. The exciting scenes of the past four days had kept her nerves strung up to the highest tensions; to a point beyond the possibility of long endurance. No matter how the difficulties might thicken as the hours grow dark, nature calls for a halt; our sensibilities become deadened, and our imaginings become weary; our fears give place to indifference, and we stop, weary with ourselves, and lie down to rest and regain our lost energies. How ever much we may feel is still before us, yet we must submit to the inevitable, and we drop into a kind of submissive composure.

Though her sleep was somewhat troubled, yet when she awoke in the morning, she felt refreshed and strengthened. Looking back upon the past few days, they seemed to her an age of mysterious wonder. They were to her, days filled with the most stern realities, yet covered over with the darkest shadows. The events were the most real and pointed of her life, and yet wrapped in the most profound mystery. She felt that she was knowing and yet to her the days were entirely unknown. She longs, hungers and thirsts to lift the veil that covers the hidden, yet dares not to inquire.

Ella felt pleased next morning when she looked through the iron grates of her window and found that it opened out upon a public street where she could see people passing to and fro. Though each face was a strange one, yet she loved to look upon them, and to feel that she was not the only human being in the world. And thus, too, she had a good view of the river as it flowed at the foot of those hills.

The dull hours passed slowly by to her as she sat in her lone prison cell with nothing to break the monotony of the hour except the occasional visit of the old negro woman to attend to her needs, or the continual tramp, tramp of the lone sentinel as he walked upon his beat in the prison hall. It appeared to her that the whole world was shut out; not a single, familiar face, not one known voice, not a living being near her that she had ever seen before, save one, and that one of all others most

dreaded. She shuddered to think of it. Not a paper came into the room by which she might learn something of the outside world; not a single line, token, word or sign, to throw a
single ray of light upon the mysterious darkness of the past
days. Thus for three days she sat in her solitary seclusion.

On the third evening while she was pensively gazing out
upon the passers-by—some citizens, some soldiers, she saw one
ride up dressed in a Colonel's uniform. She was not surprised,
therefore, when he turned his face full toward her, to see the
face of Joseph Shelton. Nor was she disappointed in the
thoughts that his mission was with her.

He ascended the steps and knocked at her door. Ella composed herself as best she could; she dreaded to face that man,
one that she knew to be destitute of every generous impulse,
and a stranger to all those sacred emotions that make men
noble. She feared him. Not that she feared bodily harm at
his hands. She knew him to be a coward, one that only struck
his foe when he had every advantage; one who seeks revenge
and gloats in the sufferings he may bring upon those who may
be within his power.

But having seen his approach and supposing his mission,
she had collected her thoughts and composed herself, and knowing that she was in his power and must submit to what he
might say to her, she was in a degree ready for his reception.
She quietly took hold of the door and throwing it wide open,
stood before him with a calm fixedness that at once revealed
to him the same force of character mingled with the same
womanly grace that he had known in the days gone by. There
was no smile of friendly recognition, nor was there a frown of
angry repulsion. It was simply the queen-like dignity, the
cold, formal indifference that said, I know you and I do not ask
your aid, nor will I be driven by your wrath.

The man was not destitute of all perception. He read all
this in one glance, and, instead of admiring, it angered him.

"You know me?" he said, lifting his cap, and yet with a
shade of sarcasm about it.

"Yes," she replied, "I know you, you are the commandant
here I suppose, what is your pleasnre?"

Though not intended, there was a kind of cold defiance in
her words. So well did she know him, that she felt that, how-

ever it might be in his power to help her, he would not
upon any terms she could accept. She would, therefore, give
him to understand that she had no terms to make with him.

They stood facing each other for a moment, and then
breaking the silence that followed her answer, he said, with
some degree of sternness in his manner:

"Ella Herbert, do you know the nature of the crime for
which you are here imprisoned, and the results that must follow your conviction?"

"I understand," she said, "that I am charged with carrying letters to the Southern army, and if this be a crime, I am
guilty."

"But," he said, carrying letters through the lines is the
work of a spy, and to be found guilty of that, is death. The
evidence against you is clear, and you even confess your guilt.
A court-martial will, therefore, have little to do but to pro-
nounce sentence against you."

"I understand," she replied, "what significance a military
court will attach to my conduct, and that if the rigors of a
court-martial are enforced, what the result will be, and I am
prepared for the worst. I counted all the cost when I engaged
in this work, and shall not shrink from the task that it may
impose."

A man possessing any other nature than his would have ad-
mired and honored the cool, dispassionate, calculating and
brave character which Miss Herbert displayed. But not so
Colonel Shelton. The manifestation of that very character
maddened him. He would have seen her a crying, cringing,
pleading, begging sycophant at his feet.

"I had," he said, "hoped to have found your nature somewhat subdued by this time. You know I once sought your
hand and how you spurned my every offer and treated with indifference my petitions. I could help you now, could I hope for
a reversal of your decision, and a change in your conduct."

"Mr. Shelton," she said, drawing back in her noble womanly dignity, "you know that I have treated you with every respect that a lady could show to a gentleman. You were not
and could not be the object of my choice, you demanded that
which I could not and would not give, nor would generosity re-
quire; and, now, knowing you as I do, my decision can never be

reversed. I should prefer death a thousand times to that of linking my fortune with yours."

This reply threw him into a rage.

"I know," he said, "that you would have been mine but for another, who, despite my protestations, and merely to ruin my happiness, sought and won your pledge. I have sworn that you shall never be his. I had hoped to meet him and let my vengeance fall upon his own head, but thus far I have failed. But you are now in my power and I will see to it that he and you shall never meet again."

Turning upon his heel he was gone before she could give reply. And she felt that it was as well, as no answer she could make would have bettered her condition.

Ella now clearly understood that she could expect the worst. She was not only in the hands of an enemy, but of a bitter, vengeful, cowardly, unrelenting foe. Ah, indeed, to her, the future looked dark. No friend, no counsellor; not a single being in whom to confide. O the bitterness of these lone hours, and how unendurable the suspense. She knew not how to communicate with the outside world. If she could get word to some friend; if George Tracy only knew. If Captain Grimes was not in the same sad condition as she, and she could just get him word. Or if Sam, poor boy, was just in reach of her.

The very next morning, and just after the guard had been changed, while she was revolving these things over in her mind, for they were thoughts that never left her, she saw a colored boy coming up the street in a kind of halting, hesitating gate, stopping and looking around and then moving on as if lost, or sadly bewildered. His walk and appearance looked familiar, yet not definitely so. She could not exactly place him, yet she could not keep her eyes off of him. When he reached a point nearly opposite her window he turned his face full toward her, and it seemed to her that her heart leaped into her throat; she was choking with emotion; her heart beat wildly; her emotions were almost beyond control. It was, indeed, the ever faithful Sam; there was no mistaking it. The possibility of this had never entered her mind before and it was almost like an apparition. She must see him and have a word with him, and how should she? She feared that if he recognized her, he would, on the impulse of the moment, betray the relation between them, and that would ruin all the prospects of a conference; she could not speak to him without betraying this herself, and yet something must be done and that quickly. He would soon pass by and maybe the last opportunity for seeing him would be gone. "*He must know that I am here,*" she repeated over to herself. She thumped heavily upon the window pane, and put her face as close to the glass as the iron bars would allow. Sam stopped again and began looking about as though he thought he was called. The knocking was repeated again, and he turned his face, looking directly at the window. A look of deep anxiety pictured upon his features, then a start, a smile, a quick motion of the hands as he clasped them together. Ella knew she was recognized, and by a quick motion of her hands she bade him be quiet. Had she have known, Sam was on his guard.

She then opened the door of her room to see who was on guard. She found it to be a colored man, who, while doubtless not very well versed in the laws of responsibility or military order, yet had a kindly face and showed a sympathetic nature. She had managed to keep her money except what had been spent for necessities, concealed in the folds of her dress, it all being in paper, and had just that morning taken some of it out for the purpose of getting her a "house girl" to make a small purchase for her. She understood its power and persuasive virtue with those who knew or cared but little for the strict observance of military law, and taking a five dollar bill and placing it in the hand of the guard, she asked him if he would call the colored boy across the street, and let her have a private word with him. Making the excuse that she wanted to send him on a little errand. The guard supposing him to be one of the many boys about town, and having no special interest in the affair any way, readily consented. Ella stepped back when the guard called and motioned to Sam to come, but cautioned him to be quiet. Ella was glad to note that Sam caught on to it all, and that he came in acting very much as though he was a strange negro.

Ella asked the guard to let him come into her room and remain a while, promising to remember him (the guard) for his kindness.

"He can stay," said the guard, "till de officer ob de day comes roun', den he mus' hide."

"But," she questioned, "where will he hide?"

"I will jes keep watch here an' when I knock on de flo dis way," pounding with the butt end of his gun, "let him come to me quick, an' I show him wha to go."

Ella thanked the guard kindly and then entering her room and closing the door, was alone with her devoted servant.

Never were two people more overjoyed to see each other, and Sam could hardly restrain his emotions. But he had had a bitter experience in the last few days. He not only knew his own danger but that of his dear Miss, who was more to him than all others. But their emotions were such that for a time neither could speak. At last Sam broke the painful silence.

"I thought," he said, "dat dem Yankees had done took you an' you was gone for sho."

"Well, Sam, they did take me," she said, "and I am here in jail as you see, but I am still living. But, Sam, how did you get here?"

"O," replied Sam, "I des come."

"But," questioned Ella," "did they not get you and put you in jail?"

"O yes'm," was the answer, "dey git me and dey put me in jail, an' dey say dey would shoot me if didn't give 'em de mail and tell 'em all about it."

"Well, you gave them the mail, didn't you?"

"No'm," said Sam very emphatically, "I couldn't."

"You could not?" again questioned Ella, "why could you not?"

"'Cause," was the reply, "jes as I got down to de ribber, who should come along but Captain Grimes, an' he took de mail, and said dat de Yankees was after him hard, and dat you an' me mus' go through as bes' we could, and meet him about Corinth."

"Oh, I am so glad," said Ella. "Captain Grimes got away with the mail safe, did he?"

"Yes, Miss, dat he did," said Sam, "an' I so glad too; dey do like dey would kill me for it, an' I 'fraid dey done kill you."

Ella's faith in a providential hand was strongly confirmed in this, for nothing else she felt had prompted her actions that evening in preparing it for transportation and sending it to the river. Nothing else could have so exactly thrown it out of the hands of the enemy and into the hand of the one to convey it to its destination. "Yes," she said, "God is in this matter, and I shall yet trust Him."

She now learned that Captain Grimes had indeed been captured by the Federal authorities soon after leaving her that morning in St. Louis. And that, really, when she took the boat he had not left the place.

The detectives had been upon his track from the commencement, and knowing that he had a great many friends in St. Louis, whose sympathies were with the South, they determined to send him to Alton, Ill., for safe keeping, until his case could be thoroughly investigated. Not that there was doubt or lack of proof of his guilt, but they desired to know who were his assistants in the matter.

The captain was an old river pilot, and understood all the crooks and turns of the great Father of Waters. He perfectly understood boating, and was at home on such a craft.

The night after Ella left, they put him under a strong guard, as they knew he would escape if it was possible for him to do so. He was not a stranger by reputation, at least to the authorities, and they determined to make sure of their game this time. In order to make assurance doubly sure, they put handcuffs on him and then chained him to two soldiers and put them on top of the boat.

They thought by this that they had made escape impossible. The sequel shows how little they knew of their wiry prisoner. The Captain knew that the success of his undertaking depended upon his immediate escape. He knew that the mail and Miss Ella Herbert were all in danger of capture, and that he must act at once. He knew that if he would accomplish his purpose he must take desperate chances. He, therefore, determined that if possible to prevent it he would never reach Alton.

Soon after they embarked on board the boat, it being about 10 o'clock at night, the guard spread down their blankets for a night's rest, feeling that as the prisoner was chained to two of them, and must sleep between them, he was safe. Thus, feeling secure, they were soon in a sound slumber.

But there was no sleep for Captain Grimes; he lay watching

the stars till the boat had passed the mouth of the Missouri river and was puffing up the Mississippi toward the prison in prospect. It happened that the Captain had a very small hand and a plump tapering wrist; he could compress his hand into a very small compass. Nor was this the first time he had worn such ornaments since he had been engaged as mail carrier. He had never suffered any uneasiness so far as the hand-cuffs were concerned.

He very easily slipped the cuffs off his hands and then watching till the boat swung around close to shore, he quietly slipped out from between the sleeping guards and sprang off from the top of the boat, far out into the river, and then swam ashore. He never stopped to inquire as to how long before it was discovered that he was gone, nor of the consternation of the two soldiers when, on awaking, they found the empty hand-cuffs lying quietly between them; he simply pressed his way as rapidly as possible to Memphis. Meeting with friends he put on a disguise and was hurried on. Just above the place he boarded a skiff and floated down to the landing.

Sam, with the mail had left Ella Herbert safe, as he thought, at the hotel, and as she had directed him, had given it in charge of the old negro woman, whom he called grandma, and had gone down to the wharf to see if he could hear or see anything of Captain Grimes. They were both delighted and surprised to meet each other. The Captain inquired of Miss Ella's safety and of the whereabouts of the mail. Sam, all unconscious of what was going on at the hotel, informed him that she was safe and well, and of how she had arranged the mail, and of its whereabouts.

The Captain was delighted to learn that all had worked so well, and that everything was so well ordered to his hand, for he knew that the Federal authorities were hot in pursuit of him, and nothing more likely than they were making for that place. Therefore, it behooved him to make his stay there a short one. He knew that he was in danger every moment that he spent in Memphis. He took the mail into his skiff, and directing Sam to tell his Miss to arrange to meet him at Corinth, and directing, as best he could how to proceed, he was off in the darkness.

Sam was just returning to the hotel to inform his Miss of

the good news when he met the detective coming down the steps.

The detective knew him at once, and the truth of what had become of the mail flashed upon him. Seizing the boy by the throat he demanded of him in the most peremptory manner the whereabouts of the letters. The poor boy was indeed frightened out of his wits; he was so bewildered and confused, that he could tell nothing. The detective hustled him off to jail and after a vain endeavor to get some information from him, he shut the door and left him alone in the darkness. Never had such rude hands been placed upon him before; never had he received such treatment from anyone. Always kind and obedient, perfectly trusting and confiding, he had known nothing but kind words and good wishes.

Strange that those who are opposed to slavery; are abusing the master for supposed brutality, and yet, when the opportunity offers, they themselves resort to that very measure of which they so bitterly accuse others. Those who know the negro, only know his human nature. Had he have treated the boy kindly, he might have learned something. But as it was, the sight of a Federal only filled him with fear.

No wonder that the boy was beside himself now. Alone in the darkness, what a dreadful night to him. Next morning they learned enough from him, one way or another, to know that some one had met him and had taken the mail and was gone. This was the reason they had made no further effort to extort from Miss Herbert its whereabouts.

After keeping the negro a few days and seeing the impossibility of using him to any advantage and believing him idiotic, as indeed he did appear, but only from fright, they turned him loose. They did not intend that he should ever see his mistress, and their idea was that if turned loose he would never find her. But he had more intelligence than they gave him credit for. Having spent some time at the hotel before, and making himself handy, it was not much trouble for him to get a place as a kind of waiter upon the guests. This very good luck gave him the opportunity of hearing and learning something of passing events. By listening at the conversation of the guests, he learned that his mistress had been sent to Fort Pillow and was there a prisoner. He at once determined to find her, and being a kind of voluntary substitute, but little attention being paid to him any way, he very easily made his escape and, by taking boat, reached Fort Pillow. He was, therefore, looking for just what he saw, when he caught sight. of Miss Ella's face at the window. He had had such a taste of the authorities as taught him that he would have to be cautious. He knew it would not do for him to inquire for her and he had just determined to hunt for her. He had been wandering about considerably that morning, and his delight could not be expressed when he saw the object of his search before him. Learning what he had in the past few days, he was prepared for the signs she gave him to be quiet.

Time flew rapidly, and Ella had not had the time to say anything to Sam about her own condition when the signal sounded for him to retreat. Quickly he obeyed, for each understood that their safety depended upon their not being discovered.

The guard sent Sam into the back yard to cut wood for cooking purposes just as if he belonged to the place, and sure enough no notice was taken of him by the officer of the day.

When the officer had completed his rounds and had found all, as he supposed, safe, and had gone, Sam was recalled, but the guard informed Miss Herbert that he.could not stay long, as his time on guard would soon be up. She therefore proceeded to state to Sam her own condition and the danger she was in of being put to death.

"Now," she said, "Sam, you must go through the lines to the Confederate army and see your mars, George Tracy, and tell him where I am, and that I may be put to death at any time, but may be they will delay and he can help me. And be sure to tell him that Joseph Shelton is in command here.

She gave him money to be used as he needed to further him on and all the instructions she could as to how to go, sending him to Corinth, Miss., and then in the direction of Tuscaloosa, Ala.

She told him to go mostly among the negroes, and that there would be but little suspicion of him as it was supposed by the Federal soldiers that the negroes were all "loyal subjects."

"Yes, Miss," replied Sam, "I'll go and I'll fotch him here, I'll git de whole army to come, dey shant hurt you for sho, you 'pend upon dat."

"I shall depend upon you, Sam, you have so far acted your part well, and I shall trust you to help me now. And now I must say good-by. Go, my dear boy, and God speed your way."

The guard was calling to hurry and Sam was forced to say a hurried good-by and was soon gone from sight, but not lost to memory.

CHAPTER XXIV.

THE GREAT RELIEF—THE DETECTIVE BE-COMES A FRIEND. HOW JESUS SAVES.

Although Ella was still enclosed in her narrow house and looked out from behind prison bars, and a sentinel stood guard at her door, yet she felt that a great burden had been removed; the doors of the past dark and dreadful days had been unlocked and everything seemed brighter now. She had learned that Captain Grimes had passed through perils too, and that he escaped; that the precious treasures enveloped in those letters had gone on their way to gladden the hearts of the weary and battle-worn soldier. That the captain would finally reach the Confederate camp she had not a shadow of doubt. And she felt that surely there was an unseen hand guiding all. Man may propose, but there is a God that overrules all and works all as He will.

"Yes, indeed," she would say, "He holds all in His hands and in His own good time and way He will bring it to pass. He will not forget me, His poor, lone, defenseless child."

"And," she mused, "Sam, the poor boy, has borne it all so well, and has shown himself so faithful." She had never, for one moment, doubted his devotion to her, but she had never before known his courage, nor had she guessed his persistent efforts in her behalf. She now understood that he would do all in his power for her. "Yes," she said, "he will carry the news of my imprisonment to the Confederate camp, if it be possible for him to do so; I have no doubt of it."

If strangers to slavery ever doubted that there was an attachment between servant and master, between mistress and slave akin to brotherhood, they were greatly mistaken. Sam would willingly have laid down his life to deliver his mistress from her peril. There were no dangers that he was not ready to face; no difficulties that he would not strive with all the energies of his being to surmount, for the rescue of her whom he almost worshiped. To him she was the one object of affection. Her word was his law, and to gratify her wish was the one object of his life. Knowing this, she had no fears that he could, by any possibility, be made to prove false to her wishes. "He will reach the camp," she said, somewhat triumphantly to herself as she thought the matter over. "It may be impossible then for me to be rescued, but Sam will do his part and the others will do all that it is in the power of men to do, and we must leave to God the rest. It may be that my mission in this life is ended and that the Master will call for me, but be that as it may, I shall trust Him for deliverance."

That night she slept sweetly and dreamed bright dreams of better days. Next morning the sun seemed to shine with a new brilliancy, and the waters of the great river looked so sparkling and the springtime flowers in the gardens and lawns in front of her windows looked so gay, that it seemed that all nature smiled and bade her be of good cheer.

She took up her Bible, that blessed treasure that had yet been left her, and turning to the 103rd Psalm, she read:

"Bless the Lord, O my soul; and all that is within me bless His holy name. Bless the Lord, O my soul, and forget not all His benefits; who forgiveth all thine iniquities, who healeth all thy diseases, who redeemeth thy life from destruction, who crowneth thee with loving kindness and tender mercies, who satisfieth thy mouth with good things, so that thy youth is renewed like the eagles."

This Psalm was indeed a sweet morsel to her, and she felt that a gentle, kind and loving hand was near her, even in her prison home. "O," she said, "why should I ever doubt Him? How can I doubt the fulfillment of every promise?" And she read on.

"As the heaven is high above the earth, so great is His mercy toward them that fear Him. O, the height of His goodness, the boundlessness of His mercy and the depths of His love."

The guard was surprised more than once that day at hearing her break forth into singing some of those sweet old songs that had cheered her soul in other days. Her heart was merry and her soul was glad. She hardly knew how to content herself.

> "Jesus, all the day long,
> Was her joy and her song."

A few evenings after this, there was another great surprise for her. The guard informed her that a soldier, an officer, wished to see her. She inquired if it was Col. Shelton, and on being informed that it was not, she bade the guard admit him. But who could describe her astonishment when she saw before her the very detective who had watched her at Memphis and who had brought upon her all this trouble. Unconsciously a frown passed over her face as the recollection of that dreadful night came to her, and a kind of a vague suspicion took possession of her that more mischief was being devised against her.

But the detective took off his cap and she saw at once, by the sad face, that something greatly troubled him or he was practicing deception to perfection. His face was pale and his eyes had a pleading, pitiful expression that betokened deep sorrow, and that hungered for sympathy and consolation. Her heart at once softened toward him.

"Miss Herbert," he said, in the most pleading tone, "I have a word for you that I do not wish another to hear; may I ask your confidence and to intrude upon your privacy for a few moments?"

Miss Ella hesitated to reply. She read those eyes again and again, and viewed that sad face once more. Was this real, or did he dissemble. Was he trying to gain her confidence so as to complete her destruction, or was he really seeking comfort?

It often happens that men are most severe with those they have wronged, that they leave nothing undone that will complete their destruction. Men often try to hide one wrong by doing another. They cannot endure the presence of the wronged, that is ever a reminder to them of their great sins. King Charles, of France, on the night of the destruction of the Protestants, cried, "Slay them all, let none escape to torment me." So men often think that "the dead know not anything," nor do they tell any tales. They forget that there is a great day of reckoning when all will stand before Him, whose eyes are over all, and who "readest our thoughts afar off." Ella understood something of wicked human nature and she hesitated. The detective saw it, and in a low tone he said:

"I know I do not deserve this, but I will yet prove to you that henceforth I am your friend."

She bid him come in, and as the room was not bountifully supplied with chairs, she gave him the only one it contained and she sat upon the bunk, having closed the door.

"I know," he began, "that you look upon me with suspicion and you have a right to do so. It may be that you despise me, and I cannot blame you for that. You know the life of a detective, that it is to practice deception, but before this is over, I will show you that I am capable of being a friend."

Ella determined to listen without committing herself till she heard his message, and she merely gave assent by the nod of her head. The detective continued:

"Since I last saw you, I have been one of the most miserable beings living—have been in perfect torment. There has been no peace for me, and I could not be content till I saw you and co fessed to you my great sin and begged your pardon. To this end I sought for and obtained a position on the commandant's staff and hence am here by his permission and authority. I must tell you that I never, till the night I saw you through that little window, fixed on purpose for your betrayal, saw the enormity of my crimes, nor understood the greatness of my sins.

I had pious parents once, and a sweet, good mother, devoted to my interests and my welfare, both in this life and the one that is to come. She taught me that there was a God and my obligations to Him, that He gave to me my being, watched over my life and took notice of all my actions. But that was in the long ago, when I was a boy. She is gone now. She crosssd the river before I became a man, and entered the rest she so beautifully pictured to me. In the rapid years passing by, the good lessons were forgotten, the good examples buried, and the sacred injunctions were cast aside. The truth is, the lessons were never heeded as they should have been. I took them more as the natural affection springing out of a mother's heart than as solemn realities.

My father gone, mother gone, and I, left alone, the only child, set out in a cold, dark world, to battle for life. I felt that this world was simply a stage upon which every one was acting, and that he succeeded best who best acted his part; that each was running a race through the world for the world, and he got most of it who ran best.

It mattered not what the part was, so it was acted well, or how we ran, so the running was to win. Each seemed to me to be striving for all they could get of the world, and I simply entered the race for my part of it.

The war came on, and I thought too much of life to throw it away in battle, and so great was my greed for gain, that I was willing to obtain it, though I did so at the expense of others. I saw an opening in the profession in which I have been engaged and so I set myself a watch upon the lives of others. In that line, shame upon one, I have been a great success, if success it may be called. I have betrayed many, brought sufferings and death upon hundreds and saddened a thousand hearts. My heart was hardened in the work; I rejoiced at the sufferings of others, for their loss and misery was my gain. My heart swelled with pride when I had a poor victim in my power. I even manufactured testimony and hunted my victims. My pride was to stand at the head of my profession. I felt that the greater the number of victims and the more intricate the cases, the greater my laurels, and the more my pay. I have received thousands for the betrayal of the innocent. O, my heart had become steel, and when I first looked at you through that window, though I knew you were the very picture of innocence, yet I gloried in the thought of my conquest, and the success of my iniquity. Had you have stopped there, all the prize would have been taken at once, and you would have been led off a prisoner.

But when you had finished your task and knelt down to offer up your devotions to God, when you lifted those hands to heaven in prayer, somehow, I know not why, the picture of my own dear mother came before me. I remembered how I had seen her upon her knees, and had seen her lift her hands like that in prayer for her "own dear boy, her only child." Yes, the words echoed through my ears as if I had just then heard them spoken, "Lord, bless my dear child, save my poor,

Elizabeth Ustick McKinney

lone boy, make him a mother's delight and a father's joy.
May he honor Thee in his life by being Thine own servant, and
his life proving a blessing to others, and dear Father, at last
take him home to Thyself in the glory land."

And then upon her finger was a ring, just such as you
wear. That ring was one of the last tokens of her love that
she had given me before she said that last good-by. O, I feel
so ashamed of myself. That ring, it is true, I had kept, but it
was hidden away in some cotton folds and had been almost
forgotten—I had not seen it for years. If I thought of it at all,
it was only as a kind of a keep-sake that must be kept as a
matter of course. But that night when the light shone upon
the ring upon your hand, my own dear mother's ring, came
vividly before me. I could not, I dare not go where you were.
And yet I was too cowardly to act the noble part. I thought I
was acting cowardly to fly from you and to shrink from your
arrest. But no, had I been brave, I would have confessed all,
warned you of your danger and helped you to fly while you
might. It was only that I shrank from the scoffs of the commandant that forced me to face you at last.

My mother wanted me to be good and to do good to
others. My life has been the very reverse, I have done others
nothing but wrong. I feel that really I have not a single true
friend upon earth, nor do I deserve one; the name detective is
hateful to me. True, many have flattered and praised my
cunning, but they have despised my life, they encourage when
they can use me to their own advantage, but they would
despise me as an associate. But above and beyond all this,
what hope can I have of the mercy of God, what is to become
of me when I am called to give an account to the Great Judge?
What can I do to atone for my great crimes; to wipe out the
innocent blood that cries to heaven against me? O, the
thought of it destracts me. I stand upon the very verge of
hell and devils sometimes seem to gloat over my destruction.
I have prayed, I have begged, I have cried for help, I have
pledged and promised a better life, but still that innocent blood
cries out from the ground against me; my days are full of
weeping and my nights of fear. O, if the past could only be
wiped out. But no, no; in spite of me there are those dark
lines ever before my eyes. O, the thought becomes unendurable. O, how I long for a mother's prayer for me once more!

And now, my dear lady, you, who have brought to my thoughts the memory of my own sweet mother, I have risked my life for this opportunity of seeing and appealing to you, not only for your forgiveness, but for an interest in your prayers. Can you tell me what I must do to be saved, or if it be possible that salvation is for such as I?"

Ella was touched with this appeal. The earnestness of it forbade the idea of hypocrisy or deception. The man frequently broke down, so intense were his feelings, and many were the tears of contrition that dropped from those sad eyes. In her sympathetic sorrow Ella found her own eyes frequently dimmed with tears during the sad recital. She waited a few moments before making reply that her own feelings might become more calm and that the detective, who seemed so overwhelmed with grief, might become more composed. Then she broke the silence by saying:

"There is *hope* for you

"Hope for me," he epeated, "How? In what? My life is a crime, my whole being is one black spot without a single redeeming quality. I have lived a lie; justice would have slain me long ago; God is just, and I cannot see how He can save me. Hope for me! Impossible; my sins will not down and I cannot undo them."

Indeed, the detective presented a picture of deep despair, and Ella's heart was touched with tenderness toward him.

"Calm yourself," she said, "and I will try to tell you how Jesus saves."

"But," he said, "can you tell me how He saves a sinner like me? I can see how He saves good people, but sinners such as I, I cannot see how that can be done."

"That," she replied, "is just what I want to tell you, how Jesus saves sinners."

"But," he interjected, "sinners like me?"

"Yes," was the answer, "sinners like you."

"That is good," he said, as if communing with himself: "Sinners like me; Jesus saves sinners like me."

Ella continued: "That was the great mission of the Saviour into this world to save sinners. You have heard those words of the poet,

"'Not the righteous, not the righteous,
Sinners Jesus came to call.'

"'The whole need not a physician, but they that are sick.' 'Jesus came not to call the righteous, but sinners to repentance.' If men were good they would not need a Saviour. The Lord says, 'Come, now, and let us reason together; though your sins be as scarlet, they shall be as white as snow; though they be red like crimson, they shall be as wool.' The Lord cannot justify you in your sins, He saves you from them. He does not deal with us after our sins, nor does He reward us according to our iniquities."

"But," broke in the detective, "what becomes of His justice? I know He must be just, and to be just I cannot see how He saves."

"True," said Ella, "He must be just, or He cannot be merciful. Justice first, mercy afterwards. God does not and cannot justify sin. He justifies the sinner.

"All men may not have lived the same life that you have lived; some have spent life in one line of sin, some have spent it in another line, but all have sinned. Every natural life is a life of sin in its line. God looked down from heaven to see if there were any that did good, and the answer was, 'No, not one.' Paul thus describes men in their lives and as they all appear in the eyes of God. Taking up her Bible she read (see Rom. iii: 10.) 'There is none righteous, no, not one. There is none that understandeth, there is none that seeketh after God. They are all gone out of the way, they are together become unprofitable; there is none that doeth good, no, not one. Their throat is an open sepulchre; with their tongues they have used deceit. [That is I, broke in the detective], the poison of asps is under their lips; whose mouth is full of cursing and bitterness, their feet are swift to shed blood, destruction and misery are in their ways, and the way of peace they have not known. There is no fear of God before their eyes.''

The detective looked up with sorrow and despair pictured upon every feature.

"That," he said, "is a correct history of my life. Can it be that that great Apostle had me in his mind? I have had no fear of God; no, He was not in all my thoughts. And oh, what misery has been in *my* ways. Of a truth the way of peace I have not known. But do you tell me that such as that can be saved?"

Ella replied, that "If such as that cannot be saved, then none can be saved. Does He not tell you that such is the condition of all?"

"Do you mean to say," said the detective, "that everybody is as mean as I am, that that is the life history of all; that there are none good?"

"That," replied Ella, "is just the way the Book reads—there is none good. That is, 'in us,' as Paul says in another place, 'dwelleth no good thing.' As I said before, every man's sins lieth in his own line. Your sins are in one direction, somebody else's sins are in another direction, but all are sinners, and there are none good but by the grace of God. Yes, there are good lives, bright lives, glorious lives, but the grace of God has made them so."

"But," argued he, "has not God a law, a standard of right by which He judges men? And can He set that law aside and maintain His own power? Would this not argue that His law was worthless?"

"Yes, indeed," said Ella, "God has a law, a just and holy law, a law of eternal truth, a rule of perfect right. Here is wherein our condition appears so deplorable. Not only have we sinned, but by our great sin we have fallen under the curse of that law, and by it have come into condemnation. That law justly and rightly condemns us, nor can we escape that just condemnation by anything we may or can do. Turn as we will, promise as we may, there stands our sins black as ever, and a just law showing how guilty we are. An action once done is done forever; when we commit an offense against the law of God, and fall under its curse, it is done for eternity; we cannot take away the guilt nor remove the curse. The sins you have committed you are powerless to remedy, and the broken law you cannot amend."

"Yes, yes," he said, "that is it. I have tried every way possible, and instead of amending, the more I look at my sins the blacker they have become; and the more I have seen of God's justice, the more I have felt that I cannot be saved. You have told me my case exactly, but what I seek to know is, can I be saved and God be just?"

"From your point of view, then," said Ella, "you cannot be saved. You have broken God's law by your great sin, and you feel sure that you cannot remedy it. You thus feel that you are indeed lost?"

He replied, "that is just it, that is just it; I *am* lost, so far as anything I can do, is concerned. It seems to me that I have done all that any poor mortal could do, and yet my great sins instead of growing less, grow in magnitude. I do not mean that the more I look at my sins, the more I sin, but that the more I look at those sins already committed, the worse they appear."

"Well," said Ella, "You have read of the Saviour's coming into the world, of His great sufferings and death; think you that He would have endured all this had not the condition of sinners have been a deplorable one? The Master did not suffer for pastime or just to give us a lesson in misery, or to rescue us from a little peril, O no. David said that he was in an *horrible* pit. HORRIBLE! mark the expression. Is it not that way with you?"

"Yes, yes, that is it, that is it, 'in an *horrible* pit.'"

"Well, the Lord's mercy reached David and he took him out of that pit. The Lord's mission was to seek and to save the lost, mark you, to *seek* them and to *save* them. I emphasize the word *lost*. So far as law and justice are concerned, powerlessly and hopelessly *lost*.

"But," continued Ella, "sinners are not saved by the deeds of the law. Let us read Paul a little further upon that subject. Having described man's condition as above, he thus proceeds to deduct those legitimate conclusions.

" 'Now we know that what things soever, the law saith, it saith to them that are under the law, that every mouth may be stopped and all the world become guilty before God. Therefore, [that is a great truth resulting from this condition of things] 'by the deeds of the law, there shall be no flesh justified in His sight; for by the law is the knowledge of sin.'

"We should not have known sin but by the law of God. Not that the law makes us sinners, but it reveals to us what sin is; it gives us the knowledge of sin. It is simply the measure of our conduct. And when we thus measure we find that we fall short; that being weighed in the balance we are found wanting. God, by the law shows us that He hates, and justly condemns, sin. He gives us a measure of how unclean our lives are in His sight; but by His grace He shows us His love of sinners.''

"O,'' he said, "I feel and know my condemnation, and that it is just. I also believe that God is good and merciful, but how He can be merciful at the expense of justice, I cannot see.''

"Then,'' said Ella, "if you see so clearly the justice of God in your condemnation, the more glorious will His grace appear in your salvation. God does not save at the expense of justice. Christ Himself has satisfied justice for us; He has taken our law place; 'He who knew no sin was made sin for us.' 'He was made under the law'; that is, He was Himself a law subject, 'that He might take us from under the law;' that is, relieve us from its dreadful curse. He was made sin for us, or He was made a curse for us, that is, He bore the curse for us.

"More than that, He took our sins upon Himself. The entirely Righteous One took our guilt; filled our law place in every sense of the word. Are you poor? behold His poverty. He who was infinitely rich in the eternal world, not only gave up the riches and the glory of it for our sakes, but He assumed our guilt, took upon Him our debt to the law of God to pay it for us, and thus to satisfy its claim and save sinners. At one bound He comes from a world of unfading glories and endless joys, to one of sorrow and of grief. Are you poor? Come with me to Bethlehem, and let us look into the manger at that innocent Babe. Never before were beasts so honored, never did rags wrap so grand a form. Here lies the King that rules the skies wrapped in swaddling clothes; look at them, how filthy! The beasts have been rubbed down with them; they are too filthy for decent hands, and yet they wrap the glory of all worlds. Are you poor? here is the picture of your poverty on Jesus. The poverty was not His own, it is *our* poverty upon Him. For our sakes He became poor.

"Do you sorrow and weep? 'Jesus wept,' not for Himself: these are tears of poor suffering humanity. He was the man of sorrows and acquainted with grief. No tears were like His; no sufferings and buffetings like His. Do you feel lone and forsaken? Jesus in the last trying hour had not a single friend. Do you suffer remorse, sorrow and misery on account of sin? the terrible weight of them killed the blessed Lord. 'He was delivered for our offenses,' not for His own. Look at Him sweating, as it were, great drops of blood in that fearful agony in the garden; look at the darkened sun and the shaking earth as nature joins its groans to the dreadful agony of those three fearful hours upon the cross, when to consummate the fullness of bitterness, He cries out, 'My God! My God, why has Thou forsaken *me?*' When God lays upon Him the iniquity of us all, and His blood, for the remission of sins, pours in a purple stream from His side; Jesus bears our sins in His own body upon the tree of the cross. Now look at all these, and tell me, was not justice satisfied? What more can He do? What more is needed to be done? What more can justice ask? Believe on the Lord Jesus Christ as your righteousness, justification, sanctification and redemption, and you shall be saved. Jesus having magnified the law in our behalf, opens to us the door of mercy, of pardon full and free. Now He says, 'Look to me, oh, ye ends of the earth and be saved. Do not look to yourself nor anything mortal, look to Jesus; yes, 'Jesus saves, Jesus saves!' Can *you* not look and live?''

Ella had become eloquent and earnest in her pleadings, and they were not without their reward. A glow of peace and joy lit up the detective's face and springing to his feet in perfect raptures of delight, he exclaimed ''Glorious! And can it be true that I am not to atone for my own sins?''

"It is true," replied Ella, "that you *cannot* atone for them, and Jesus has done for you what you cannot do for yourself. He has atoned for your sins.''

As if yet half doubting, half believing, half praising, and yet half questioning, he said, "What! for *my* sins; for such a great sinner as I?''

"Yes," replied Ella, "for *you;* salvation is personal, special, and particular. If such is not true, we have no personal interest in Jesus. He was delivered for *our* offences. Not for offence, but for our offences, covering them all.

> "'Jesus paid it all,
> All to Him I owe.'

"Peter told those people who had even murdered the Lord to repent and believe on Him, and they should be saved. Can you not do this?''

"O yes, yes," he said, "I do repent and I do believe. O, here is that glorious grace that I never could understand before; Jesus has met justice for me, and I only trust Him, believe on Him. Now I see He leads the blind in a way they knew not. Glorious! Glorious! O, the abounding mercy of God; I will praise Him as long as I live."

But here the officer of the guard made his appearance, and while the detective could show his full authority for being found in company with the prisoner, yet he feared to prolong his stay. Some suspicion of the true purpose of his visit might be aroused and thus all that he had designed to accomplish be defeated.

The detective, after holding a short conversation with the officer, returned and said to Miss Ella:

"I hope you will now regard me as a friend."

She replied, "After what I have seen and heard, I can not doubt your friendship."

He then told her that he was sorry the conversation could not be prolonged. "But," said he, "I was sent here upon another mission." What selfish beings we are. But it was not altogether selfish. "I did not feel that the purpose for which I was sent would be an agreeable one to you, nor is it to me, but by that mission I have had access to your presence, and through it I hope to prove of benefit to you. I am really ashamed to mention the business for which I was sent, but the God whom you serve will strengthen you to bear it.

"I must tell you now that in the commander of this post you have an inveterate enemy, one bent upon your destruction unless you accept of his terms."

"I know, I know," she broke in, "and I know his terms. Death is preferable. . Never, no never, my vows are to another and I shall be faithful."

"You have rightly guessed," replied the detective, "I see that you understand, but here is a message from him that I promised to deliver, and I have your reply. To-morrow the court-martial will set and he will appear against you. There can be but one result—they will find you guilty.

"But do not despair, escape is possible; that good Lord will help us. I shall do all in my power to that end and I think you need not fear."

"Yes," she said, "I know what the result of the trial will be, and one thing I ask of you, and that is, if you have any influence with the court to have them put off the day of execution as long as you can."

The detective promised to do all that he could, and with an assurance that she should hear from him again, and thanking her for the comfort she had given him, he took his departure.

CHAPTER XXV.

THE TRIUMPH AND THE OVERTHROW.

Ella Herbert took the message given her by the detective, ind was not in the least disappointed in its contents. It ecited the fact of the meeting of the court, and the case going)efore it, of the testimony against her, and that when once the :ourt had made its decision, there would be no retreat. That f she rejected this last opportunity for conciliation, that she lid so at her peril, and after fair warning.

The terms were such as she had anticipated, but such as ihe could in no wise accept. So degrading was it to her woman nature, that she tore the missive into a thousand pieces ind gave it to the winds as they whisked by her window.

Next day the court-martial set, and Ella appeared before .t. Col. Joseph Shelton appeared as judge advocate. It is 1eedless to enter into the details; there was simply the form)f trial. Ella confessed to the carrying of the mail and was sent back to her room. As to the judge advocate's testimony against her, that was with closed doors, Ella heard none of it. The result was as expected, she was found guilty of the charges against her, and nothing was left now but the fixing of the time for the execution of the sentence. Col. Shelton urged the immediate carrying out of the sentence of the court, or at least that it should be put into execution the next day. But here the detective came in with his work and he could do so with effect. He was one of the prime movers in her arrest and the chief witness to the things charged in the indictment. He had been employed by the authorities to make the discoveries; he had made them and it was his right to plead for mercy. He said that she was but a woman, and she was away from all her friends, so that there was no danger of an escape from that direction. The post they then occupied, was far away from any enemy, and was well guarded with gun-boats and a strong force, so that there was no danger from that quarter; hence, he argued that the court could afford to be merciful. It had a certainty that its decree could be carried out at any time. Besides, he argued that it was desired beyond all things else to capture Captain Grimes, the main instigator of all, and if Miss Herbert was left in prison he would be sure to search for her and then he, too, would be captured, and who knows but the court can save this innocent woman, in the event they get possession of him who has brought her to this.

His argument had the desired effect upon the judges who were too glad for an excuse to put off the evil day; and despite the threats and pleadings of Col. Shelton, they determined not to fix a day at that meeting.

It may be argued that the detective is still practicing deception, and hence, the profession of contrition and deep convictions for his crimes is unworthy of belief. To an extent this is true, but his deceiving Col. Shelton is not for his injury, or that of any one else. As chief witness, he was compelled to appear in court, and he has testified to the facts. He is not shrinking the responsibility of the position assigned him. He is simply doing now all that is in his power to do to correct the wrong that he feels that he has done the prisoner. He had no idea of the relation that had previously existed between Col. Shelton and Ella Herbert, or that the Colonel even knew her. He had hoped by enlisting the Colonel's sympathy to obtain Ella's release. He was perfectly taken back, therefore, when he discovered the facts about it. And this he fortunately did without giving the Colonel the least intimation of his own purpose. He had heard the Colonel in an outburst of passion, declare: "I will humble her haughty pride." Till then, he had never known the real character of Col. Shelton, nor anything of the viper he had to contend with. If he would do the prisoner any good, he was compelled to keep his motives hid from the commander of the post. But at the same time he must be upon friendly terms with him.

Although the Colonel stormed and raged at the detective's pleadings for mercy, yet he knew so little of human nature, that he never suspected for a moment that he was really the prisoner's friend. He had simply accepted of the fact that as the detective had discovered the plot and was the chief witness against her, that he was really in favor of her conviction and that his pleadings were for the mere sympathy he had for the suffering.

The next day the detective sought the prisoner and informed Miss Ella of the results of the court-martial. She was not disappointed at the news of her conviction; it was what she had fully expected. She very graciously thanked the detective for the part he had taken, and was rejoiced that the date of execution had not been fixed.

"There is no question," said the detective, "but that Colonel Shelton will urge upon the court the necessity of putting their decree into execution as speedily as possible. You seem to be a rebuke to him while you are here, and he hungers to reek his vengeance upon you and his hated enemy, as he calls George Tracy. The plain upon which he moves is purely a selfish one. He does not conceive that others have feelings and aspirations that reach out and beyond mere selfish motives to the broad plain of true devotion and filial affection. But such is the man, and the best that can be done now is to watch his movements, and if possible, thwart his plans and purposes."

Ella had not informed the detective of her prime reason for delay in the execution of the court's decree, nor anything of the mission upon which she had sent her servant. Partly because she feared that her confidence might be misplaced and partly because she did not think it would be of any benefit to him to know, as he could not co-operate with the Confederate force outside. And then she hoped that he might invent some plan of escape in case the outside failed. She, therefore, determined to allow him to act from his own convictions. And really this was the one fixed purpose of the detective; from that very day he began to lay his plans to that end.

After a little further talk upon the condition of things, the detective said: "Miss Herbert, I know your troubles are such that you do not feel like talking upon other subjects, but the theme upon which we conversed when I was last with you was so glorious to me, and the Scriptures were opened to my understanding in such a new light, and the grace of God in the salvation of poor sinners appeared to me so soul-cheering, that if it would not be asking too much, I should be delighted to hear more upon that subject."

"O," said Ella, "I never tire of talking of my Lord and His boundless love to poor, lost and perishing sinners; and the greater the danger that surrounds me, the more I think of Him. I have realized so much of His goodness in my own case. He is my stay and comfort. In the lone hours, when none else is near or hears, I have my God and my Bible as my everlasting portion. With Him as my Friend, death has no terrors. True, I do not say I want to die, that is contrary to our nature. I want to live as long as it is God's will for me to live. I want to live to serve Him, and that I may do good to others. I pray God to bless all my labors to the good of men, and that I may live to be to the praise of His glory. And I feel that even in your case God has used my troubles to your good, and through them has answered a good mother's prayers in your behalf. Yes, indeed, He maketh the wrath of man to praise Him.

"But I feel that when my work here on earth is done, my mission ended, and the good Lord calls for me, that I want to go, and He only will know that time. True, I have a dread of the darkness and of the pain of death, but then my Saviour died, and has robbed death of its sting, has sweetened the bitterness of parting with this life, and gloriously perfumed the grave with the incense of heaven. And then, looking over the darkness, I think of the bright, the glorious beyond when all is over.

"Yes, yes, I delight to talk of Jesus and His love. And I did want to show you just how Paul's argument coincided with the argument I set before you in your last conversation. In that we had shown to us how that by the deeds of the law no flesh could be justified in His sight. The question then to be considered is, how are men justified? Let us read the conclusion:

"'But now, the righteousness of God without the law is manifested, being witnessed by the law and the prophets.'

"That is, the law bears testimony to the fulfillment of all its claims in Christ, and that in Him and by Him it has been satisfied. Therefore it has no further claims, but grants a perfect and absolute release to all represented in the sufferings of

Christ. The prophets also bear testimony to the same truth, witnessing and testifying that Christ should come and suffer for us. Men are saved, then, not by works of righteousness which they have done or can do, for we have seen that men could not satisfy the claims of the law, but they are saved by what Christ has done for them. I repeat those sweet words, 'Jesus saves.' "

"In this same line of thought, Paul continues the argument. 'Even the righteousness which is by faith of Jesus Christ unto all, and upon all them that believe, for there is no difference.' That is, there is no difference in the condition of men as sinners. I do not mean that there is no difference in sins, some sins are more aggravated than others, but I speak of men's condition as sinners; all are guilty, all are condemned, all are under the curse of God's law and by that law none can be justified. Hear Paul: 'For all have sinned and come short of the glory of God.'

"In plain terms he then tells us how we are justified. 'Being justified by His grace through the redemption that is in Christ Jesus, whom God hath set forth to be a propitiation through faith in His blood, to declare His righteousness for the remission of sins that are past, through the forbearance of God; to declare, I say, at this time His righteousness, that He might be just, and the justifier of him that believeth in Jesus.' Here you see set forth how God by giving His Son as a propitiation for our sins, satisfying the law for us, maintains His own justice, and at the same time is enabled to justify them that believe on Him. Not that He justifies them in what they have done, but He, having redeemed them from the claims of the law, justifies them by what He has done. As Christ has taken our place in fulfilling the law for us, He gives us His place as our righteousness. Paul therefore further concludes, as to our peace and eternal happiness, that, 'Being justified by faith, we have peace with God,' we become united to Him and are one with Him."

The detective had given the most marked attention to all this, and his soul seemed filled with perfect delight. He repeated over and over again, and again, "How glorious! How glorious!" But still there seemed to be a kind of shadow of doubt, a something he could not understand. After reflecting a few moments, he said:

"Miss Ella, does religion entirely discard good works?"

"No, no," she replied, "Religion is made up of good works, there can be no religion without them. But in point of salvation that question cuts no figure at all. With man as a sinner, it is not a question of what he shall do in his sins, but as to how he shall be delivered from them.

"Take my own case for illustration. Here I am condemned, and you tell me this morning that sentence has been passed against me. Now it is not a question of how I shall behave myself while here in prison, but how I shall get out of prison; not a question of how I shall act between now and the execution of the law's sentence, but how shall I escape the execution of it! (I shall not argue the justice or injustice of human law, but proceed upon the idea that it is just.) I have no complaint to make against the law, nor the court that did the findings. I had a perfect knowledge of what that law was, and of the results of my disobedience if my guilt was discovered. I cannot claim ignorance of that. I have by my own free will chosen to set that law at defiance; my guilt has been discovered, as you know, and here I am under sentence of death. Now it is not within my power to undo anything I have done, or to satisfy that law except by suffering its penalty. I may escape, but not lawfully, the law will not be satisfied. If I escape, it must be at the expense of justice, that is, supposing the law and the sentence to be just. The only possible way for law to be satisfied and for me to be justified, is for some one to suffer for me; that is, to give me his place and he take mine. Then it would be justified by his act and not by my own. This no mortal can do, because he himself is a law subject. No one can satisfy law save He who is above law. He who is altogether righteous without law. Hence, the sufferings of the Law-giver.

"You see now that it is not a question as to how I shall act while here in prison. Everything demands my becoming behavior at all times, but here I am in this fearful dilemma, and how shall I get out of it? Such is the condition of men, they have willfully broken God's law and are under its curse, and justly so; they can make no complaint against the law; they knew its claims; they have put themselves in a condition from which they are powerless, by anything they can do to get out.

"But here comes in the goodness and mercy of God. Of His own will or mere good pleasure, the great Law-giver suffers for us; takes our place; pays our debt, and simply says to the poor sinner in the sink of sin, 'Trust Me and I will take you out; give me your hand and I will lift you up.' So you see it is not a question of good works."

"O, yes," he said, "I see it all now, good works are all right, but they do not take away our bad ones; it is required of us all to be good at all times, but that cannot change our bad works; good works cannot save from suffering th e consequence of bad ones; they cannot save."

"That is it," replied Ella, "Salvation is of the Lord; have faith in Him, trust Him, and all is well."

"And now I see," said the detective, "how it is that by His mere mercy and grace He saves. We have willfully and knowingly sinned, done despite to His laws and set at defiance His will. Yes, it is by grace we are saved, through faith in His name. Glorious salvation," and he added, "if I knew you could escape this prison and get free I could almost thank the Lord for your imprisonment. The last few days have been glorious to me and the way brighter and brighter. I now can see Christ as my Saviour, and can praise Him for His abounding grace. The only thing is your own sufferings."

"O," said Ella, "the Lord will provide."

"Yes, the Lord will provide," was the reply, "and now I shall look about and see what the provisions are that He has made. How much the Lord provides for us if we will only hunt up the provisions. The decree of the court must not, it shall not be carried out, said the detective, vehemently; from this time on I shall not rest till you are safe from this place."

Ella thanked him for his kind, good wishes, and with an assurance that she would hear good news from him in a few days they parted.

The detective set to work from that hour for the liberation of the prisoner. He asked leave of absence for a few days, with the purpose in view of finding some friends on the outside that would help him in his undertaking. He knew the country to be filled with Southern people who would be too glad to help him when they understood the case.

The Colonel readily granted leave of absence, not because

Yours
A H P Colvin

he took pleasure in doing the detective a favor, but because he saw that he was in the way of his carrying out his purpose. He had determined upon the death of the prisoner and that as speedily as possible. With the detective gone, and the fact that the other officers were under his command, he thought he could force them into measures. And well he succeeded.

The very next day, after the detective left, the court was convened, and by threats and intimidations, they were induced to set the day and the hour of the execution of the prisoner. Miss Herbert was notified that evening, that the next evening at 6 o'clock P. M., the penalty of the law would be enforced; the death sentence was read and she was told to make her preparations for that solemn hour.

While she knew that the Colonel was seeking her destruction, and that he would bring it about as quickly as possible, yet she was not prepared for the sudden change. The detective had left her the morning before, full of hope and cheer, and that he was working some scheme for her escape, she had no doubt, and she rightly attributed this change in affairs to his absence. She was given till the next evening, and she cheered herself with the thought that there was yet hope. The detective would be back soon, may be that very night, with deliverance. Besides, she had now been looking each day for news from Sam's expedition in some way. It might come yet. "God," she said, "can work wonders." After the excitement of the moment had passed away, she became composed and prayed to the good Lord to make her perfectly resigned to His will.

She spent most of that sad night in writing to home friends and the dear ones, telling them of what she had suffered, of God's goodness to her and of her hope in the bright beyond. "It may be," she said, "that to-morrow will be my wedding day. I shall become a *bride;* wedded to my dear Lord forever. If it be so, how glorious! Though enemies follow me to my grave, angels will be my attendants at the marriage altar, and though the dread roll of musketry may announce my death, the shouts of angels will announce my marriage to the Lamb. O sweet, happy exchange."

She then slept a few hours—sweet, happy sleep. When she awoke next morning, the sun was just looking above the top of the eastern hills and sending a bright radiance over river and forest; looking out upon the brightness, she could but picture the glory of the rising of that Sun that never sets, and the sweetness of its radiance over the waters of life and the evergreen trees on the eternal shore. She took it as a bright omen of some good in store for her. May be her crossing the river, may be her deliverance.

The chagrin, mortification and even rage of the detective can hardly be imagined when he came into town early on the morning of the 12th of April, having perfected his arrangements for the escape of the prisoner the following night, and learned that the court had set the time of her execution for that very evening. To reverse the decision now would be impossible, and to hurry up his own arrangements was equally impossible. What he was designing to do was to be done under cover of darkness, and the prisoner would be dead before that hour came. But he must see her; she must know how earnest his efforts had been in her behalf, and then they must arrange to take desperate chances. "She must not die," said the detective in his fixed determination.

Just before reaching the prison, he met Colonel Shelton, and forgetting that he was a subaltern and at the mercy of this vindictive tyrant, he at once charged him with being a contemptible coward, making war upon and seeking the destruction of poor, defenseless women.

The Colonel, in his rage, threatened the detective with vengeance and declared that he would "humble the proud queen," and that George Tracy should feel the sting of his whip. He had rode by the prison that very morning, that he might mock the poor prisoner within, and that she might see that he rejoiced in her sufferings. He was just in the act of turning back and ordering the guard to arrest the detective when an orderly dashed up to him excitedly, and handed him a message. He read it over hurriedly and the detective noticed that he turned pale. He whirled his horse in the direction of the works and was gone.

The detective left free, and the guard having no instructions to the contrary, he entered the prison unmolested. He found Ella in tears, yet in a measure composed. He explained to her his plans for her deliverance, and how it was that he knew nothing of what was going on until he came in that morning, and then tried to encourage her with the thought that there was yet hope.

She fully understood and appreciated his efforts. "I do not mind to die," she said, "if it be the Lord's will, but to die at the hands of such a man! I could have gone to the place of execution without a murmur could I have been spared the mortification of witnessing the triumph of that man.'"

"But," she added, "all hope is not gone yet, the Lord has never forsaken me and He never will. Of this one thing will I be confident. Let the day close upon my life here as it may, I feel that its ending will be glorious. When I awoke this morning and caught the first glow of the bright sun as it sent its radiance over those hills and away across the waters to the glowing valley beyond, it betokened to me good. I took it as the shadow of better things. It may be of the brightness on the evergreen shore, but I can but think it means deliverance. I cannot realize that I shall die this evening. It may be as you say, we shall have to take desperate chances, but be that as it may, we shall succeed."

She continued: "Have you noticed that the gun-boats are all gone, and that a part of the infantry force have been taken away? What a nice time for that eagle-eyed Forest to dash in and capture the place."

This brought the detective's mind to the message that he saw handed to the Colonel that morning, and though he thought little of it then, the whole scene came fresh before him now; the excited condition of the orderly, the Colonel's turning pale and his strange actions, and he sprang to his feet so exultingly as almost frightened Ella, as he fairly shouted, "*Forest is here, now.*"

As they were shut out from a view of the ditches, where they were, the detective ran out of the prison and looked over the hills. Sure enough, everything was in a stir; the men were rapidly filing into the trenches and the officers were flying everywhere trying to encourage the men.

The paper that had been handed to the Colonel in the presence of the detective, was nothing more or less than a demand from General Forest for the immediate surrender of the place. The Colonel was too cowardly to surrender. He

knew that he had not the force to hold it, but he dare not surrender. He knew that as soon as Forest entered the place he
would find out all he had been doing, and the coward supposed
all men to be like himself, destitute of every generous impulse,
and only filled with envy and spite. He knew that the gun-
boats would be back that evening, and in the vain hope of
delaying the attack until that time, he began hurriedly to form
his men into line, and asked General Forest for a parley.

Forest, from his position, had noticed every movement and
he was determined not to give the foe any advantage.

Just as the detective had began to take in something of the
situation, the loud crack of a cannon rent the air and he came
darting back into the prison. At the same time, a soldier came
dashing up the street crying, "Forest and his cavalry! Forest
and his cavalry!" The detective was about to go out again,
but Ella told him to stay with her and he would be safe.

"I have been looking for this," she said, "it is no disap-
pointment to me."

"Why? How?" questioned the detective.

"You remember the servant of mine that hid the mail bag
and that you all took to be a kind of idiot, do you not?"

"O, yes, yes," was the answer. "Well," continued Ella,
'I have seen him since I have been here and this is the result
of his work. Before another hour, I will see him again, the
proudest boy living. Now you know the reason I asked for
delay."

But their talk was cut short. Crack, crack went the guns
in rapid succession; boom, boom the roaring cannon, and then
a long, loud deafening yell, mingled with the roll of the rattling
muskets. Shout followed shout, cheer after cheer went up
from all the hills, mingled with that sharp crack of guns and
pistols and the roar of tramping horses. The very air seemed
filled with the noise of battle, and all the hills covered with
charging men. Louder and louder grew the din; more and
more shrill the yells of the victors; nearer and nearer rolled the
great wave of deafening noise. The very earth shook neath
the tread of the charging squadrons. Looking down the street,
they see a great surging wave of flying fugitives. Down, down
the hill they came, like the swine on the hills of Gadarea,
pouring on toward the river as though they would seek refuge

beneath its turbid waters, and still the death shots fell thick and fast. Looking up the street, in the opposite direction and waving proudly above the flying mass of frightened fugitives, is the Southern cross. A regiment of cavalry comes sweeping down like a whirlwind, dashing through the flying foe and shouting victory as they come.

The roar of battle was so exciting, the charge so terrible, the revenge so swift, the carnage so dreadful, and the victory so glorious, that Ella trembled with emotion. What tumultuous thoughts filled her heart! Snatched as it had been from death and given a new lease of life; the overthrow of her enemies and the meeting of friends, all presented a scene so strange, so glorious and yet mingled with its sadness, that Ella stood through it all as one in a trance, but drinking in all its realities.

She heard a voice cry out, "Dar she am! Dar she am!" And looking down on the pavement below, she saw Sam, already dismounted and making rapidly for the stairway, followed by two cavalry men.

Without ceremony, Sam came bursting into the room crying, "Miss, I got 'em, you's safe! You's safe!" The two cavalry men were none other than George Tracy and Captain Grimes. The welcomes and greetings of that glad meeting we shall not attempt to describe. We could not, if we would. After the impassioned moments were over, Ella explained briefly the presence of the detective, and how he was her friend.

As for Sam, he was the hero of the occasion. He kept a respectful distance noting the rejoicing of others till all had become somewhat quiet, and then he sprang to his mistress. His joy knew no bounds, and he manifested it in many ways. He grasped her hand and kissed it again and again, while he fairly washed it with his tears. And then he would laugh and leap up for joy, exclaiming, "My Miss, my dear good Miss is safe now." He dropped to the floor and caught her by the feet and embraced them. Ella patted his cheeks and rubbed her hands over his head and called him her dear, faithful Sam; and when at last she sat down, he claimed the right to stand behind her and play with her curls.

The detective noticing it all, at last said, "And this is slavery?"

"Yes," said Ella, "this is *slavery*. A boy that will risk his life for his mistress."

But, reader, we will linger here no longer. The revenge had been swift and terrible. Many that had laughed at night, thoughtless of danger, lay cold in death. And among these were Colonel Shelton. With him gone, the tragedy is over. That evening, instead of marching to her death, Ella is in a carriage with Sam, driven on her way to the Southern army, with Gen. Forest's cavalry as a guard. The detective is along too, as his profession was gone and he had determined a new life.

Since we have seen how well Sam succeeded on his mission, we shall not follow him in his wanderings. He reached the Confederate camp just the evening before Captain Grimes reached it at night. The captain had been delayed by a hurt he received in getting from the boat the night he sprang into the river; that grew worse after he left Memphis, and, also, by waiting about Corinth to get some word from Miss Herbert. Finally, supposing she had gone on before him, he went on to the command.

When Captain Grimes learned of the condition of things, and knowing where General Forest and his men were stationed, he at once looked to them for help. It was a strange coincidence that when Captain Grimes and his company reached Forest's command, they found him just on the eve of starting to attack the place. He had, by his scouts, been watching his opportunity, and had just learned of the departure of the gunboats and the weakening of the force, and although he knew nothing of the prisoner, or the fate that awaited her, he had determined to sweep down upon the garrison and destroy the stores. All that Captain Grimes and his company had to do then, was to fall into line and march with the dashing, victorious cavalry.

CHAPTER XXVI.

HOOD'S MARCH INTO TENNESSEE. BAT-
TLE OF FRANKLIN AND DEFEAT
AT NASHVILLE.

Atlanta, Ga., was entirely abandoned by the Confederate army on the night of the 1st of September, 1864, and on the 5th of that month Sherman's army fell back from Jonesboro to that place, while Hood's army went into camp at Lovejoy Station. This ended the struggle for "the gate city." The Confederate army lay in camp at Lovejoy Station till the 17th, when they had orders to cook two day's rations and be ready to move. On the 18th, they took up the line of march, swinging to the left of Atlanta, in the direction of Palmetto Station, on the "West Point and Montgomery R. R., and near the Chatahooche River." The army arrived at that place on the 20th and began fortifying.

While at this place, President Davis and some of the authorities at Richmond, visited the army under Hood. What the purpose of the visit was, the writer does not know, but it seems that a new plan of campaign was inaugurated. General Hood was to entirely abandon Gen. Sherman's front, swing around to his rear, and by cutting off his supplies, compel him (Sherman), if possible, to follow the Confederates back into Tennessee and Kentucky. In accordance with this plan, the Confederate army received orders, on the evening of the 28th, to cook three days' rations and be ready to move at 10 o'clock next morning.

On the evening of the 29th, the army moved by the left flank and crossed the Chatahooche River, about thirty miles below Atlanta. The army lay in camp on the 1st of October, where General Hood issued an order to his men, stating that he would strike the railroad in the rear of Sherman's army near Big Shanty, and that if he would meet him in open field he would give battle; if not, he would move north, tearing up the track as he went.

On the evening of the 2d of October, the army again took up the line of march, and passing to the north of Lost Mountain, reached the railroad on the evening of the 3rd, capturing Big Shanty with sixty or seventy prisoners and began tearing up the track of the road. General French, with his division, moved to the right, tearing up the railroad to within three miles of Kennesaw Mountain. Gen. Loring turned to the left in the direction of Acworth, capturing the place and tearing up the track some distance beyond.

On the evening of the 11th, Gen. French received orders to move with his divisions, consisting of Generals Sears, Young and Cockrell's brigades with twelve pieces of artillery, and attack Altoona next morning at daylight. Before light, on the morning of the 5th, Gen. French had gained a position within three-quarters of a mile of the works and began skirmishing with the enemy. By the time it was light the brigades had taken position. The artillery, supported by a portion of a regiment of Young's Texas Brigade, was posted on an eminence south of the town, and the Fourth Mississippi Regiment of Sears' Brigade was detached to attack a block-house on one branch of the Hightower river. With the remainder of his force, Gen. French moved to the north and rear of the enemy's position, which was now discovered to be very formidable, consisting of strong forts and heavy redoubts running in all directions. After having secured his position in the following order, Gen. Sears to attack and carry a strong fort on the left, Gen. Cockrell, supported by Gen. Young, to attack and carry the heavy redoubts in front of a strong fort on the right, Gen. French dispatched a flag of truce demanding an unconditional surrender of the place. Before the bearer of the flag had reached the Confederate lines on his return, the firing of a cannon gave the enemy's answer. General French was thus, also, informed that the enemy had evidently been re-inforced. This proved true. The re-inforcements had reached the place just in advance of Gen. French, consisting of five regiments from Rome, Ga. The garrison already consisted of three regiments, in all a little over three thousand men, while French's division numbered not over two thousand five hundred. When General French heard the reply of the enemy, he immediately began to prepare for action, determined if possible to take the place by storm.

When the roar of the first cannon was heard rolling out from the top of Altoona Mountain, every soldier in the army understood that it meant battle. And when they looked at those frowning works they understood that somebody would taste of death before the summit was reached. But there was manifest a grim determination to make the desperate attempt. At the command, "Attention!" every soldier sprang to his feet, ready for action. At the command "Forward men!" the Missourians, with a yell peculiarly their own, sprang forward toward the works. The enemy fought like men and when within twenty yards of the entrenchment so deadly was their fire, that the line halted and the contest seemed doubtful. Here many of those brave men, officers and privates, fell to do battle no more. But another deeper, louder yell, and Gen. Young's Texans joined the charging ranks and the men leaped over the breast-works. Here sabers clashed, bayonets crossed, and clubs and rocks were hurled back and forth in the desperate struggle Texans and Missourians joined hands, or stood shoulder to shoulder in the battle. The Mississippians came gallantly up from the left, and the field was won. The Confederates were now in possession of all the works, except a strong fort on the right. This fort was the strongest of all, being surrounded by a deep, wide ditch with no approach but the draws. The Confederates were compelled to rest, reform the line and get a fresh supply of ammunition. While this was being done, and preparation being made to storm and carry the last remaining fort, Gen. French received a dispatch from Gen. Armstrong, commanding cavalry, that the enemy was advancing 10,000 strong, by way of Big Shanty. This made it necessary to withdraw; for if this be true, before preparations could be made and the last works taken, the enemy would be upon the Confederate army and in its rear. It turned out that the dispatch was a deception, the enemy was not so near as reported. But it robbed the Confederates of a great victory, greater indeed, than they had anticipated, for here was stored the greater portion of the rations that was to feed Sherman's army. Had it have been taken it is more than likely the "march to the sea" would not have been made.

Here is where Gen. Sherman, from the heights of Kennesaw Mountain signalled that noted order, "Hold the fort, I'm coming"; and none more than he understood the importance of holding it.

Not only did the men who had fought so grandly, turn away sadly, but the failure cast a gloom over the whole Confederate army.

Falling back from Altoona, French's division joined the main army at New Hope Church and on the evening of the 6th, started in the direction of Rome. Leaving that place to the right, the army crossed the Etawa River at Quinn's Ferry on the 10th. Marching rapidly, they struck the railroad about three miles south of Resica and began tearing it up. French's division was about six miles north of this place. On the morning of the 13th, the army moved up the road to Tilton, which place was garrisoned by a Federal regiment. This, after a little skirmishing, surrendered.

Dalton, garrisoned by 3,000 men, surrendered on the 14th, to a portion of Hardee's corps. On the 15th, left the railroad and moved in the direction of Decatur, Ala. On the 16th, passed through Summerville, Ga.; on the 20th, passed by Lookout Mountain; on the 22nd, camped near Black Wayer River; on the 23rd, passed through Summit, Ala ; and on the 26th, reached the neighborhood of Decatur. Here there was some skirmishing with the enemy which continued till the 29th, when the whole army moved in the direction of Tuscumbia or Florence, Ala. Arrived at Tuscumbia four miles from Florence, on the 30th.

Here the army took a few days' rest and received a supply of clothing. After throwing up some earth works on the Tennessee River, the army was put in motion on the 20th of November, crossing the Tennessee River on a pontoon bridge.

On the 22nd, General Hood issued an order to the troops, congratulating them upon their past conduct and informing them that the fruitful fields of Tennessee were before them; that at times they might be short of bread, but only for a short time; they knew endurance. This news was welcomed by the men and the army moved on.

On the morning of the 27th, they reached Pleasant Hill, which had just been abandoned by the Federal forces. This was a door to one of the most beautiful valleys of Tennessee, and the people manifested their joy at once more seeing the Confederate army. On the march to Columbia, the most beautiful scenery was presented on every side, rich lands and beautiful blue-grass pastures. When the army reached Columbia, they found it still occupied by the Federal forces. That night the enemy withdrew across Duck River and threw up a line of entrenchments. On the morning of the 29th, Gens. Cheatham's and Stewart's corps crossed the river about seven miles above Columbia, Cheatham in the advance with orders to strike the turn-pike at Spring Hill, and, if possible, cut the enemy off from Nashville.

The army moved rapidly, with no baggage and only eight pieces of artillery. About half an hour by sun, firing began in front and the continued booming of artillery in the rear told that the enemy had not yet left Columbia. One of the brigade commanders in front stopping, needlessly to bridge a creek, caused a delay so late that the enemy could not be pushed from Spring Hill that night. Had Hood's order have been carried out, the enemy would have been driven from the pike and thus cut off from Nashville and more than likely captured. As it was, the Confederate force lay that night in one-half mile of the road, and a portion within a few hundred yards of it. Even then, had the Confederate force have been active, the enemy being scattered, they might have been driven from the road and all their baggage and artillery captured. As it was, the enemy passed, burning a part of their army supplies and wagons in their hasty flight.

At about ten o'clock on the evening of the 30th, the enemy was found occupying some heights about ten miles from Franklin, a pretty village situated on the west bank of Harpeth River. Gen. Stewart's corps, now being in front, filed to the right, flanking the enemy's position and compelling him to fall back, thus allowing Gen. Cheatham's corps to pass directly down the pike, Gen. Lee not yet having arrived from Columbia.

The enemy now took up his position inside the fortifica-tions around Franklin. These were in two lines and very formidable. The second and main line of works were well arranged and thoroughly guarded, the men almost completely protected from the fire from their front by deep ditches and strong earthworks, with a head-log all along on top. In front of this was a cotton field almost level, running out some three or four hundred yards. The men behind the works, by putting their guns under the head-log, could sweep the whole field in front of them. General Hood at once made arrangements to storm these works. Gen. Cheatham took up his position on the left, his left wing resting on Harpeth River below, and his right reaching around crossing the turn-pike at the center. Gen. Stewart occupied the right, extending from the pike to the river above. Gen. Loring's division, of Stewart's corps, occupied the extreme right, Walthall's next, and French the center. Of Cheatham's corps, Gen. Gavan occupied the center, Tucker next, and Granby the extreme left.

Gen Cheatham's men were mostly Tennessee troops and many of them were near their own homes, from which they had been separated for many long days. Some of their families were inside these fortifications. They had everything to stimulate them on to victory; they were indeed, fighting for their homes and their firesides.

It was near sundown when the lines were formed and the army ready to advance. (I quote from the "Civil War," page 241.)

"It is said the dropping of a flag by Gen. Cheatham was the signal for the charge. With a characteristic yell and a tremendous force onward they advanced, stopping not nor halting, however obstinately the enemy might resist and however thick might be that awful, bloody field of carnage with their own dead. The attack in the center by Gen. John C. Brown, of Cheatham's corps, with Bate on his left, swept on with a force which seemed almost irresistible. General Brown, Edward Johnson, Manigault, Quarles, Crockrell and Sears were wounded; Gen. G. W. Gordon was captured inside the enemy's works with a part of his command. On the right, Gen. Stewart's corps fought desperately; Gen. John Adams' brigade of Mississippians, of Loring's division, received a fearful, enfilading fire from the enemy's fort on the opposite side of Harpeth River; but onward to the charge they went. In the act of leaping his charger over the enemy's works General Adams was killed and fell within the entrenchments, and 'Old Charlie,' his horse, was also killed, his form powerful in death, striding the enemy's works, his legs reaching to the bottom of the ditch, his head on the parapet, as if still breathing defiance at the foe. This was the last battle of the gallant Cleburne Generals Gists, Granberry, Carter and Strahl fell in this bloody conflict. On that crimson battle-ground many a knightly soul went out within sight of the firesides where the wives and little ones were praying and watching for the absent soldier's return.

"A pathetic incident of this battle was the mortal wound, at the very threshold of his home, of young Carter. * * * Though the gray dawn of the next day, saw the Federals flying toward Nashville, the victory was dearly bought. The sacrifice these soldiers offered on the altar of their country was great."

Col. Elijah Gates, commanding the Missouri brigade, was severely wounded. I shall not undertake to tell who were killed in that fearful charge: it would be easier to tell who were not killed. The Confederates lay in heaps in the ditches in front of the works, officers and privates in one mangled mass.

The firing was kept up till about one o'clock at night, when the enemy fell back toward Nashville.

The next day was indeed a sad one to the Confederate army, and especially to the Missourians. Far away from home the few survivors of that once grand brigade, now depleted, buried their friends, their comrades in arms. This was the first time in the whole history of that brigade that it had made a charge upon the enemy and failed to drive them from their position. Other portions of the army may have failed, but this brigade never. And this is said with no disparagement to other troops; the recorded facts bear testimony to the truth of the statement.

They were as proud and noble a set of men as ever shouldered a musket, each man fighting for a principle. Some idea of their courage, and of how well they had borne their part, may be given when it is remembered that when they crossed the Mississippi River, the two brigades, now consolidated into one, numbered near 8,000 men, and yet on the day of the battle of Franklin, they only numbered 610 men for duty. There had been very few desertions, and not many had died from sickness; their graves were scattered over Mississippi, Alabama, Georgia and Tennessee, and the wounded found shelter in the hospitals of these States.

The writer has not the statistics of the loss of the different brigades. But those which lost heaviest were: Cockrell's Brigade, 492; Gavon's, 319; Tucker's, 414; Granberry's, 363. It is thus seen, that out of a number of 610, on the morning before the battle, the Missouri Brigade, lost, killed and wounded, 492; leaving 118 for duty. In the company to which the writer belonged, there were thirty-two men reported for duty that morning, and of that number, eight were killed dead and sixteen wounded, leaving eight unhurt. Throughout the brigade this was the proportion. This has been termed a hard-fought battle, we term it a slaughter. In twenty minutes from the time the men crossed the first line of works, the brigade was swept away. O, how sad the task of these few survivors to put away their comrades in their last resting place on that bloody field.

The first day of December was spent in burying the dead. On the next day, the army moved toward Nashville, the capital of the State. Contrary to all expectations, the army had been supplied with an abundance to eat, but nearly one-third of it was bare-footed and destitute of a sufficiency of clothing. The sufferings of these were great, unparalleled since the commencement of the war. Snow fell and covered the ground with ice and sleet, and the men in this condition were compelled to occupy the ditches. The army was in poor condition to do battle not only from their destitution, but from the great loss they had sustained, they were disheartened and discouraged.

Cockrell and Gates being wounded, the command of the brigade, now reduced to a mere company of 118 men, fell upon Col. Flurnoy. On the 10th, he was ordered to take his little command and proceed to the mouth of Duck River and build a fort to prevent the gun-boats from coming up the Columbia River. Having marched within eight miles of that place, he was compelled to halt, on account of heavy rain and high waters. While here in camp, about the 18th, he received a dispatch from Gen. Hood, stating that the enemy came out, on the 15th and 16th, and attacked his position completely routing his army and capturing sixty pieces of artillery, and ordering the Colonel to fall back and join him at Florence, Ala.

Col. Flurnoy, with his handful of men began his march toward Florence, Alabama, on the morning of the 19th, and on the 26th reached the main army, four miles above Florence, with all his baggage and artillery complete. The worst apprehensions of the brigade were realized; the army of Hood was demoralized beyond description. Only Gen. Forest and his men were in perfect order and doing battle like Trojans; and to these must General Hood owe the salvation of his army. Beaten from the field, half-clothed and barefooted, these once grand veterans presented a sad sight, and each felt from this on it was impossible for the South to maintain the unequal contest. The failure was not from the lack of courage upon the part of the Southern soldiery, it was the overwhelming numbers and fine equipment of the other side.

On the night of the 27th, the brigade crossed the Tennessee River and by early dawn on the morning of the 28th, the whole army was safely over. Nothing of interest taking place, the army moved by slow stages, and on the 27th of January, 1865, went into camp at Varona, Mississippi.

CHAPTER XXVII.

THE BATTLES ABOUT MOBILE, SHIP ISLAND, AND THE FINAL SURRENDER.

After remaining at Varona a few weeks, the army under General Hood was transferred to the East and sent after General Sherman, except the division under Gen. French. Hence, for the remainder of this history the scenes will be changed to another field.

General French's division was ordered to report at Mobile, Alabama. At this place the men enjoyed a rest for a season. On the morning of the 24th of March, the division received orders to cook three days' rations and to be ready to move. At three o'clock that evening the command was placed on transports and conveyed to the east side of the Mobile Bay, near its head, and landed at Fort Blakely, moved out some six miles to meet the advancing column of the enemy under General Canby. His force was variously estimated at between fifteen and twenty thousand. On the morning of the 26th; heavy skirmishing began, the Confederate forces falling back. The Confederate forces were divided, a portion being sent to Spanish Fort and a portion to Fort Blakely. From the 28th to the 31st, there was heavy fighting around Spanish Fort. Cockrell's and Sears' brigades had been sent out on different roads to guard the approach to Blakely. On the morning of the 1st of April, Cockrell's brigade had been called in to where the two roads joined, and halted, waiting to be joined by Gen. Sears, when it was the design for all to fall back within the fortifications.

While waiting here, a horseman dashed up and informed the brigade commander, who was now Col. McCowan, Gen. Cockrell being in command of a division, that the Federal cav-

E. G. Williams + Wife

alry had cut through the brigade of Gen. Sears, and would soon be upon them. If this proved true, Cockrell's brigade was all there was to defend the fort. Col. McCowan sent all the brigade to the ditches except the third and fifth consolidated regiments. Hardly had those orders begun to be obeyed when the Federal cavalry, one thousand strong, hove in sight.

The little regiment formed in a narrow ravine which ran across the road, fixed bayonets and prepared to receive the cavalry charge. On it came like an avalanch, but so destructive was the fire of the Confederates, that they were compelled to halt and to fall back. It happened that they were in supporting reach of the artillery at the fort which opened upon the wings of the cavalry thus preventing the little regiment from being surrounded and compelling the enemy to rapidly fall back.

On the 2nd, the enemy began approaching the works around Blakely, 3rd and 4th there was continued skirmishing along the lines. On the evening of the 4th, about one hour by sun there begun a heavy artillery duel at Spanish Fort which was taken up by the Confederate gun-boats and extended along the line to Fort Blakely. This terrible roar of cannons was kept up till after dark. Fighting continued till the evening of the 8th, when the Confederate force in attempting to evacuate Spanish Fort was assaulted. But most of the garrison escaped.

There were not men enough at Blakely to man the works, but they scattered along as best they could to keep up appearance till the force could be withdrawn. Cockrell kept up the fight all day, the 9th, till about an hour by sun when the Federals advanced upon the works all along the line, capturing the entire garrison.

It will be noted that the battle of Fort Blakely was fought the very day that General Lee surrendered to General Grant at Appomattox Court House, April 9, 1865.

On the 14th, the Confederate prisoners were put on board ship and sent to Ship Island as prisoners of war. They were kept on this sandy, barren island for thirteen days, in the broiling hot sun during the day, and the cool, chilly winds at hight, with no shelter from sun or storm, and but few blankets. Besides, a regiment of negroes to guard them who took great pleasure in shouting at every supposed misstep of the prisoner,

"Look out dar, white man, de bottom rail on top row." While here, the news of Lee's surrender was received, also of the assassination of Abraham Lincoln, the President of the United States. There is a book entitled, "Fifteen Years in Hell." The Confederates called this thirteen days in that hot climate, hot more ways than one. On the night of the 28th, the Missouri Brigade was put on board the steamer "Clinton" and started for Vicksburg. On the way the news of the surrender of Lee was confirmed and also that of Gen. Joseph E. Johnston.

The brigade arrived at Vicksburg on the 2d day of May, and were paroled as prisoners on the 4th. On that day the Mississippi Department surrendered. The Missouri Brigade moved out to Jackson, Miss., and on the 13th, received their final parole. "The war is over, the brigade is no more, the men are scattering in all directions, and our history is ended."

Closing Address.

In closing this volume, the writer feels that he can find no more befitting words than those found in an address to the people of Missouri, written by him immediately after the surrender at Jackson, Miss., and approved by that part of the brigade present at the time, and designed to have been published in *The St. Louis Republican*, but which that paper thought best to withhold.

To the People of Missouri.

FELLOW CITIZENS:

After four years of the most desperate and bloody war known to the annals of history, the struggle has ended. In this contest questions of the greatest moment to the American people were at stake. Upon the part of the South the question of "State rights" or sovereignty, and upon the part of the North consolidated power in the General Government. Those holding with the South had obtained the pre-eminence, and this had been the principle that had governed the great body of the American people from the days of Thomas Jefferson, till Abraham Lincoln took his seat as President of the United States. Being the true principle of all Democratic Government, it was impossible of overthrow till made so by thrusting upon it the question of slavery. Had it have been fully understood that the question of slavery was designed to overthrow this great principle of American liberty, the results of the war would have been different.

We are now told that this great question of State Sovereignty has been settled by the sword, and that when we lay down our arms we must accept this as true. We deny that the war had settled any living and eternal principle. We accept it that by force of arms you have robbed us of our property, and we give it up forever, but that eternal principle of true Democratic Government can never be taken from us. "Truth crushed to earth will rise again." War may force submission, but might never makes right. We believed in the rights of the States when we enlisted in the war; we fought for them, and while the results of the war force us to accept a consolidated government, and the bayonet has robbed us of those rights which were once ours, and for which we fought, yet it is still a living principle to be held and contended for as long as Republican Government lasts.

Being nursed in the School of State rights, and believing, as we still believe, it to be the true principle that should govern the American people, we early enlisted in the cause; when we saw war was inevitable we took the side our conscience told us was right; at Boonville we flung our first Southern banner to the breeze upon the battlefield, and we can say without boasting that from that day to this, it has never trailed in the dust; from that day to this we have met our enemies in noble, *honorable* battle. Though future historians may never do us justice; we feel proud of the part we have taken, and shall ever, cherish the cause for which we fought. We must say that we love the South. In her misfortunes we love her more, and had it simply have been the North against the South, our flag would have been waving as proudly to-day as at Manassas or Arlington Heights. But our enemies brought their men from the world's graneries, yea, even put our slaves against us, and by overwhelming numbers compelled our submission.

We once numbered near eight thousand; to-day we could not muster five hundred for duty. Where are those missing sons of Missouri? Go ask the bloody battle-fields of Missouri, Arkansas, Mississippi, Alabama, Georgia and Tennessee; their bodies lie buried in the soldier's grave. The once honored and glorious flag which we have borne so long, has been surrendered; the bright and glorious star whose rising we hailed as the rising star of liberty has set in night, and we have been compelled to accept your terms of peace. Our homes must be with you. Our fathers, our mothers, and all that we hold dear upon earth, are there, and you necessarily compel us to be there. We asked for separation; it was not granted. We, therefore, present ourselves to-day acknowledging we have been beaten upon the battle-field. Our duty, in the future, shall be to submit calmly to the powers that be. While there was hope for the South, we fought as men who honestly differ with their fellow-men; now that the war is over, we return to the homes of our fathers. Shall we be received as citizens or shall we be rejected? We do not get down upon our knees to beg your pardon, or implore your reception of us. If you are men you would scorn such humiliation. But we come as men with a clear conscience, believing we have fought for the right, but acknowledging your triumph.

For our country, mid waste and suffering, we rejoice at the beams of peace, but the eternal principle of right, we shall never surrender; that principle no sword can destroy.

Loved ones, we shall be with you again in a few days, where we hope we shall all work shoulder to shoulder for the good of our now common country and have war no more. May a day, bright and prosperous, open up before us and our life be strewn with the flowers of peace; the past be buried as the irretrievable past, and all hearts be united for the welfare of our common people.   JAMES BRADLEY,

Company K., 3rd and 5th Regiment, First Brigade, Missouri
    Infantry, C. S. A.

————

Some time after the close of the war, Mr. George Tracy and Miss Ella Herbert were married; and since then have shared life together, having around them a respectable family of children. Capt. Grimes became a merchant in St. Louis; the detective became an efficient, gospel minister, and the faithful Sam still lives a near neighbor to his loved mistress and enjoys telling of his adventures.

PART SECOND

INTRODUCTION

THE CONFEDERATE HOME

ITS ORIGIN AND OBJECTS

——BY——

MRS. ELIZABETH USTICK McKINNEY

BIOGRAPHY

AND AN EXPLANATORY INDEX TO ENGRAVINGS

Introduction to Second Part.

In the foregoing pages, when the work was first undertaken, it was the intention of the author to only give a history of the two brigades, with an appendix, giving the names of all the members of these brigades and a little sketch of the part that each took in the great struggle. But upon examination of the muster-roll it was found that such a list would, in itself, make a large volume, and that of names and dates uninteresting save to the individuals named. The cost it was thought would be more than the worth of such a book. The idea, therefore, of this appendix was abandoned. It was never the design of the author to write the history of any particular men, but that of a *body of men*. He wished it recognized that each soldier of these two brigades was fit to command and, that the name of one in that action that made them famous, should not be placed above another. For this reason, the officers are not named only as it was necessary to designate the commands.

When the idea of the appendix was abandoned, it was suggested that in place of it there be given a sketch of the origin and objects of the Confederate Home at Higginsville, Mo., and especially the part taken by the Daughters of the Confederacy in its purchase and maintenance. Mrs. Elizabeth Ustick McKinney was selected to do this and has done her part well.

That each Confederate soldier might feel that he was represented in the work and that it was no intention of the author to disparage the courage of any loyal Confederate by giving the history of these two brigades, it was designed to have an engraving of all the officers of the Home. Of this there was not a complete success, some seeming to have the false idea that it was a species of vanity and a seeking of notoriety. The truth is, that we should be glad to leave to the generations to come some token of our lives, and feel that these friends will look with gladness upon our faces when we are gone. It is simply an act of kindness to others.

The author is thankful to those who have contributed and only regrets that, owing to the great cost, which he feared the undertaking would not justify, the field of illustrations could not be enlarged. To those who have furnished their pictures the author has given an explanatory index telling who they are and the stations they have filled, and he feels that these will all be appreciated by their friends and the people generally.

He has also given the picture of some of the noble women of the Confederacy, and regrets that this field also could not be enlarged.

No one can look upon that noble face, grand in old age, of Mrs. McLure, the mother of the Daughters of the Confederacy, and not feel proud to call such *Mother*.

The author of this work cannot close this account without returning his thanks and heartfelt gratitude to those who have so kindly encouraged him in the work and lent him a helping hand. G. N. Ratliff has rendered substantial aid, and in inquiring after the old comrades. Mrs. E. U. McKinney in her history has given invaluable service, and Miss Bell Morris has been exceedingly kind in getting together the gallery of pictures and a biographical sketch of many of the Daughters of the Confederacy. And now the author will feel doubly grateful to every friend who will help him in the introduction of the work into every family and to all friends to whom he hopes and believes that it will not only be instructive, but prove a blessing.

The author feels that he can close this short address with no better words than a little gem that speaks volumes of truth, and that will find an answering "amen" in every Southern heart, taken from the *Confederate Veteran*, published at Nashville, Tennessee.

Echoes of the South contains a pathetic story of a little Southerner with his mother in a Brooklyn theater, when the play was "Held by the Enemy."

During a brief intermission he asked: "What did the Yankees fight for, mother?"

"For the Union, darling," was the answer.

Just then the curtain fell, and the orchestra struck up "Marching through Georgia." An expression filled with painful memories, brought up by the air, swept over the sad face of the mother.

After a brief pause the little fellow asked: "What did the Confederates fight for, mother?"

The second question was hardly asked before the music changed, and the ever-thrilling strains of "Home, Sweet Home" flooded the house with its depth of untold melody and pathos.

"Do you hear what they are playing?" she whispered. "*That* is what the *Confederates* fought for, darling."

Then he asked quite eagerly: "Did they fight for their *homes?*"

"Yes, dear, they fought for their *homes.*"

Was it the touch of sorrow in the mother's voice? was it the pathos of the soft, sweet notes of "Home, Sweet Home?" or was it the *intuition of right?* No matter. The little boy looked up at his mother with adoring eyes, burst into a flood of tears, and, clasping his arms around her protectingly, sobbed out: "O mother, I will be a Confederate!"

The mother's tears mingled silently with those of her true-hearted boy as she pressed him to her heart and repeated softly:

> "Yes, they stood for home and honor;
> Yes, they fought for freedom's name."

Ex-Confederate Home.

"Peace hath her victories no less renowned than war."

The ex-Confederate Home of Missouri, located at Higginsville, in LaFayette county, erected in 1893, by the women of Missouri, stands to-day, as an example of one of the proudest victories of peace, and is an enduring monument to the princely generosity of this great commonwealth.

Every State in the Union (save Kentucky), which furnished organized bodies of troops for the Confederate army, has established a home, where her worn-out soldiers may spend their declining years. Missouri alone bears the proud distinction of having erected and furnished a home for her old veterans solely by voluntary contribution, which speaks far more eloquently than words, of the generosity of her people. All great enterprises are born of great needs, and as the ex-Confederate soldier in the prime and vigor of manhood, met his older and less fortunate companion in arms, after years of separation, toil and hardship, seeking to regain lost fortune, his quick, observant eye and sympathetic heart knew that in a few more years his comrade would be unable to care for himself and provide for his dependent family; for the once proud and manly form was now bowed with age, and the hand-clasp, once strong and cordial, was growing feebler and more tremulous with every passing year; and he longed to do something for his old companion in arms, to smooth his pathway as life's shadows lengthened. Many of them were destined to find shelter in the Poor House, at no distant day, unless otherwise cared for. The proud spirit of every true Confederate soldier felt humiliated and saddened at the thought of being cared for by public charity.

That friendship which is born amid the stormy scenes of war and nurtured in the vicissitudes of the bivouac, is changeless and deathless.

Years pass on, and memories flit and fade, or lie buried under the great white tomb of the past, but time cannot obliterate the sacred memories that live in patriot hearts, or cause to burn less brightly the fires of friendship kindled on the tented field, where men shared each other's blankets and divided their scanty rations. The feeling of the ex-Confederate soldier is touchingly expressed in a pathetic and beautiful poem, composed for dedication day at the Home, by one of its inmates, Captain Warner L. Briscoe, of the 13th Missouri Cavalry. It fittingly bears the title—

"IN MEMORIAM."

"We yield obedience to the statute laws
  That govern this broad land to day;
  We're loyal, yes, but we *still love* the cause
  We fought for when we wore the gray.
  We march e'en *now* (in dreams) to that old air
  Called 'Dixie's Land,' and see the barred flag fly
  'Bove battle's smoke, fringed with the blinding glare   .
  Of sheeted flame that showed how brave men die.
  Place immortelles above the unmasked graves
  Of those who died for country, home and right,
  Salute the flag that now no longer waves,
  Then furl and fold it in your hearts from sight.

Farewell, 'Lost Cause,' now buried in the Past,
From which we turn with reverence away
To face the future, yet, while our lives last,
We'll never blush for having worn the gray!"

When old comrades meet again in brotherly reunion, the sound of *reveille* wakes again a martial spirit, and they talk over their camp life, its joys and sorrows, sacrifices and hardships, during the four long years of civil strife. As the white wings of peace overshadow them, they sit once more about the glowing camp fires, recalling reminiscences of other days. Ever and anon, tears glisten in the eyes of sun-browned faces as they recount thrilling and pathetic experiences of their soldier life.

There are tender memories which touch the heart, memories that are sacred, and we refer to them only when in the presence of those whom we love best, as the fond mother takes from its hidden place the golden tress of hair, or the dainty garment worn by her dead darling, weeps over them silent tears which bring sweet relief to the bereaved heart, then lays them away tenderly between the leaves of her Bible; so the old soldiers of the South, heroes of many battlefields, experience a melancholy pleasure in recalling the sad memories of other days, but this is no time for moralizing and brushing away the gathering tears; he turns from the sorrowful past, to the busy, practical present, and obeying the kind, philanthropic promptings of his generous nature, the desire to assist his fellow soldier has materialized in a splendid ex-Confederate Home, with attractive and beautiful surroundings.

The history of the origin of the Home is best told by Captain W. P. Barlow, of St. Louis, who has been identified with its history since its very inception, having acted as Secretary of the Confederate Home Association since it was organized. In an article which appeared in the *Higginsville Leader*, August 26, 1893, he says:

"It was something like ten years ago that prominent Confederate soldiers like Major John S. Mellon and Judge Thomas A. Portis began talking about a soldiers' home. Finally, the Southern Historical Society, of St. Louis, appointed a committee, in 1889, to secure a charter. This Committee secured the charter and reported it to the annual reunion of Confederate soldiers at Higginsville in August of that year. The Historical Society turned the charter over to the Ex-Confederate Association of Missouri, whose officers were elected to corresponding positions in the Home Association. This Association has a Vice-President in each congressional district, and this constitutes the Executive Committee of the Home.

"After working experimentally for one year, $10,000 were in the treasury. It was then resolved at the Nevada reunion in 1890, to proceed at once and build the Home. By the following February, some $18,000 were on hand, and bids for the location were solicited. The offers were numerous. A committee of six spent a week traveling over the State, examining the various pieces of property offered.

"The committee separated without any one member knowing the choice of another. Two days later the committee met in St. Louis and Higginsville was unanimously selected for the location of the Home. This committee consisted of the following members: James Bannerman, Harvey W. Salmon, F. P. Bronough, A. G. Anderson, W. C. Bronough and W. P. Barlow. The gentlemen who represented Higginsville, A. E. Asbury, M. L. Belt and J. J. Fulkerson offered a donation of $5,500 to secure the Home at this place.

"In March, 1891, the Home farm of 373 acres was purchased of Grove Young for $18,600 cash. There were two nine-room houses available. Contracts were immediately let for ten three-room cottages, and other buildings were soon filled with destitute soldiers and their families.

"Having thus made a start and shown the people of Missouri that the Association really meant business, the first hard work of raising money in large quantities began. Each Vice-President canvassed his own district. Hon. Henry Newman and Capt. W. P. Barlow made a running canvass of the State, extending over fifteen months, speaking at nearly all of the county seats, organizing county associations and in every way arousing enthusiasm in this long deferred charity.

"The liberality of the people of this grand old State was manifested by cash contributions of over $70,000 in less than three years."

About this Home, the patriotic Southern women of Missouri, learning the purpose and plans of the Confederate Association, to establish a home for worn-out and helpless soldiers, became deeply interested in the work, and desired to lend a helping hand to the cause which had so long lain very near their hearts. With an enthusiasm born of devotion to Southern principles, they began raising funds in various parts of the State, by giving dinners, ice-cream socials, etc., to swell the fund for the purchase of a home

Mrs. Abner C. Cassidy, of St. Louis, a lady of wealth, influence and much financial ability, has the honor of originating the organization known as "DAUGHTERS OF THE CONFEDERACY." She gave liberally of her means and time to the cause and did much toward making a success of the Society in St. Louis.

With regard to the origin of this patriotic band of Southern women, I quote from the first annual report of Mrs. E. R. Gamble, Secretary of the Daughters of the Confederacy of St. Louis, submitted in February, 1892. She says:

"One year ago, Mrs. A. C. Cassidy conceived the idea that the ladies of St. Louis could and would, if given the opportunity, contribute their mites in aid of the Confederate Home of Missouri. Her first step was to select a fitting name; the next to find a President to fit the name, and whom the women of the city would delight to follow. Both selections were happy. The name "Daughters of the Confederacy" appealed at once to all who had suffered for that cause for which so many heroic loved ones had laid down their lives, and the venerable Mrs. M. A. E. McLure, then eighty years of age, was requested to accept the leadership. Upon the promise that she would be relieved from the hard work as much as possible, Mrs. McLure cheerfully consented to serve, and a meeting was called at the parlors of the Southern Hotel, on January 27, 1891. Ninety-seven ladies responded to this call. The meeting was called to order by Mrs. A. C. Cassidy, and Mrs. Minor Merriwether was elected Temporary Chairman, with Mrs. R. K. Walker, Temporary Secretary. After the objects of the meeting were explained, the following officers were elected to serve for one year:

"*President*—Mrs. M. A. E. McLure.

"*First Vice-President*—Mrs. A. C. Cassidy.

"*Second Vice-President*—Mrs. Randolph R. Hutchinson.

"*Third Vice-President*—Mrs. T. H. West.

"*Fourth Vice-President*—Mrs. Leroy B. Valliant.

"*Fifth Vice-President*—Mrs. Thos. J. Portis.

"*Sixth Vice-President*--Mrs. Jas. Bannerman.

"*Treasurer*—Mrs. Jno. D. Winn.

"*Recording Secretary*—Miss Iola Harwood.

"*Corresponding Secretary*—Mrs. A. C. Robinson.

"Upon the resignation of Miss Harwood, Mrs. E. R. Gamble was elected Recording Secretary.

"Another plan, from the fertile brain of Mrs. Cassidy, was the sale of tickets, each representing a "brick in the Confederate Home," costing ten cents. This simple device has produced in this city alone, so far, $1,048 and $322.80 from the country, making a total of $1,370.80, with many reports yet to come in. In appended list of auxiliary societies will be found credits for brick funds remitted.

"Much encouraged by these successes, it was then determined to give a grand ball on Thanksgiving Eve, and in this we were again gratified by an unexpected triumph, the ball being in a social sense, the finest ever seen in St. Louis. The net proceeds amounted to $4,351.46. A similar ball will probably be given annually.

"At this time the cottages at the Home were completed, and we assumed the duty of furnishing four of them, which was done at a net cash cost of $395.05 —aided by liberal donations from various business houses whose names are given below. We also expended $255 88 for furniture for the main building, making a total of $650 93 expended from the proceeds of our Strawberry Festival. For this we were given the privilege of naming the four cottages, and they were designated in honor of the memory of Generals John S. Bowen, W. Y. Slack, M. M. Parsons and Henry Little. The sum of $397.10 was sent to us by the Ladies' Auxiliary Societies of Edina, LaGrange, Lewiston, Newark and Monticello; and from this fund $108 was used in furnishing a fifth cottage, which was named by the ladies of Knox county in honor of General Martin E. Green."

During the year societies were organized in twenty-six towns and counties of Missouri, and many of these became auxiliary to St. Louis, others, preferring to work independently, turned their funds over to the Confederate Association, while a few of the societies paid for the erection of cottages, with the privilege of naming them. For these cottages $500.00 was paid into the treasury of the Association.

After the cottages were occupied, it soon became apparent that these, with the two houses already on the farm, when purchased, were inadequate to accommodate the old veterans who sought admission to the Home; besides, the expense of keeping up so many individual homes, was much greater than keeping the same number in a larger building. Many old soldiers had to be turned away until accommodations could be provided, hence, it was determined to proceed at once to erect a main building.

The success of the women of Missouri in raising funds was phenomenal, and a strong desire was felt by many to pledge the amount necessary for this work. Quoting again from Mrs. Gamble's report of the first year's work, she says:

"Our treasurer's report shows $11,618.06, being over one-third of this sum, now in bank, and we have unofficial reports of $4,339 in the hands of Ladies' Societies not auxiliary to our own, which swells the total of women's work in Missouri to $15,957.61. Reports from those societies not auxiliary to ours have been collected by the Secretary of the Confederate Home. A sufficient number of auxiliaries have now joined with us to make it probable that the women can alone pay for the main building, and this we are resolved to do, leaving the endowment fund to be raised by the men."

Captain Barlow, in alluding to the promise made by the Daughters of the Confederacy in his report says:

"Upon their guarantee that they would pay for this building, contracts were let last fall for a building to cost, with fixtures complete, $24,000, which amount is the aggregate D. O. C. contribution. The gas, engine and fixtures, with the furniture and general outfit, cost some $4,200 more, the payment of which was assumed by the D. O. C., thus giving them the proud satisfaction of paying for everything connected with the main building."

Thus the work moved grandly on, and many societies which had hitherto worked independently, now became auxiliary to St. Louis, the parent society. Although many organizations were small, and worked under many disadvantages, yet an enthusiasm and zeal characterized their efforts, and the result far exceeded the expectations of the most sanguine.

The thoughtful and far-seeing mind of Major James Bannerman, President of the Confederate Home Association, who has labored with faithful heart and tireless hand for the interest of the Home, conceived the idea of calling upon every school district in the State to contribute $10 to the Home, and by April 6, 1892, a circular letter was in the hands of the county clerks all over the State, who, regardless of party affiliation, responded promptly to the call, giving their work freely and gratuitously for the cause. The amount realized from this source aggregated to $13,000.

It is but just to mention the generosity which has characterized many persons whose sympathies during the Civil War were with the Union army, and many who were in the army have contributed without solicitation. Several G. A. R. Posts in the State have also given liberally to the Confederate Home.

These kind offerings, given voluntarily, have done much to establish a fraternal feeling between the old soldiers of the two armies, and unite them in bonds of enduring friendship.

Prominent business firms and individuals in St. Louis, Kansas City and various portions of the State, responded nobly to the call for donations and cash contributions. Thus, the ladies have been encouraged and assisted in their undertaking since their organization, by princely gifts from generous hearts, until on the 9th day of June, 1893, they were enabled to present to the Confederate Home Association, the main building complete in every part. The formal presentation took place with very imposing ceremonies, witnessed by many hundred people from Lafayette and adjacent counties, and was participated in by prominent citizens from all over the State.

Many a heart thrilled with pride, and many a face beamed with joy, while tears of gratitude fell from eyes unused to weep as Rev. P. G. Roberts, of St. Louis, in an eloquent address on behalf of the "Daughters of the Confederacy," formally presented the handsome structure to the Confederate Home Association. Major Bannerman, president of the Association, responded in appropriate words. A large delegation of members of the Daughters of the Confederacy were present to witness this fitting culmination of their faithful and arduous labors.

Among the number, none wore a brighter smile than the venerable Mrs. M. A. E. McLure, president of the Daughters of the Confederacy, who, although eighty-two years of age, had come from St. Louis to be present on this occasion. Her faithful labors and unflagging interest in this noble cause has been an inspiration, not only to the Southern women of St. Louis, but all over the State.

DESCRIPTION OF THE HOME.

Upon the summit of a gently rising knoll, two miles northwest of the progressive and beautiful town of Higginsville, near the center of Lafayette county, stands the Confederate Home. It is a two-story brick, built in the Colonial style of architecture so frequently met with throughout the Southern States. Spacious porches and broad sweeping verandas are striking features of the exterior. It is constructed in the form of a double L, which forms an open court in the rear of the building. There are general apartments for 120 inmates, and separate rooms for the accommodation of forty more. The outside trimmings are of stone, and it is covered with a slate roof. The interior is handsomely finished in hard wood. The building throughout is lighted by gas and heated with steam. The main building fronts the east, and has a broad veranda two stories high extending the entire length. On entering the spacious hallway and turning to the right, one enters the office. This is a memorial room, in honor of Gen. John S. Marmaduke and Capt. William Parkinson McLure, a son of the honored president of the St. Louis Society. Life-sized portraits of these adorn the walls, and also a picture of Mrs. McLure, presented by the St. Louis ladies, by whom this room is elegantly furnished. The clock which is the gift of Mrs. McLure, to whom the Home is indebted for much of the elegance of its furnishing, is said to be the handsomest in the State. The parlor is also a memorial room, in memory of ex-Governor Claiborne F. Jackson, and was furnished by the ladies of Hannibal and Marshall, at which places Mrs. C. L. Lamb and Mrs. Anna B. Perkins, daughters of the dead Governor, reside. Neither pains nor money have been spared to furnish the building elaborately throughout.

Mr. J. B. Legge, a prominent architect of St. Louis, with that spirit of liberality which characterizes noble natures, donated the plan of the building, in honor of his wife who is a member of the St. Louis Daughters of the Confederacy,

The cottages are arranged on either side of the street or avenue, and the lots have a frontage 100x200 feet deep. To avoid any invidious distinctions. they are built after the same model, and have a back and front porch, and three rooms. Each cottage has a nice grass-plot and room for flowers in the front door-yard, while back is a fertile garden spot so that every one can raise his own vegetables. Beside the cottages built by the State organization, the following countries have paid for cottages through the ladies of the D. O. C.: "Soldiers of Jackson county," by the Independence D. O. C., "Benjamin A. Rivers," Ray county D. O. C.; "John B. Clark, Sr.," Randolph county D. O. C. There are also two unnamed cottages, one of which is built by "Camp Holloran" of Independence, and will be named by that camp. At the south end of the street or avenue, stands a neat frame chapel built by the ladies of Lafayette county, at cost of $1,200, where preaching service is regularly held. Men of families occupy the cottages, and enjoy the quiet retirement of domestic life, just as though they were in their individual homes. Children over fourteen years of age are not permitted to enter as they are old enough to earn a livelihood. Those of school age are sent to school. Since the establishment of the Home, 194 persons have been admitted. The officers of the Confederate Home Association are:

President, James Bannerman, St. Louis.

Vice-President, Harry W. Salmon, Clinton.

Treasurer, H. A. Ricketts, Mexico.

Secretary, W. P. Barlow, 3849 Cook avenue, St. Louis.

Superintendent, T. W. Cassell.

Surgeon, J. J. Fulkerson, M. D.

SUPERVISING COMMITTEE.

GENERAL:

H. W. Salmon, Thos. P. Hoy, Blake L. Woodson.

LOCAL:

A. E. Asbury, Chairman.   A. Wade, M. L. Belt.

EXECUTIVE COMMITTEE.

1st District, K. F. Peddicord, Palmyra.

2nd   "   F. L. Pitts, Paris.

3rd   "   A. C. Cook, Plattsburg.

4th   "   Elijah Gates, St. Joseph.

5th   "   Blake L. Woodson, Kansas City.

6th   "   W. C. Bronaugh, Lewis Station.
7th   "   Thos. P. Hoy, Sedalia.
8th   "   Robt. A. McCulloch, Pisgah.
9th   "   W. H. Kennan, Mexico.
10th   "   Henry Guibor, St. Louis.
11th   "   W. C. Green, M. D., St. Louis.
12th   "   Frank Gaiennie, St. Louis.
13th   "   Edmond Casey, Potosi.
14th   "   O. H. P. Catron, West Plains.
15th   "   C. T. Davis, Nevada.

The surrounding country about Higginsville is in a high
state of cultivation and a view, from any direction, presents a
beautiful picture, diversified with hill and dale, prairie and
woodland, where the old soldier of the Confederacy may feast
his eyes upon the restful scene, and enjoy the rural beauty of
his peaceful home, without a care. Nature has been lavish of
her gifts in this productive country, and under the skillful
hands of M. L. Belt, past superintendent, who had all the hard
initiatory work, and T. W. Cassell, the present superintendent,
art is still bestowing additional charms to this beautiful home.
The yard is enclosed with a neat picket fence, and in front of
the main building, a Macadam driveway 435 feet long, has been
constructed. Fruit and ornamental shade trees, have been
planted and the grounds otherwise beautified by landscape gar-
dening. The old farm house has been converted into a hospital, and the farm well stocked, and everything is being done
with an eye to economy and comfort in the maintainance of the
home, hoping in time to make it self-supporting, or as nearly
so as practicable.

The D. O. C. of Higginsville, are doing a noble work for
the Home. Their committees visit it twice each month, for
the purpose of issuing necessary stores, visiting and caring for
the sick, and taking a general supervision of the needs of the
various households. There is now a plan projected to uniform
the men, which will doubtless prove successful, as Kansas City
and St. Louis have both entered heartily into the work, and no
doubt, every old veteran will be comfortably clad in a neat
suit of gray before the year closes. Several other auxiliaries
will assist in the work   Kansas City has worked independently, and has accomplished much, but as her funds have not

passed through our treasurer's hands, we do not know the
exact amount realized. On last Christmas this society presented the Home with a handsome piano, costing a thousand
dollars.

We must not close this brief sketch without a passing
tribute to the dead. About 300 yards west of the main building, beneath the shade of forest trees, are fifteen grassy
mounds.

> "Step lightly near this sacred spot,
>   And move with solemn tread,
> For *this* is consecrated soil,
>   Where sleep our honored dead!
> The sunlight shimmers through the boughs
>   Of shadowy forest trees,
> Nature weeps here, her silent tears,
>   A requiem sighs the breeze,
> When the tall grasses gently wave,
>   The wild flower lifts its head,
> As if its tribute sweet, to bring
>   To our Confederate dead,"

Who sleep the sleep that knows no waking, "Under the sod
and the dew, awaiting the judgment day." Once a year kind
hands scatter fresh, fair flowers over the graves of these
departed heroes,

> "But the ranks are growing thinner
>   With the coming of each May,
> And the beards and locks once raven,
>   Now are silvered o'er with gray;
> Soon the hands that strew the flowers
>   Will be folded, still and cold,
> And our story of devotion
>   Will forever have been told."

THE FIRST EFFECTIVE WORK FOR THE HOME.

The first real effective work for the establishment of the Confederate Home took place at the Eighth Annual Reunion of the Ex-Confederate Association of Missouri, held at Nevada, on August the 21st and 22nd, 1890. Showing the will and determination of the people, one year from that time the Home had been located; the ground purchased, and the institution was a fixed fact.

I quote from the Secretary's report of the reunion at Nevada, Mo., in 1890, the eloquent appeal of Hon. W. H. Kennan, of Mexico, Mo., in behalf of the Home. And how well it was received and how hearty the response, is told in the work of the year that followed.

Following the appeal of Mr. Kennan, is the address of Judge David DeArmond, showing the spirit of patriotism and manly fortitude of the Confederate veteran

SPEECH OF W. H. KENNAN.

Comrades: I scarcely know in what terms to address you. I came here without any anticipation or expectation of making a speech in behalf of the ex-Confederate Home of Missouri. If I should not know, gracefully, how to make acknowledgments to you for this honor you have conferred upon me by asking me to address you on this most important matter, I trust you will take the assurance of a plain and unassuming native Missourian and ex-Confederate soldier, that I thank you from the bottom of my heart for this manifestation of your respect for me.

It gives me great pleasure to look into this multitude of intelligent upturned faces—the faces of soldiers who, as soldiers, were as brave and as enduring as the columns led by Napoleon into the sunny, flowery land of Italy, who never there suffered defeat, and as gallant and true as the army led by the same invincible dashing spirit over and across the bleak and barren mountains of Russia into Moscow, whom only fire and the turbulent elements could subdue.

Since your surrender you have, in the civil pursuits of life, exhibited that same aggressive spirit which, perceptibly, characterized you, and made you the acknowledged best and truest soldiers of your age.

The God of Nature, aided by your indomitable energy, skill and perseverance, has blessed the greater portion of you with a goodly portion of this world's goods. Unfortunately, there is a small portion of our number who, by disease, accident and other causes, are unable to care for themselves. Our better natures call upon us in tones to which we cannot turn a deaf ear. It is our bounden duty as true ex-soldiers, citizens and Christians, to give cheerfully and uncomplainingly a moiety of this world's goods, with which God, in His infinite mercy, has blessed us, and use all of our best energies and persuasions to cause others to give bountifully, in order to establish and maintain a Home for the unfortunate and disabled portion of our comrades. I make this appeal to you as an ex-private Confederate soldier; one who stood shoulder to shoulder with you, and carried his musket at "right shoulder shift" and took the "route step" with you, poorly clad and still poorer fed, on the long, weary and fatiguing march, and paced on the sentinel beat with you beneath the "keen full moon" and the bright and shining stars of heaven, when naught could be heard save the quiet, deep-breathing sound of the tired soldier as he lay dreaming of home and battles fought, and the hourly outcry of "All is well" from neighboring posts.

The question is: Will you respond to this appeal? Will you go home and organize ex-Confederate County Associations in your various counties and appeal to the good people of your several localities in this populous, rich and fertile State and ask them to aid you in this highly laudable and charitable cause? All who will agree to this will please hold up their hands. [Then the speaker paused, and a great number of hands went up with a cheer, signifying that they would faithfully carry out the request of the speaker.]

You, as tried and true soldiers, know that you never began to win victories until you were thoroughly organized and officered; so it is in this very important matter to these poor unfortunates of our number, in soliciting and collecting for the Confederate Home. You can accomplish practically nothing for the Home until you organize. Organize—with a president of your County Association and a Vice-President in every township in your counties; make permanent organizations, and at the head of them place thorough-going, active business men. Do this, and the Confederate Soldiers' Home of Missouri will not be a thing talked of, but will be an existing monument of the humane generosity of the great people of the great State of Missouri, and a permanent home beckoning to the unfortunate of our comrades to come within its walls and under its roof to find a warm reception and succor in their declining days, during the remainder of their years. [Applause.]

My comrades, it is merciful to be charitable and to give cheerfully of what God has blessed you with. "Mercy is not strained; it droppeth as the gentle dew from heaven upon the place beneath. It is twice blessed—it blesseth him that gives and him that takes."

> "Cast thy bread upon the waters—
> Out upon the waves alone;
> You will find it drifted to thee
> After many years have flown."

Then let us all be "up and doing" in this, the greatest and grandest of our undertakings. Let us as soldiers continue the battle of life in doing this good, with all the other good we may do in this world.

> "Do all the good you can,
> To all the people you can,
> In all the ways you can,
> Just as long as you can."

Let us subdue and control our worst passions and cultivate to the highest our better, and help to control, by word and example, the evil passions of others. To accomplish this will be greater than any victory we ever won on the blood-stained field of battle.

Having done this and accepted with simple child-like faith a risen Redeemer, together with the precious promises contained in the Holy Writ, we can then have the pleasing assur-

ance that there is a Home for all in the great beyond, "not
made with hands, eternal in the heavens." Then

> 'So live, so act that every hour
> May die as dies the maternal flower;
> A self-reviving thing of power;
> That every word and every deed
> May bear within itself the seed
> Of future good in future need."

[Loud applause and waving of handkerchiefs by the ladies.]

JUDGE DeARMOND'S SPEECH.

Judge David A. DeArmond was called upon to speak, and
in the course of his remarks said:

This scene and these surroundings carry me back in
memory to the stormy days of '61. Beyond these grizzled veterans I see the chivalrous youth of the Southland, rushing to,
the front in response to the bugle's earliest blast, and I see
Southern matron and maid, with more than Spartan fortitude
cheer them on.

I see the citizen soldiers in grey in the first scenes of the
awful drama, fighting in the hope and confidence of victory.

Later, when the mighty North, out of her vast resources,
had poured her wealth of men to bear down the Confederates
by weight of numbers, I again behold the devoted soldiers of
the South fighting with less hope but with matchless daring
and endurance.

And later still, when only the light of despair shone in the
hollow eyes of the wasted men in grey tatters, I see the
unequal struggle still going on—the pride and heroism of the
Confederate even more conspicuous than in better days.

And when the end came and the cruel war was over, behold the soldier of the Lost Cause, poor, hungry, almost
naked, dropping back in the gloom of defeat to the spot where
his home once was. Flower-wreathed banners did not float
over him as over the conqueror in blue. His way was not car-
peted with flowers. No sweet strains of music were wafted to
his ears. Instead of passing proudly under triumphal arches,
the way of the defeated Confederate was through somber woods
and across devastated plantations. Over the old homestead
had swept the scourge of war, if not, indeed, the full tide of

battle. Friends were in lonely graves on the battle fields. Other friends, broken and maimed, were to be nursed and supported without governmental aid. Hearthstones were buried in the ashes of once stately mansions. Over the sweet flower gardens, where women and children had laughed and sung, the briers grew and the rank weeds nodded.

Amid these scenes of desolation the lot of the Confederate veteran was cast. Rich was the harvest of glory which he reaped in the field of battle, but his victory in the peace which followed the surrender at Appomattox was grander than man ever won in warfare. The civilization of the century is elevated in the grandeur of his superb life.

In the world of business, in the social circle, in education, charity and religion, his influence and energy have been on the right side. Of the Government he has asked no favors, but he has demanded and is still demanding, for himself and for all his countrymen, the protection of just laws, impartially and economically administered. He cannot be content with less and remain a good citizen.

With pleasure I see these Federal soldiers—your foemen once, your friends now—joyously commingled with you in this great reunion.

There is something touching in the kinship of gallant spirits. In the fight hero may grapple with hero, but when the smoke lifts and the conflict is past, the survivors are brethren, and each has a share in the common stock of glory.

It is pleasant to note the pride and tenderness of the veteran as he hails a revered leader. And all must rejoice that here are to be seen such leaders as Shelby, Bledsoe, Barlow, Guibor and others.

Long live our heroes, whether of the Blue or the Grey, who glorified the American name in war and ennobled the American nation in peace. They inspire us by their devotion and guide us by their experience and example.

And as countrymen let us never forget that while Grant and Thomas were of the Federal army and Lee and Jackson were Confederates, yet all were Americans—the North and the South are united in the glories of war and in the triumph of peace.

This little gem of a speech was listened to with wrapped attention, and loudly cheered at the conclusion.

I give the address of Mr. Bannerman, the President of the Association, not only for its value as an official document, but for its intrinsic merit as giving the facts of history that should be preserved for the children of future ages.

MR. BANNERMAN'S ADDRESS.

Comrades, members of the Missouri State Confederate Association, Ladies and Gentlemen: Ten years ago, when time had softened the asperities engendered by five years of the bloodiest Civil War in the history of nations, and true men who wore the grey could get together and discuss these troublous times calmly, your Association was formed. It had not to insure its success the prestige of a victory won, or the probability of indefinite pecuniary reward for duty voluntarily undertaken and presumably cheerfully performed. We met our comrades in arms to renew in the midst of smiling peace and plenty recollections of those dark hours spent together. When I look around upon your smiling, well-fed faces, I feel like asking, do you remember the times when you went three years without coffee? You boys from the First Missouri can recall the first time in three and a half years that you tasted Lincoln Green, and there were only thirteen grains each for you. When you drank it weak and black without sugar the next morning you thought it was nectar, didn't you? If some of the good wives I see around me should overlook the cream and sugar some morning, the chances are the neighbors would think that the war had broken out again.

The first reunion was held at Moberly, and on that occasion among the honored guests of the day were Gen. Jo. Shelby and Col. Thomas T. Crittenden. This was not the first time that they had met, however. Crittenden, a Union soldier, addressed you that day; your votes made him Governor. That was the largest reunion of the eight you have held. This was natural, as it was the first, and comrades met for the first time in fifteen years.

The gatherings at Jefferson City, Sedalia, Mexico, Higginsville, Clarksville and Marshall held since, have served each year to bring together the old guards. Friendship formed under such circumstances as were ours, are not lightly forgotten. Year after year hand meets hand in warm and honest embrace beneath the flag we would to-day die to defend from a foreign foe, and a heart-felt salute meets the few, the very few of our gallant old leaders that are still spared. But the memory of Price, Parsons and Marmaduke of that grand army of soldiers who were gentlemen and gentlemen who were soldiers, still lives with us.

Your own ranks are thinning, and each year we miss the kindly faces of those dear old "boys" who survived the tempest of battle, the fever-tainted terrors of the Southern swamp and bayou, and the horrors of military prison. Happy were they to die surrounded by their children; loyal citizens of the greatest country on the globe, followed to their last resting place by mourning friends, happier their lot than that of those who filled unmarked graves on the gory battle fields of the South land. We are getting old, and our ranks grow thinner each year; we have no subsidiary organization to keep our existence in memory. We meet as friends, who suffered together, and together give our thanks for the blessings of the peace we now enjoy.

It was my purpose to briefly review the achievements of Missouri troops in the war, but before I proceed farther I want to say a word in explanation of my remarks about the horrors of military prisons. In a neighboring city there is an institution moved from Richmond, Va., brick by brick, which is exhibited to visitors much as are the torture chambers of the Inquisition in the Old World. I mean Libby Prison. There was another prison in the South, and it was called Andersonville. The man with the bronze button, who served so gallantly in the quartermaster service, waxes eloquent whenever he hears of Andersonville, and the man who draws a pension for a chivalric diarrhœa or valorous piles, has not words to express his horror.

Some of you "boys" out there knew something about Ship Island and Johnson Island. Now, I do not wish to stir up any harsh feelings at this late day, but in the interest of truth I want to say that the least said on either side about this prison life the better.

From the official figures prepared by the United States Pension Bureau and published in every reputable political almanac,

I find that the number of United States troops who died while prisoners was 29,724, and the Confedrate troops who died while prisoners was 26,778, and this leads me to remark that the impartial history of the war that is to be written will, despite the best efforts of the government, be rather one-sided unless our people come to the aid of the bureau having in charge the annals of the rebellion with all the information of a statistical line at hand. So far as the Union army is concerned they have figures at hand. In the table furnished by the United States Pension Office I find figures that are misleading.

The grand total of Union soldiers killed in battle, died of wounds and died of disease is given as 279,376, but the figures of the losses to the Confederate army are given simply on the number of soldiers died from wounds and disease as 133,281. This must be exclusive of killed in battles. A friend of mine who was looking over these figures suddenly seized a pencil and figured for a moment and exclaimed: "Can it be possible that we chanced them two to one?" If I was not very careful to avoid saying anything that might be construed as out of order, I would say that a glance at the pension roll to-day looks as though we chanced them a little the rise of two to one.

But I won't say any more about that. The chances are that if we had got there we would have taken care of our own.

The history of Missouri in the Confederacy has not been fully written as yet. My friend, Col. Tom Snead, has in his books, and his splendid articles in *The Century*, told most of the story. And Missouri's gifted son, John Edwards (God bless his memory), has surrounded the efforts of Shelby and his men with all the glory his magic pen could impart. My friend, Capt. Joe Boyce, has written the history of the First Missouri, Bowen's old regiment, the marvel of discipline, the pride of the Confederacy, a regiment that loaded and fired by number at Shiloh while under a heavy fire, a regiment that went into the service with 1,400 men and surrendered less than 150. In a way the Southern Historical and Benevolent Association is helping out this work, but the papers submitted are all of a personal and reminiscent nature, without special historical value. What I want is the records of Missouri's troops followed from Wilson's Creek to the surrender, battle by battle, on both sides of the river.

The war in Missouri began at Wilson's Creek. Boon-ville, Carthage, and Lexington were skirmishes, bloody and important. I would commence when Price took hold at Springfield with Rains and Clark, Weightman and Kelly as able allies. This battle of Wilson's Creek was the first battle of the war fought west of the Missis-sippi, and for the number of men engaged, it was the bloodiest. With 5,521 Missouri troops engaged we lost 175 killed, and 557 wounded—a total of 732. I doubt if there was a bloodier battle than that, unless it be Franklin, Tenn., where Hood threw 12,000 Confederate troops against the fortifications and lost 6,800 of them in twenty minutes. Here the First Mis-souri was slaughtered. I asked an old veteran of Wilson's Creek one day how they came to fight so hard, and he replied: "I guess because we were so green." But that I hardly admit. Parson's brigade was not green at Pleasant Hill, and through-out the war Missouri men on both sides of the river were at the fore of the battle, for out of 13,000 that left the State, I doubt if 5,000 ever got back.

The total Confederate loss at Wilson's Creek was 279 killed and 951 wounded, the full force being 10,000 men.

The Federals had 268 killed and 873 wounded. That was your baptism. Next, on August 25th, came Lexington, where you lost 25 killed and 72 wounded, but killed 37 and wounded 120 of your opponents. Pea Ridge next claimed 203 killed and 980 wounded. And among the latter was "Old Pap" himself, this being his second injury. Here Gen. W. Y. Slack and Col. B. A. Rivers were killed. In the meanwhile the battle of Shi-loh and Bowen's Missourians bore off 98 killed and 490 wound-ed. Out of a total of 1,728 killed, Missouri gave up 98. I must hurry on to the retreat from Van Buren to Little Rock, during which occurred the battle of Prairie Grove, where we lost 1,251 men in killed and wounded. On July 4, 1863, as the Federals were marching into Vicksburg, we made a foolish, futile assault on Helena. Under Price, Parsons, Fagan and Marmaduke were 7 646 men, and they were repulsed with a loss of 173 killed and 687 wounded.

Then on the retreat and the operations around Little Rock, 67 Missourians were killed, although Steele, the Federal com-mander reported a loss of 137 men. All the Transmississippi victories of the Federal troops were dearly bought. After Little Rock came the terrible two days' fighting at Pleasant Hill in the Red River campaign. We lost 3,976 men in that dearly bought victory. Parson's brigade went into Pleasant Hill with 2,200 muskets, and 200 more Missourians bit the dust.

There is no accurate record of the losses sustained by Gen. Price in what some historians have been pleased to call "Price's Missouri raid." It was not a raid. It was an invasion of a State in the hands of an enemy. The battle of Pilot Knob was one of the most important engagements of the war, as upon its issue depended the fate of St. Louis and its vast supply of munition and treasure. Gen. Price wrote himself of that "raid": "I marched 1,434 miles, fought forty-three battles and skirmishes, captured and paroled over 3,000 Federal officers and men, captured eighteen pieces of artillery, 3,000 stands of small arms, sixteen stands of colors and destroyed $10,000,000 worth of munitions of war, wagons and other supplies of the enemy."

Thus have I briefly referred to Missouri in the war. Modesty forbids me to say more of my old brigade—Parson's brigade. You have all heard of it. We surrendered at Shreveport when the war was over.

Missouri Confederates you may well be proud of your record as soldiers. The Confederacy was proud of you and your opponents held you in the respect that bravery always commands, at the hands of brave men.

THE ORATION OF THE DAY.

At the reunion at Kansas City in 1891, the Hon. Wm. H. Hatch, of Hannibal, Mo., delivered the address of the day which is worthy to be preserved for future ages, as he was an actor in some of the most momentous and important events connected with the Civil War.

ADDRESS OF WM. H. HATCH.

Gov. Francis then introduced Hon. Wm. H. Hatch, of Hannibal, stating that "he was a gentleman who needed no introduction to a Missouri audience, and would be the speaker of the Fifty-second Congress of the United States." Congressman Hatch said in brief:

Mr. Speaker and Citizens: I have only pleasant and joyous words for you to-day. I never dwell on gloomy subjects. I never talked gloomily during the war, nor have I since. The ablest men of the nation had failed to settle the great questions at issue in the halls of Congress, and it was left to the sons of America on the battlefield. It was settled, and as we have never apologized for our conduct, we do not apologize to-day. [Cheers.] We claim as honest and brave men to have buried all animosities. I surrendered my sword on the terms accepted by our great leader at Appomattox, Robert E. Lee. [Cheers.] We surrendered to the noble boys in blue, who wore haversacks and fed us across the line for so long when we were hungry.

Serious criticism has been made upon the conduct of Mr. Davis and Gen. Lee in that great struggle for three or four months, when it was a foregone conclusion that we would be compelled to surrender. My friends, let me give you a bit of history. In February, 1865, when the dark shadow of that event which transpired in Appomattox in April was hovering about Richmond and the army of Northern Virginia, I was selected by the Secretary of War to escort through the lines that celebrated peace commission of A. H. Stephens and R. M. T. Hunter, of Virginia, to devise ways and means of a peaceful termination of that struggle. On a bright winter's Sunday, after three hours' resting in Petersburg, when a flag of truce was established upon the lines, and Gen. Grant was notified of the coming of the commission and gave his orders to receive them, I carried them through the lines. I was met upon the other side by a member of Gen. Grant's staff. That first conference was held on that Sunday morning, and early Monday morning their credentials were submitted to Gen. Grant and the Secretary of War of the United States. Gen. Grant, in the most emphatic and determined manner stated to the commissioners that it was absolutely futile to go to President Lincoln upon the instructions in those letters. He said: "This army will never have a settlement based upon those instructions." At 8 o'clock on Monday morning I was dispatched back to Richmond by this commission with a letter to President Davis. I made my way to Gen. Lee's headquarters, and before 8 o'clock I placed that package in the hands of Mr. Davis. I shall never forget that scene. That great man, with all of the responsibility of that great struggle upon him, as commander-in-chief of its armies and President of the Confederate States, calmly and deliberately opened that package and read the message; read it a second time, deliberately folded it and asked me half a dozen leading questions, and said to me:

"Col. Hatch, meet my cabinet in this room to-morrow morning at 9 o'clock."

I was much younger than I am now [laughter], but felt the responsibility of my position. I was a Missourian and a Missouri soldier. I determined at any rate to break the ice and make a single suggestion. I said: "Mr. President, I will obey your order with great pleasure, but permit me to suggest that if this matter is postponed until to-morrow morning at 9 o'clock, an answer will reach the commission too late. Can't you send me back with a reply to-night?"

He looked at me for a moment. I first thought in anger, but in the tones of his voice, as quiet and gentle as a woman's, he said to me: "It is not necessary. Come to-morrow morning."

I went back the next morning, and was cross-questioned by the cabinet for two hours, but the cabinet did not return from that cabinet-room until after the middle of the day. No reply was ever sent. Why? I have simply related this to impress upon you that no power on earth could have written a diplomatic settlement that would have been acceptable to either. It had to be fought upon the battlefield. The army under Gen. Grant, victorious up to that hour and knowing its power, would have accepted nothing but absolute surrender. In Gen. Lee's army 99 per cent. of it would have hung to the limb of a tree any Confederate who would have dared to surrender until their chief had sheathed his sword. [Cheers.] No, the war was a necessity. We bore our parts in it as became brave and valorous men. We are entitled to these reunions in Missouri and throughout the length and breadth of the land—wherever the sun shines, wherever brave men are loved by noble women, wherever valorous deeds are known and recorded—Confederate soldiers can be found to shake hands.

I could indulge in these reminiscences for an hour. We all know them by heart. They are carried in our heart of hearts, and the memory of them will never die while reason holds its seat. But, my friends, in these reunions we have even a brighter record at which to point than at our deeds upon the battlefield.

Our wives welcomed us to our desolated homes on our return. That more than compensated every brave soldier. I left a bride and came back to my wife. I know she would rather have worn the weeds as a widow of a Confederate, than to have been the wife of a coward. [Cheers.] We have had all the compliments and encomiums that any people could want. We have a prouder record still here in Jackson—in every county in Missouri. The magnificent courage, the splendid conduct of our comrades in the battles of peace, throughout the agricultural districts of the land, in the harvest-field, in the work-shop, in the office, in the pulpit; aye, everywhere Confederate soldiers have won plaudits for patriotic conduct and magnificent citizenship. I do love to dwell upon this part of our record; I congratulate you that your cheeks have never tingled with shame, that your women have never been called upon to blush at the dishonorable conduct of the great body of Missouri soldiers. The building up of our churches, the building up of our schools, our seats of learning, the administration of State and county affairs, all attest this magnificent record. We have shared with Federal soldiers the honors, the benefits and the prestige in the rehabilitation of this most grand domain of the United States of America.

I look back, my comrades, to that point in 1865, when we were called upon to close that great struggle. The scene which I witnessed then determined for all time to come, my position as an American citizen. I have alluded to one incident that happened upon the line the day after the surrender and before Gen. Grant's commissaries' stores could reach the land. I want to convince my friend, the Governor of the State, and all the young men present, that we Confederates of Missouri are simply bearing in mind and memory the honorable and better deeds of that struggle, and not its animosities. I am the last but two on the Confederate side who was selected by Gen. Lee to act in the second interview with Gen. Grant, when the final terms of surrender were made. Accompanying my superior officer, I went by order of Gen. Lee not only as witness of that great scene, but to receive certain orders that would go through the lines.

I was present at that scene with the two armies on either side of the little stream of Appomattox. I saw the last meeting between those two great generals. I witnessed, my comrades, the magnificent, the soldierly, the most chivalrous bearing of that American soldier, Gen. Grant. [Cheers.] It softened my heart then. No man loved our chieftain better than I did. As a soldier I idolized him. I knew, of course, what would transpire to such a great soldier at a time like that, but the bearing of Gen. Grant to Gen. Lee on that occasion settled forever my feelings toward that great man, and in the political campaigns of 1868, 1872, and down to the time of his death, and from that great hour to this no living man has ever heard a word pass my lips in criticism upon that eminent citizen and great General, U. S. Grant. [Cheers.]

The struggle is over. Those issues were settled by the arbitrament of arms—settled forever; and upon the ninth annual reunion in Missouri we have a more pleasant duty to perform; we have a noble charity, we have a magnificent work; we have one in progress here under the shadow of your great city, for which all good men and women pray, and for the success of which every Confederate soldier in the State of Missouri should work so long as there lives a Confederate soldier who needs a home, a resting place—that blessed place that carries us back to the days of infancy and early childhood when, nestling at the mother's side, we learned wisdom and character. It is the end of a journey—a home for the weak, for the weary and the footsore and tired of that little band. Those heroic hearts, like muffled drums, are beating funeral marches.

My friends, lives there an ex-Confederate in Missouri who will not share the providence that God has bestowed upon him in the establishment of this Home? It is certain of success. How it warms the heart of every Christian soldier to be able to have the privilege of contributing to this Home. What Christian man or woman who does not remember the most consoling promise of the Saviour when upon earth, He said to His disciples: "In my Father's house are many mansions. I go to prepare a place for you." My friends, we are hastening to that home. Those of us who are surrounded by the comforts and luxuries of homes of our own making, certainly will not refuse to extend a helping hand to that noble band that is struggling, few in number, that has held out until the last hour of strength and health was spent.

My friends, I am sure if every man in Missouri were to sew up his pockets that Home would be built by the noble women. Our wives and daughters would do it—those who stand by us in struggles with their delicate hands and heroic hearts. It is simply a privilege to help them. Friends, wives, daughters, ex-Confederates and fellow comrades, I thank you for your earnest attention.

Auxiliaries.

The MEXICO AUXILIARY of the Daughters of the Confederacy began its existence July, 1891, and the daughters, strongly united in their efforts, after a year and a half of organization, forwarded to the mother society $322.46 in cash, realized in the face of many difficulties.

The ladies feel pride in the success of their work and pleasure in the thought of the accomplishment of their object. All through their difficulties they had the sympathy of the State organization and written congratulations from many sources on a success made in the face of a narrow, stupid and utterly inconsistent opposition. Miss Belle Morris, President, and Mrs. R. M. White, 1st Vice-President, grand-daughters of the Confederacy, are energetic little women, who have worked successfully together in many charitable enterprises, and are representatives of prominent families in the State.

Many of the Auxiliary Societies through the State have realized very handsome sums, notably Sedalia, Hannibal, St. Louis county, Marshall, Louisiana, Moberly, Paris, Richmond, Independence and Macon. Kansas City is an independent society, well organized and kept in full accord with the spirit of the work by Mrs. R. E. Wilson and her energetic helpers. The St. Louis Society holds that the Moberly record is a valuable illustration of woman's work and gave a full account of all the business of that society in their first Annual Report of the Daughters of the Confederacy. The St. Louis Society has had unprecedented success in its noble work, due to the efforts of the many energetic women who are members of it. The venerable Mrs. M. A. E. McLure, who holds the leadership, Mrs. A. C Cassidy, ever ready with plans for social and financial successes, Mrs. C. C. Rainwater, one of the greatest charity workers in the State, Mrs. W. P. Howard, the able Treasurer, Mrs. E. R. Gamble, the faithful Secretary, Mrs. Gen. Bowen, Mrs. Pickett and Mrs. R. K. Walker, are only a few of the Daughters who have rendered valuable services for the Confederate Home.

Biography.

MRS. M. A. E. McLURE.

Margaret A. E. McLure, the beloved President of the Daughters of the Confederacy, is a superior woman of great force of character, intelligent and refined, and so gentle and kind in her disposition, that no one can know her without loving her. She is a devoutly religious woman and her teachings are manifest. Her loving words and tender acts, her unselfish devotion to "the lost cause" for which she was banished, have brought forth a thousand-fold. Her integrity of character has adorned her life and shed upon it a light of unfading luster.

MRS. ELIZABETH USTICK McKINNEY.

Mrs. Elizabeth McKinney, whose maiden name was Ustick, belongs to one of the oldest and best families of LaFayette county. Her parents, Charles Taylor Ustick, and Susan E., his wife, were Virginians, and soon after their marriage, determined to seek their fortunes in the West.

In the fall of 1837, they came to Missouri, when the journey was a long and tedious one, and two months were occupied in making the trip. They passed through a large portion of the State, only making one stop, at the home of Mr. Clark, at Jackson, Cape Girardeau county, then the county seat. Mr. Clark was an old friend and a native of Virginia also, and assisted in constructing the boats for Lewis & Clark in their famous exploring expedition up to the head waters of the Missouri River. Mr. Ustick, in searching for a pleasant location for a home, with attractive and beautiful surroundings, found no part of the State so inviting as the rich and productive county of LaFayette. They located at the then thriving little village of Dover, which was surrounded by a fine agricultural region just ten miles east of Lexington, the county seat. LaFayette county was first settled by a substantial and progressive class of people, made up largely of Virginians, Kentuckians and a few families from Tennessee. At this time, no town in the State could boast of more cultured society or a more hospitable people than resided in and around Dover.

Mr. and Mrs. Ustick were the parents of six children who had never known a sorrow until in the spring of 1856, when death crossed their threshold and took from the happy home the kind father and devoted husband, leaving Mrs. Ustick a widow at the early age of 37. She continued to reside at the old homestead until all of her children were educated and married. Though many years have passed away, the memory of Charles T. Ustick is still revered and honored, and the record of his noble life has been a golden legacy to his family.

Elizabeth was the fourth child, having two sisters and an only brother older than herself. Mr. Ustick supplied his family with good books and excellent magazines, so that early in life they developed a fondness for reading. It is rather unusual to meet with a whole family of literary turn, but this may be owing to the fact that in this case it was partly inherited, as the poets, Watts and John Greenleaf Whittier, were both relatives of the Ustick family. Two of Mr. Ustick's brothers bore the middle name of Watts.

The celebrated naturalist Audubon was a cousin of Mr. Ustick's mother, whose maiden name was Hannah Taylor. She was also a cousin of Gen. Zachary Taylor. As writers of both prose and poetry, Mr. Ustick's daughters have contributed much for the press of this and other States. During the war, Elizabeth, who was then a school girl, was the author of a number of patriotic war songs, several of which were composed for special occasions. Under the *nom de plume* of "Claire," she was a frequent contributor to the Lexington papers. In the fall of 1867, she was married to L. W. McKinney, a lawyer of Fulton, Mo., where she resided for a period of fifteen years; during this time, her articles in prose and poetry were published in the Fulton papers and other papers and journals in the State, sometimes under the signature of "Clyde Campbell," and sometimes over her own initials.

A book entitled "Poets of Missouri," is soon to be issued

by "The American Publishing Association" at Chicago, in which will appear some of Mrs. McKinney's writings, and also poems by two of her sisters. She has received prizes in various contests for addresses, essays and poems. Also a native Missourian, her sympathies have always been strongly enlisted for the South, and during the scourge of yellow fever there, she wrote a poem called the "Stricken South," which was published in *The St. Louis Republic* and copied by many papers in the South. At present, she is a regular contributor to the *Southern Home Companion*, published in New Orleans.

In 1881, Mr. McKinney removed to Colorado, but after a residence of three years in Denver, they returned to Missouri and located in Moberly, where, with their family of four sons, they have continued to reside. Wherever they have lived, Mrs. McKinney has been identified with all kinds of charitable and church work. From its very beginning, she has taken an active interest in the establishment and completion of the Confederate Home, and was the first President of the "Daughters of the Confederacy," organized at Moberly, in Randolph county.

H. A. RICKETS.

H. A. Rickets, of Mexico, Missouri, is treasurer of the Confederate Home at Higginsville.

MISS BELLE MORRIS.

Miss Isabelle Oberia Morris, is the daughter of Mary Belt and George A. Morris, formerly of St. Louis, but for some time residents of Mexico, Audrain county, and their beautiful home Lakeview, one mile south of Mexico, is one of the handsomest country villas in Missouri. Miss Morris is a refined, cultured lady and is a graduate and post-graduate of Mrs. Cuthbert's Seminary. She has an extensive acquaintance and her rare accomplishments and lady-like ways never fail to fetch her admirers. Miss Morris was the modest winner in the race for the most popular young lady in Missouri, under the auspices of the Confederacy and her friends were legion.

MRS. R. M. WHITE.

Isabelle Dinsmore Mitchell, daughter of Sophie Bayless and Leander C. Mitchell, and the wife of Col. R. M. White, the popular editor of the *Mexico Ledger*, was born in Ohio, but came to Alton, Illinois, in her infancy. She was graduated from the Alton high school and took a post-graduate course at St. Mary's, Knoxville, Illinois. Mrs. White is a brilliant musician and was considered quite a prodigy at the age of five years, playing many pieces. She studied with Lavitsky, Beethoven Conservatory and has published a few of her own compositions. Mrs. White is the vivacious mistress of a beautiful home, and quite the pet of the Missouri Press Association.

J. M. ALLEN, M. D.

Dr. J. M. Allen joined the Missouri State Guards, May 1, 1861; in the same month he was appointed surgeon 4th Regiment of Cavalry, B. A. Rives, commanding. In Dec. 1861, while camped at Osceola, Mo., Cols. B. A. Rives, J. D. Pritchard, Finly Hubble, James Kelsey McDowell, Dr. J. D. Wallis, St. Hi. Faulkner, George Simpson, and ten others whose names have been forgotten, joined the Confederate States' army and went into camp on Sac River. These formed the nucleus of the First Missouri Brigade. Dr. Allen was a private in Company E., and was appointed surgeon of the 3 Reg., and by seniority was Brigade Surgeon. He served in this position until August, 1863, when General Joseph E. Johnston appointed him Chief Surgeon of Mississippi and East Louisiana. He served in this position till the war closed. He was paroled at Granville, Alabama, May, 1865.

In August, 1865, he returned to his native county, Clay, and resumed the practice of medicine and surgery at Liberty, Mo. In Nov. 1866, he married Miss Agnes McAlpine, of Port Gibson, Mississippi. In 1868, Dr. S. S. Laws, then president of the University of Missouri, selected him to deliver a course of lectures on the Gastric Intestinal Canal to the senior students of the medical department of the University. In 1882 he was appointed to the Chair of Theory and Practice of Medicine, in the University Medical College of Kansas City, Mo., and in

1888 was made president of the college. In 1884-5 he represented his county in the State Legislature.

COL. RIVES.

Col. B. A. Rives was born in Virginia, a descendant of the Rives family of that State. He was a graduate of Liberty College, with the degree of A. M. Also of a Medical College with the degree of M. D. Shortly after his marriage, to an accomplished Virginia lady, he moved to Missouri, and settled in Ray county. He soon relinquished the profession of medicine, and began farming. About 1856, he was elected to represent Ray county in the Legislature. In April, 1861, he organized a company of cavalry and was elected Captain. At Lexington, in May, 1861, he organized a Regiment and was made Colonel.

He joined the Confederate army at Osceola and went into camp on Sac River. He, with seventeen others, was the nucleus of the First Missouri Brigade. He, and Col. James A. Pritchard were the first to urge Missourians to join the Confederate army; indeed were the leaders in that direction. Rives was elected Colonel of the 3rd Regiment and Pritchard, Lieutenant Colonel. Col. Rives was killed at Elk Horn Tavern, Ark.. while repelling a charge of the enemy near the close of the battle. He was a thoroughly educated gentleman of decided literary tastes. He was one of the best public orators in the State, a vigorous, convincing speaker. In the interests of the South he gave all the enthusiasm of his nature. As a commander and soldier he had no superior in Missouri, and had his life been prolonged, it would have been marked with high distinction. In command he had the entire confidence of Gen. Sterling Price, as well as all the other officers of rank. He was always counseled in the movements of the army. He was a bold, independent thinker on any subject presented, and never hesitated to give his convictions.

As a soldier, he was brave, aggressive and dashing. As a commander, a splendid organizer and disciplinarian, yet kind and thoughtful of the comforts of his men. He was the idol, not only of the third Regiment, but of the whole brigade of C. S. A.   A.

JAMES KELSEY McDOWELL.

J. K. McDowell was born in Ohio, in 1838, moved to Ray county, Mo,. in 1858, where he taught school till 1861, when he inlisted in the M. S. G.s, and was elected Lieutenant of Rives' company. He was one of seventeen that joined the Confederate army at Oceola, and went into the C. S. A. camp on Sac River. He was elected Captain of Company A. 3rd Regiment, First Missouri Brigade. At the re-organization, he was elected Lieutenant Colonel in 1863. He was killed on the battlefield leading a charge, near Atlanta, Ga. He was a brave, kind, generous gentleman.　　　　　　　　　　　　　　　　　A.

G. N. RATLIFF.

G. N. Ratliff was born and raised in Macon county, Missouri, the date of his birth being the 28th of February, 1843.

He joined the M. S. G. at the commencement of the war, and continued with them till the Confederate Brigade was organized, when he joined Company K., 3rd Regiment, at Springfield. He served in this company, when able for duty, until the close of the war. At the battle of Baker's Creek, he had his arm broken above the elbow by a Minie ball. When Gen. Grant closed his lines around Vicksburg, the wounded of the Confederate army were left in the Confederate lines. He was left nine days without medical attendance. Notwithstanding this, he recovered and was able to join the command soon after they reached parole camp, at Demopolis, Ala.

At the close of the war he settled in Randolph county, and after laboring on the farm for two years he determined to go to school. His education had been very limited and he now began his first days of school. He laid to with such a will and untiring determination that in a few years he was able to teach school successfully. He served several years as superintendent of schools; he was afterward elected sheriff of the County, which office he filled for eight years. He was then elected to the office of Collector, and is now closing his second term in that office.

ED. G. WILLIAMS.

Ed. G. Williams was born August 8, 1844, in Bedford county, Virginia. He lived there and in Montgomery and Floyd counties. In 1858 he went to Lynchburg and was in the commission business till the commencement of the war. In 1861 he enlisted in Company E., 11th Va. Infantry and served in First Brigade, commanded during the war by Gens. Longstreet; Clark, Emel, A. P. Hill, Kamper and W. R. Perry. He was in all the battles, under Longstreet and Picket, as follows: First battle of Manassas, Gainesville, Fredricksburg, Gettysburg, Antietam, Boons Mountain, seven days battles around Richmond. Second, Fredricksburg, Belmont, N. C., Wilderness, and at the battle of Drewry's Bluff, on the 16th of May, 1864.

He was wounded and had his left leg amputated above the knee.

In March, 1867, he came to Missouri and lived in Rolla until the twelfth day of February, 1869, when he was appointed Deputy Clerk of the Circuit County, and Probate Courts of Pulaski county, Mo., and served as such for four years. He was then elected Clerk of all the Courts and served as such for four years. He was re-elected County Clerk in 1882, and has the office at this date, and the renomination for the office for the next four years. He served as Vice-president of the Confederate Home for four years, and is in full sympathy with every effort for the care of Confederate veterans.

FRANK L. PITTS.

F. L. Pitts, the subject of this sketch, was born in Shelby county, Missouri, April 25, 1841. When he was four years of age, his parents moved to Hannibal, Mo., where he lived until January, 1860, when he moved to Paris, Mo., and engaged in the saddle and harness business.

In the spring of 1861, at which time Gov. Jackson made his call for six months' troops, he enlisted in Company A., of Col. Brnce's Reg., Missouri State Guards. After the six months had expired he enlisted in the 2nd Reg. Confederate troops commanded by Col. Burbridge. He served with him until the reorganization at Corinth, Miss., at which time F. M. Cockrell was elected Colonel.

He served under Gen. Cockrell in all his marches and battles until Nov. 30, 1864, at the battle of Franklin, Tenn. Here he lost his right arm in a charge upon the enemies' works. He fell into the hands of the enemy and was taken to Nashville, Tenn., and from there to Camp Chase, Ohio, where he remained until the close of the war.

When released from prison, he returned to Paris, Mo., and re-engaged in the saddle and harness business. In 1872, he was elected Sheriff of Monroe county, serving four years. In 1876, he was elected Collector and served in that capacity ten years, being honored with five consecutive terms.

He is one of the organizers of the Confederate Home Association of Missouri, being Vice-President for the Second Congressional District. He is active in this work and has succeeded in raising a handsome fund in his district for this worthy cause. In 1892, he was a candidate before the Democratic Convention, for nomination to the office of State Treasurer and was defeated by a small vote.

O. H. P. CATRON.

O. H. P. Catron was born near Lexington, Mo., December 27, 1842. He belonged to Company C., Gordon's Reg. Shelby's Brigade. He was educated at the common schools of the county and at Shelby College, near Waverly, Mo. He inlisted in the M. S. G.s on the 16th day of June, 1861, at Camp Holloway, near Independence, in Capt. Carl J. Kirtley's Company, Grave's Regiment, Weightman's Brigade, Rains' Division. Graves' Regiment, was re-organized after the battle of Wilson's Creek, and Capt. Ben. Elliott was elected Colonel. He took part in the battles of Carthage and in the advance on Springfield, from Cowskin Prairie, Wilson's Creek and Lexington.

In December, 1861, he was discharged at Oceola, and returned home sick. But in August following, he reinlisted for the war in Company C, Gordon's Regiment, Shelby's Brigade, and was in active service until the surrender at Shreveport, La., on the 16th day of June, 1865. He participated in the following engagements: Coon Creek, Newtonia, Prairie Grove, Springfield, Hartville, Cape Girardeau, Brownsville, Bayou Meeter, Little Rock, Neosho, Marshall, and all the skirmishes of Shelby's raid. In the fall of 1864, he went into Missouri in advance of Price's army, with Col. Rathburn and fifty others recruiting, and joined his regiment again at Lexington, and was with Shelby in the running days fightings near Fort Scott, where Gen. Marmaduke was captured and Shelby's Brigade saved Price's army at Newtonia.

The promotion of Col. Shelby to General caused a vacancy in Company C, by the promotion of Capt. G. P. Gordon to Major. This caused an election for Lieutenant in Company C, and O. H. P. Catron was chosen, and from that until the surrender he actively assisted Capt. Spinder in commanding the Company.

He arrived home, near Waverly, Mo., on the 3rd day of July, 1865. On the 29th day of January, 1867, he was united in marriage to Miss Mattie E. Goodwin, daughter of James Goodwin, who now lives in Waverly, aged 90 years. He engaged in farming in LaFayette county. until the Spring of 1869, and then moved to Alma, Mo., and engaged in the Mercantile business. He was the first post-master of Alma. In 1882, he moved to West Plains, Mo., and engaged in the real estate business, and in 1883, with three others, organized the West Plains Bank and now resides at that place.

HON. W. H. KENNAN.

W. H. Kennan was born on a farm in Boone county, Mo., on the 15th day of September, 1837. His father's name was Samuel Kennan; that of his mother before marriage, Harriet Ragan. He was educated at the common schools and the Missouri University at Columbia. He read law for a time with Judge James M. Gordon, and soon after, he entered the Confederate army as a private soldier and surrendered as first Lieutenant and Adjutant of the Battalion of Sharp Shooters, at the close of the war in 1865.

After returning home he pursued the study of law, in connection with teaching, and in 1869 was admitted to the bar by Judge G. H. Buckhart. In the same year he located in Mexico, Mo., and began the practice of law and soon entered into a successful and lucrative practice. In 1871 he was married to Cordelia P. Jenkins, daughter of Maj. Theodrick Jenkins, late of Boone county, who was an estimable lady. She died in November, 1893, greatly lamented by her family and a host of friends, leaving three daughters and one son, Churchill B.; her oldest daughter, Mary Hardin Kennan, a lovable character, having died six years before her mother.

In 1884, without opposition, he was nominated by the Democrats of his county, and at the general election was elected to a seat in the General Assembly of the State. He is the author of, and had passed, while in the Legislature, several wholesome laws which are now a part of the statutes. He was a member of the Judiciary and Appropriation Committees of the House. He is at present president of a local insurance company doing business in his county, and a member of the staff of Gov. Stone, with the rank of Brigadier-General. He is a member of the Baptist Church, also of the Board of Directors of Hardin College, and one of the Directors of the Confederate Home at Higginsville, Mo

MAJOR R. J. WILLIAMS.

Major R. J. Williams, the subject of this sketch, was born in Prince Edward county, Virginia, Oct. 2nd, in the year 1825. With his father he moved to Missouri in 1836 and settled in Ray county. He was a soldier in the Mexican war, belonging to the command of Gen. Doniphan. He crossed the plains to California in 1850.

After two years passed in the California gold region he returned to Missouri. He participated in the Kansas troubles in and about Osawatomie, in the year 1856; joined the Confederate army, at Springfield, Mo., in Dec. 1861, and was elected Captain of Company A., 3rd Regiment, Missouri Infantry. He was promoted to Major of the same regiment in 1863, in which capacity he served until the close of the struggle. He was once severely wounded.

Since the close of the war he has been engaged in farming and at the same time interested in banking, railroading and coal-mining. At the present time he resides on a splendid farm about four miles north of Richmond where he operates an extensive coal mine. The history of the Brigade is the history of the part he took in the "Civil War."

———

J. S. BOWEN, MARTIN E. GREEN AND HENRY LYTTLE. A JUST TRIBUTE.

The following is copied from the *Lexington Missourian*, and is a just and beautiful tribute to those who gave their lives for the cause they loved:

THERE WERE OTHER HEROES.

Mr. A. A. Lesueur in a letter to the *Intelligencer*, though addressed to Mrs. Sallie Long, speaks of the "Prices, the Marmadukes, the Parsons, the Shelbys and others, who led our Missouri divisions and brigades."

It is strange that any prominent Missourian even at this remote date will, in mentioning Missouri's Confederate leaders name only these.

Where was Bowen, a hero at Shiloh, a victim at Vicksburg; a man of heroic deed at least the equal of Price in organization, as he surely was of Marmaduke, Parsons and Shelby in tact and generalship?—a Napoleon, almost in conception, a Ney in execution.

Was he not, resisting Grant from the Bayou Pierre to Bovina, entitled to some notice? Grant had massed 40,000 men in his front and on his left flank. Bowen had less than 5,000, for he had just fought the bloody battle of Port Gibson, where, with 5,500 men he had held Grant in check from early morn till nightfall. Before this overwhelming force he marched two days and crossed Black River on a single bridge without the loss of a man or a gun. Was not this leadership?

Did Missourians ever hear of General John S. Bowen?

Alas, our politicians only have been writing history, and Bowen's friends are too few to count for much at county primaries—they fought where ofttimes the majority was left upon the field of carnage.

Then there was Brigadier General Martin E. Green. Brave old Martin Green. We can see him yet as his tall, spare form sits erect upon his gallant bay. Cool in battle as at brigade review, undaunted in the presence of danger, ever alert; always ready to lead his men where effective work could be done. At Elkhorn Tavern, at the seige of Corinth, Iuka, Corinth and Bruinsburg, he was ever in the melee of battle, ever self-reliant—always awarded the post of honor which was synonymous with that of danger.

You never hear the politicians say anything of Martin Green. Too many who know him as he should have been known are like him, filling graves in the far south land. But could you look into the hearts of those who followed him and yet survive—now a scattered remnant and scarce a hundred strong—you could read their tributes of love and remembrance far brighter, far more eloquent than those the politicians utter·

And General Henry Lyttle too—at once an army's pride and the glory of his State. Than Lyttle none was braver, none more heroic. We all loved the man as we honored the soldier, for he possessed those noble traits of character that involuntarily drew all hearts to him; and not an eye was dry that beautiful September evening, when as we rushed to battle while the roar of small arms was furious in our front and the artillery was shaking the forest trees, we heard from Price's own lips the story of Lyttle's death.

It is almost sacrilege to mention Missouri's Confederate leaders and ignore the name of brave, gallant, noble Henry Lyttle.

Cockrell still lives, and can speak for himself—but was it no honor to have led and won where Cleburne led and failed and fell? No honor when over 600 of his 884 followers were left upon the bloody field of Franklin? If that was not heroism where do you find it?

Were Mr. Lesueur the only one who is accustomed in speaking or writing of Missouri's Confederate leaders, to ignore those devoted men who fought east of the Mississippi river, this would not have been written. But the disease is chronic, and the names of many of the real heroes of the war are passed by in silence.

J. H. FINKS.

J. H. Finks has been for some time connected with banking in Salisbury, Mo., and is now candidate for Railroad Commissioner on the State Democratic ticket.